LANGUAGE IN THE CRIB

JANUA LINGUARUM

STUDIA MEMORIAE
NICOLAI VAN WIJK DEDICATA

edenda curat

CORNELIS H. VAN SCHOONEVELD

INDIANA UNIVERSITY

SERIES MAIOR
14

1970

MOUTON · THE HAGUE

LANGUAGE IN THE CRIB

by

RUTH HIRSCH WEIR

Second Printing

1970

MOUTON · THE HAGUE

First Printing: 1962

Printed in The Netherlands by Mouton & Co., Printers, The Hague.

TO ANTHONY
AND
HIS FATHER

PREFACE

The material for this study was gathered at one point in time, and in this sense it is a case study. It consists of recordings of pre-sleep monologues of a two-and-a-half year old child, alone in his crib, talking to himself. *Language in the Crib* hence is a descriptive title of the nature of the data. I have attempted to present a structural description of this language, in terms of phonology, morphology, and syntax, as well as of the language in a less restricted sense, looking at it from the point of view of its functions. Although never static, the linguistic structures in the system of a very young child are in their infancy, and are, therefore, much more fluid than in their mature state. The phonemic system is presented as static, which is true only for the particular point in time, and the same is true of all the other linguistic structures. However, this handling seemed to me best for an adequate description. Needless to say, reference is made to the stability or instability of certain structures, since their degree of acquisition varies greatly. A number of frequency counts and proportionate analyses are included as further support for the conclusions on stability. Also, rather than to consider the phoneme as the smallest unit, it seemed more revealing to analyze the phonemic system from the point of view of articulatory features, thus gaining additional insight into what the child had learned well, what he was in the process of learning, and what he had not yet acquired in comparison with standard English.

To consider syntax as the highest level of analysis seemed incomplete to me, since this would have distorted the nature of the data. I have therefore attempted a discourse analysis, selecting paragraphs as the linguistic units to be treated in such a manner as to show the hierarchical orderings of language functions.

Language in the Crib, however, may have relevance beyond the limiting nature of a case study. I have consulted a good deal of literature on child language in order to draw comparisons with data reported by other investigators and thus try to contribute further to our knowledge of language development in children, generally.

Language in the Crib is presented here in still another sense, namely, the development of inner speech. I have tried to show that the language recorded is inner speech for the child – although vocal – as this stage of development would lead one to expect. Furthermore, just as in our adult inner speech we usually imagine an interlocutor, so do the infant's soliloquies take on the nature of a dialogue, perhaps the primary form of language.

To the people and institutions whose invaluable assistance contributed to the completion of this work, I am deeply grateful. I can do no more than indicate a small measure of my appreciation here. Before and during the entire period of research I had the benefit of frequent and lengthy discussions with Roman Jakobson, who instructed and encouraged me with unfailing patience and kindness. His ideas and suggestions are incorporated in the text, above and beyond the references to his published works. Jakobson's own work on child language has become classic in the field, and it is the cornerstone of my work. Without his pioneering work on language functions, my interpretations would not have been possible. I feel the deepest gratitude to him for his support of my efforts.

I have discussed extensively most of this material with Morris Halle, and have benefited greatly by his suggestions. I owe a special debt to George A. Miller, who, in addition to inviting me to the Harvard Center for Cognitive Studies to complete my study, has kindly read the manuscript and offered his comments. I also wish to acknowledge J. S. Bruner's interest, criticism, and suggestions during my stay at Harvard.

I want to acknowledge particularly the generosity of my colleagues at Stanford University. Dorothy Huntington, Alphonse Juilland, Cornelius H. van Schooneveld, and Patrick Suppes were most generous with their time and assistance. Elise Belenky was of great help with the statistical work, devoting many hours of her time to the manuscript.

Perhaps most important, my thanks go to the unwitting subject, my son Anthony, and to my husband for his patience and his assistance in preparing this text.

This book was supported in part by funds granted by Public Health Research Grant No. MH 05120-02 from the National Institutes of Health, United States Public Health Service to Harvard University, Center for Cognitive Studies.

Stanford, California
October, 1962

RUTH H. WEIR

TABLE OF CONTENTS

FOREWORD BY A PSYCHOLOGIST

I am grateful to Dr. Weir for offering me this opportunity to record some of the impressions I formed while talking with her and while reading her descriptions of the pre-sleep monologues from her young son. Although I can claim no competence in the scientific study of child development, I have tried for several years to keep generally informed about work in psycholinguistics and am at least superficially acquainted with most of the psychological theories that have been proposed to explain how children acquire their native language. Thus I have approached Dr. Weir's work with certain prejudices and sensitivities that may, if only by their naïveté, highlight aspects or implications of this research that would not seem as interesting to the author herself. Sometimes it can be helpful merely to express surprise at the right instant. That, perhaps, is the kind of contribution I can make here.

Psychologists seem to have a special knack for discovering things about children that everybody else knew already. When Sigmund Freud forced his contemporaries to recognize the existence of infantile sexuality, their initial reaction was a shocked, "Can this really be true?" and when the evidence of every experienced nurse testified that it was indeed true, their second reaction was, "Why has no one pointed this out before?" Dr. Weir's discoveries arouse few of the emotional undertones that Freud's did and it may be stretching a point to compare her work with his, but certainly the same two questions arise, in the same order, when one reads the following pages. These two questions express the first of the surprises that Dr. Weir's book held in store for me.

Is it really true? I tried asking some discreet questions of my friends who have children around the age of two or three. They understood immediately what I was asking about and wondered why I should ever have doubted that such soliloquies occur. Even my own wife, who is an authority on how little I know about children, was surprised to hear my questions.

"*Everybody* knows that children talk to themselves before they fall asleep at night," she told me. "If you had read A. A. Milne as much as I have, you wouldn't be so surprised." And with that she produced a tattered copy of *Now We Are Six* and recited the following lines:

So – here I am in the dark alone,
　　There's nobody here to see;
　　　　I think to myself,
　　　　I play to myself
　　And nobody knows what I say to myself;
Here I am in the dark alone,
　　What is it going to be?
I can think whatever I like to think,
I can play whatever I like to play,
I can laugh whatever I like to laugh,
　　There's nobody here but me.

I'm talking to a rabbit...
　　I'm talking to the sun...
I think I am a hundred –
　　I'm one.
I'm lying in a forest...
　　I'm lying in a cave...
I'm talking to a Dragon...
　　I'm BRAVE.
I'm lying on my left side...
　　I'm lying on my right...
I'll play a lot tomorrow...
　　. . . . .
I'll think a lot tomorrow...
　　. . . . .
I'll laugh...
　　　　　a lot...
　　　　　　tomorrow...
　　　　　　(Heigh-ho!)
　　　　　　　　Goodnight.

I refuse to think of A. A. Milne as a scientist (a scientist would not describe a two-and-one-half year old child in a book entitled *Now We Are Six*) or to believe that he listened to his children with a tape recorder, but he does seem to have noticed the same kind of verbal play that Dr. Weir overheard and, in his own way, to have recorded his observations. I was, therefore, convinced. I accepted the fact that young children commonly, perhaps universally, talk aloud when left alone in the dark before they go to sleep. Dr. Weir, my friends, my wife, and A. A. Milne couldn't all be wrong.

My second surprise has not been so easily resolved. Why have I heard so little about these pre-sleep monologues from the experts on children's language? In the case of Freud's discoveries we can easily imagine that polite gentility kept the true facts about infantile sexuality out of the public eye. But that explanation will not work here. There is nothing dirty or embarrassing about bedtime monologues. Apparently they were never reported and analyzed before because nobody thought it was either interesting or important to do so. Now that I have had a chance to study

Dr. Weir's manuscript I consider that to have been a case of very poor judgment, and I wonder what factors might have contributed to it.

One possible explanation comes to mind and, although it reflects little credit upon psychology, it may be worth developing briefly. Children are very complicated things and there is simply not enough manpower available to study *everything* they do. Anyone who undertakes to study them is forced to make some very realistic decisions about what is and what is not worth his time and effort. Such decisions are not made without careful rationalization, and an important basis for that rationalization must be the general conception one holds about human nature and human development. Among psychologists in the United States there has been general agreement that language learning is much like any other kind of learning. That is to say, we have usually assumed that language learning depends critically upon a supporting environment that will respond to the child's vocalizations, that will approve or correct, that will reinforce successes and extinguish failures until the proper stimulus-response connections are established. Guided by this general conception of the language-learning process, some psychologists have even dreamed of teaching animals – chimpanzees, porpoises – to talk with us by providing the right kind of environmental support and tutoring.

Now, it seems reasonably obvious that anyone who holds this view of the language-learning process will assume immediately that nothing important could possibly take place when a child is isolated in a dark room. If you want to study the development of language, they would say, study the intimately interacting mother-child dyad where the familiar processes of teaching and learning are going forward with great energy and efficiency. In my opinion, Dr. Weir's observations clearly indicate that any such simple conception of language learning is flatly wrong.

And that was my third surprise.

After many years of reading psychological theories about the environmental events that strengthen or weaken various stimulus-response associations, I was completely unprepared to encounter a two-year-old boy who – all alone – corrected his own pronunciations, drilled himself on consonant clusters, and practiced substituting his small vocabulary into fixed sentence frames. The gap between this child's reported behavior and all I had been led to expect from the books of Pavlov, Watson, Thorndike, Hull, and other association theorists was more than I knew how to cope with. If you read Dr. Weir's report with an eye for how you might build an explanation in terms of rewarding or punishing stimulus-response connections, you may get some feeling for the difficulties that young Anthony poses for the psychological theory of human learning.

But let me not over-state my perplexity and dismay. Anthony Weir did not spend 24 hours a day in the dark by himself; if he had, of course, he would not have learned to talk. Obviously, the source of his information about the language he was learning came to him from his social contacts during the remainder of his day. But his rehearsal persisted even after social contacts were withdrawn and under conditions where only the pleasure of increased competence could have served as his reward. Moreover, his rehearsal concentrated on aspects of language – phonology, morphology, syntax – that most parents do not understand well enough to "teach" in any manner other than by example, and that could not, therefore, have been a perseveration of exercises devised for him during the day. Anthony's persistent, combinatorial play was the surprising thing to me.

My fourth surprise was a bit different in character and if I wished to preserve a semblance of sophistication I suppose I would suppress it completely. But I will confess that the magnitude of Dr. Weir's undertaking seems somewhat depressing and I greatly admire her willingness to undertake it. Admittedly, I have seen even longer accounts by linguists of the utterances of a single child, but this one is, after all, an analysis of only a small fraction of a child's total output, and for only a few months of his life. When I project this to include the full description of language learning in a single child over a period of several years, it grows to staggering size. And when I project that further to include several aspects of the child's development, or to include the verbal development of several children, the whole enterprise seems literally monstrous. To pursue those larger goals with the methods of analysis used here would be extremely expensive; someone should consider costs and estimate the eventual profits involved in so detailed and careful an approach. As I said above, psychologists characteristically try to avoid this difficulty by formulating specific hypotheses which then they try to test. Given a specific question, techniques of data reduction are possible to bring the task within reach of our resources. But part of the danger of this economy, as I complained above, is that our hypotheses often blind us to obvious facts that are not entailed by the particular hypotheses we are testing. I must admit that I see no simple solution to this methodological dilemma – the use of digital computers to handle such huge masses of data is still little more than a wishful dream – but if linguists continue along their present direction they are sure to encounter the Tristram Shandy effect.

My fifth and final comment cannot be so easily described as surprising, unless I claim to be surprised by my own ingratitude. Having just been given a clean and careful piece of work that opened my eyes and corrected some of my long-standing misconceptions, I should not immediately ask for something more. But I cannot completely suppress my desire to understand better what it is that children *know* about the language they speak. The present monologues are, after all, rather poor evidence on that score. The vocabulary is smaller than in the child's everyday speech, and so must be far smaller than the vocabulary he knows well enough to recognize when he hears it. His activities are a kind of self-imposed drill – a playful drill, admittedly – that must serve to bring what he already knows up to a level of complete automaticity; they do not enable us to see very far into the linguistic complexities that he could understand if someone else produced them. His ability to correct his own errors in the course of this verbal play suggests rather strongly that he must know a great deal more than he is actually producing for us.

What Dr. Weir overheard in her nursery has given us a revealing glimpse behind the scenes. We find some rather unexpected kinds of self-instruction taking place, and language-learning suddenly seems a great deal more complicated than many psychologists hoped it would be. Such a glimpse is both valuable and tantalizing. If we can see that much of what is going on, why can we not see it all? Is there no way to study the language the child knows by concentrating on what he can understand, rather than on what he can generate? The question is scarcely a fair one to put to Dr. Weir, for that was not her goal at all, so I address it quite broadly to the psycholinguistic community at large. How can we discover what a child *knows* about his language? What are the most sensitive indicators of linguistic competence that we can devise? The recent growth of interest in the linguistic analyses of the child's language could, I believe, profit considerably if the people doing the work would put this question higher on their list of priorities than it seems to have been in the past. But such remarks are unfairly critical at the present time, however, and ill serve to express my real appreciation for what has already been accomplished.

It was indeed a fortunate occurrence for those of us at the Harvard Center for Cognitive Studies when, through the good offices of Professor Roman Jakobson, we were able to be hosts to Dr. Weir during the final stages of her work on this book. She has opened up a new road into the mind of the young child, and we look forward eagerly to the traffic it will someday bear.

Harvard University   GEORGE A. MILLER
Cambridge, Massachusetts
July 1962

ANTHONY'S CONTRIBUTION TO LINGUISTIC THEORY

The half-dream soliloquies of the two-year-old Anthony, recorded on tape, transcribed and analyzed by his mother, the Stanford linguist Ruth Weir, lead us into a fascinating and hitherto unexplored province of language. As Vygotsky's profound investigation of inner speech has disclosed, the so-called egocentric talk of children is an "intermediate link between overt and inner speech." We have been taught that "egocentric speech is inner speech in its functions; it is speech on its way inward." In a child's development, speech proves to be "interiorized psychologically before it is interiorized physically." Anthony adds a new and apposite angle to Vygotsky's discovery: the transition from overt to inner speech displays a graduated order.

Our overt speech is directed toward an outside addressee and requires a listener. Our inner speech obviously meets with no listener and is not supposed to reach an actual addressee. Children's egocentric talk has no concern for any outside addressee, but it tolerates, not seldom even favors the presence of a listener, whereas their pre-sleep speech does imply the absence of human hearers. It is meant as a genuine soliloquy, the speaker's *privatissimum*, ready to be cut off as soon as he realizes that his solitude has been broken. Hence such verbal activities of the child in his crib bring us a step nearer to true inner speech, namely, to its most hidden and perplexing variety, the speech in dreams. The soliloquies of Anthony falling asleep give us a suggestive insight into the speech of our dreams, which in the whole of our verbal behavior plays a no less vital part than do dreams themselves in our mental life.

For linguistic study in this border zone of inner speech and dream speech, the various specimens of reduction and condensation are particularly inviting. One could hardly find a more gratifying text for the investigation of radical ellipsis on the different levels of language — fragmentation not only of sentences, clauses, and phrases but also of words used side by side in their full and truncated form: *Anthony* and *Antho-*, *dance* and [dæn-], *donkey* and [dɔn-].

Sometimes it is difficult to separate features typical of inner speech in general from those which specify the speech development in young children. Nonetheless, here one immediately detects new and valuable clues to the study of child language. According to Ruth Weir's subtle observations, the lowering of the cognitive, referential function in Anthony's soliloquies brings to the fore all the other language functions. A typical property of child speech is an intimate interlacement of two functions — the metalingual and the poetic one — which in adult language are quite separate. Although the pivotal role which in language learning belongs to the acquisition of metalanguage is well-known, the predominantly metalingual concern of the somnolent child with language itself comes as a great surprise. It shows us the ways in which language is gradually mastered. Many of the recorded passages bear a striking resemblance to the grammatical and lexical exercises in textbooks for self-instruction in foreign languages:

> "What color — What color blanket — What color mop — What color glass.... Not the yellow blanket — The white.... It's not black — It's yellow... Not yellow — Red.... Put on a blanket — White blanket — And yellow blanket — Where's yellow blanket.... Yellow blanket — Yellow light.... There is the light — Where is the light — Here is the light."

Selection of modifiers for one head word and selection of head words for one modifier: "Big and little — Little Bobby — Little Nancy — Big Nancy." Antonyms (either contraries or contradictories) follow each other: "On the blanket — Under the blanket.... Berries — Not berries.... Too hot — Not too hot." The disjunctive *or* is missing. Members of a paradigmatic set (either lexical or grammatical), joined to each other by a conjunctive *and* or without any conjunction at all, are open to selection: "Hat for Anthony and Bobo — For Bobo — Not for Anthony — Hat for Anthony." The desired choice is finally achieved: Anthony is the designated proprietor.

He practices confronting different grammatical forms of the same vocable, especially of the same verb: "*Fix* the music — Music is *fixed*.... Cobbers *crossed* the street — Cobbers always *cross* the street [with the adverb manifestly opposing the present to the preterit].... Anthony *write* — Pencil's always *writing* [pair followed and supported by a parallel couple: *smiling — smile*].... *Take* off — *Took* off.. *See — I see*.... Where *are you going — I am going*." Vocables used both in verbal and nominal function are juxtaposed: "Can bite — Bite — Have a bite.... Broke the vacuum — The broke — Get some broke — Alice broke the baby fruit [*break* is generally replaced by the alternant *broke*]. Nouns and verbs are deliberately used side by side with their anaphoric substitutes: "Take the monkey — Take it.... Stop the ball — Stop it.... Go for glasses — Go for them.... Don't jump — Don't ticklish — Don't do that."

Grammatical alternations and purely phonemic minimal pairs are purposely strung together: /tək/ — /tʊk/ — /bæk/ — /tʊk/ — /tek/ — /bʊk/... /wɑt/ — /nɑt/ — /naɪt/. *Light* and *like* or *likes* and *lights* attract each other. *Ba*ck and *we*t are blended in the portmanteau word *Babette*. Thus in the child's pre-sleep speech, lexical, morphological, and phonemic sets appear to be projected from the paradigmatic axis into the syntagmatic one.

In chains of repetitive sentences the variation within each pair may be limited to one single unit:

There's a hat
There's another
There's hat
There another hat
That's a hat.

The whimsical interchange of two syntactical operations — properly singled out by Ruth Weir as a "build-up" and a "break-down" — are patently similar to the play of Anthony's coevals who turn by turn assemble and dismantle their toys. The gradual constituting of a sentence from its originally separate and autonomous components, each with a predicative function, and on the other hand the progressive fill-up and expansion of primary sentence frames are equally instructive procedures which bring to light the mechanism of syntactical learning and training. How informative, for instance, are Anthony's sentence drafts, where the place of the noun is signaled by the article, while the noun itself has not yet been selected:

> "Anthony take the — Take the book.... This is the — This is the — Book... That's a — That's a — That's a kitty — That a Fifi here.... Mommy get some — Mommy get some — Soap."

Predicate phrases without expressed subject or with a merely deictic pronominal subject (*That's a kitty*) and transitional forms between subject-predicate declarative sentences and vocative-imperative sequences indicate how explicit two-term propositions may embarass the somnolent child. The type of sentence he prefers is a mere annex to an implied or required situation.

Anthony's bedtime play with language as a condensed summary of his day imperatively calls for further investigation — how far such self-educational linguistic games are usual among dozing children. Yet however prominent is the metalingual function in Ruth Weir's records, she is right to consider the copresence of other functions. In particular, the last and longest of Anthony's "paragraphs" discussed by his mother, with its eight times recurring leitmotiv "Daddy dance," is not only an elaborate lesson in grammar but also a moving and poignant psychoanalytic document, exploiting the child's whole inventory of expressive devices, and above all it is a true and beautiful poetic composition tantamount to the masterpieces of infant art — verbal and pictorial.

Harvard University   ROMAN JAKOBSON
Massachusetts Institute of Technology

INTRODUCTION

This book deals with certain aspects of the language of a two-and-one-half year old child. The investigation focuses on language, both as a skill, that is, in its distinctive function, and as a means of communication, that is, in its significative function. The child's language is studied as a self-contained system under special circumstances, namely, just before he falls asleep at night, and his linguistic system at the time can be called his own "idiolect".

Since the child is learning the American English spoken in his surroundings, and since the child of course speaks at other times as well, some comparisons between the child's language of the pre-sleep monologues and his day language on the one hand, and the language of the adults around him will be made.

Modern linguistic science defines language as an arbitrary system of vocal symbols by which members of a speech community communicate and cooperate. It is this system, or "langue" as Ferdinand de Saussure has called it, which is being investigated here. While the individual speech acts, or Saussurian "parole", serve as a basis for the investigation, it is only their relationships within the English system of the child which are of primary concern.

In this context, phonetics, the science of speech sounds, is only auxiliary to phonemics, that is, the discipline of linguistics which deals with the distinctive sounds features characteristic of a given language. The phonemic principle is crucial to this study since one aspect of the investigation involves the phonemic contrasts utilized in the child's language on the one hand, and the phonetic variations used in different circumstances within the child's phonemic range, on the other. Language, in all its aspects, is a patterned structure. Hence, babbling, the young child's unstructured making of sounds, is of no relevance in the establishment of phonemic contrasts; however, some babbling occurs in our data and will be dealt with separately.

In addition to the establishment of the child's phonemes, their patterning is studied in terms of clusters occurring in his speech. However, since the phoneme is a bundle of simultaneous articulatory features which appear in combination with each other, it must be assumed that the child learns these important subphonemic elements so that his phonemes can be properly actualized. It is a relevant question to ask, which of these features have been learned well by the child, which ones are still unstable, or which ones he still ignores.

The hierarchical nature of a linguistic structure imposes as the next step the study of forms and their meanings. Again, the issue revolves around the child's morphemes and words and their variants within his self-contained system, although some comparison with his day speech and the structure of forms in adult English will be made. In his morphology and vocabulary, the combinatory possibilities allow the child some freedom which had not been available to him in the phonology and he makes limited use of them, in word coinage. His selection of linguistic entities will be described in examining his linguistic system in a number of functions.

The arrangement of forms, or the syntactic constructions and sentence types, present an interesting system in the child's language, often mastered, apparently, before the forms themselves. The relative freedom of possible combinations into sentences, and the great freedom of combinatory possibilities into even larger units give the child the opportunity for a good deal of linguistic exercise.

We would, however, be remiss if we restricted our linguistic analysis to phonology and grammar, without dealing with the various functions of language. Jakobson (1960) has outlined six such functions, corresponding to the constituents of the speech events, and we will apply these to our data. In order to do that, the distinctive elements of sounds and forms must be analyzed first as the system underlying the various functions of the child's language. Freud's "sense in nonsense" (1960) in dealing with language in the description of the joke technique is relevant to an understanding of the nature of the monologues. Just as the pleasure in a joke can be derived from play with words, so does the child enjoy play with words. But analogous to the joke, where there is sense in nonsense in the deliberate use of word play, the child's word play also makes sense. The pleasure of play is structured so that it serves as a systematic linguistic exercise.

The scope of this work is a case study, dealing with the speech of one child over a limited period of time. The author intends to continue these studies with new materials from two younger children when they reach approximately the same two-and-one-half years of age.

THE NATURE OF THE DATA

The data gathered for this study consist of pre-sleep monologues of Anthony, a two-and-one-half year old child, with no adult present, recorded on tape by remote control. It was the child's habit, after being put to bed at night, to engage in soliloquies of various length. In other words, in this period of solitude, he carried on a conversation with himself. As an adult counterpart of such a dialogue, we could point to the end of *Ulysses* where Joyce reproduces a half-conscious speech of an adult. Usually with adults, this is not vocal; it is inner speech. In the case of the child, it is also inner, but vocal, speech before falling asleep, but as Vygotsky (1962) has pointed out, this is an earlier step in the linguistic development, and hence, it is still vocal. This vocal social speech then turns into inner speech at a higher developmental level. The nature of the soliloquies is not monologues *in abstracto*, but a dialogue with imaginary interlocutors or the child's assuming both roles in the exchange. Slama-Cazacu's "Le dialogue est la forme la plus normale et, en tout cas, la forme fondamentale d'existence du langage" (1961) is fully borne out by our data.

Anthony's monologues can then be characterized as consisting in part of imaginary dialogues with people he knows or with toys he owns, and partly as statements addressed to no one in particular. It is vocal speech with people or toys that exist in reality, but whom he in fact does not see. Peirce (1933) has suggested that "thinking always proceeds in the form of a dialogue" (p. 10), as has Vygotsky, who referred to inner speech as taking the form of a dialogue. The monologues are vocalized thought or inner speech, hence the primary structure of a dialogue is not surprising.

Linguistically, we ask what are the characteristics of vocalized inner speech of a child of this age when he is in his own surroundings, with his toys, by himself? Is he still preoccupied with sounds, similar to the babbling stage, or does his interest center on forms and meanings? Is he practising morphologic and syntactic patterns, with substitution lists drawn from his own vocabulary and experience? What are the functions of his language? Is there any overall structure underlying these soliloquies? We shall attempt to deal with these and other questions in this work.

Although we do not have detailed records covering Anthony's day speech over the period of the recordings, we have kept notes to make some comparisons possible. They will be utilized throughout the study, but one aspect seems pertinent to mention here, namely, the question of babbling. Jespersen (1922) has defined three stages in the linguistic development of the child: the screaming time, the babbling time, and the talking time. Jakobson (1941) in his important work on child language also carefully distinguishes between language on the one hand, and babbling on the other which he calls an articulatory exercise. Goldstein (1948) defines babbling as having no relation to the outer world, which certainly sets it apart from the nature of language.

In Anthony's day speech, babbling had ceased to occur several months prior to the recordings. In the monologues, however, babbling does occur occasionally, often soon before the child falls asleep. It is a somewhat different babbling though from the younger infant's undifferentiated articulatory exercise. This babbling is mostly confined to possible phonetic realizations of English, with the exception of a palatal stop and a palatal nasal, which otherwise also occur in Anthony's speech, but structured as variants of a phonemic system. The system remains essentially the same, but the predilections are different.

The babbling in this twilight zone is apparently a relapse to an earlier linguistic stage of development. This is also parallelled by relapses in other areas of the child's development at the time and can be partly attributed to the presence of the baby, his younger brother which caused him a good deal of anguish at the time of the recordings.

However, more generally, regression in dreams is well-known to psychologists, and since the monologues occurred just on the threshold of sleep, they can be partially likened to dreams.

The strictly solitary nature of the material is violated twice by the presence of his father in the room during the recordings and an ensuing conversation, by an occasional verbal reply of a person passing by the child's room, and several times by an adult fulfilling the child's request, for example, giving him a bottle of milk. Initially, this material was not included in the analysis, but was added subsequently to the phonemic analysis, since no difference from the phonology of the monologue was found in the sound pattern.

Another deviation from complete solitude was the child's reaction to outside noises. For example, when the dog started to bark, Anthony would react with an imitation of his barking or he would say the dog's name. Similarly, when the baby in the room next to his would cry, he would embark on a discussion of the baby.

The child's language in the recordings is completely spontaneous, that is to say he was at no time aware that his speech was recorded since he was completely unfamiliar with such a concept. He never even heard his voice played back since all transcription was made by listening through earphones. Thus the question of the child's awareness of being observed and the consequent validity of data, often discussed in the literature on child language, is not relevant here.

It should be pointed out that our corpus is recorded material under less than perfect recording conditions, in spite of the quality of equipment. Therefore, occasionally the speech is unintelligible either due to low volume or to extraneous noise, and cannot be transcribed.

THE CHILD AND HIS SURROUNDINGS

Anthony is the first-born child in the family now numbering three boys. At the time of the recordings, Anthony was between 28 and 30 months old. His younger brother, David, was an infant less than ten months old.

Anthony walked fairly early, taking his first steps unaided at about ten months. His size has been about average for his age, his build wiry, his physical strength about average. His interests and apparent mental age have always been somewhat ahead of his chronological age. Being the first-born in the family, Anthony's social adjustment has also been slightly on the precocious side, since a good deal of individual adult attention was directed toward him.

No detailed records were kept on his speech development prior to the recordings; but his development seemed in line with his progress in other areas. In addition, he appeared a highly "verbal" child – as observed by the family and others – enjoying talking and using language a great deal. Except for adding "-ie" suffixes, like "doggie", "horsie", etc., and using an expression like "night-night" for "good night", and for often avoiding personal pronouns, baby talk was not used in the home, nor in communicating with him. No peculiar language developed between him and his home environment, just the usual substitution of proper names and kinship terms for personal pronouns, e.g., "Anthony" instead of "you" or "I", "Daddy" rather than the proper pronoun, etc.

From the start Anthony's imitations were quite accurate, and his speech was readily intelligible to outsiders without undue "interpretations" by members of the family. Of course, a number of sound substitutions occurred as well as peculiar morphologic and syntactic constructions. On the whole, Anthony's speech was clear and intelligible.

In his home environment, Anthony was exposed to a variety of linguistic backgrounds, although he was addressed only in English. That was also the only language used in the home among the adults. The only native speaker of English, however, was his father who was born in the Boston area and who received almost all of his schooling there, including college and graduate school. Two characteristics of his phonemic system should be pointed out since they are relevant to the child's speech. One is his use of post-vocalic /r/ in accordance with other American English dialects, that is to say, it does occur in a word like *part*, and it does not at the end of a word like *idea*. The other is his use of a non-high back phoneme in words like *top*, *not*, rather than the /a/ which occurs frequently in American English.

Anthony's mother came to the United States from her native Czechoslovakia in 1947. Her English is definitely non-native, although she attended college and graduate school in the United States. The mother's native languages are Czech and German, neither of which she used in talking to Anthony, but they do mark her English. Particularly characteristic of the non-native features of her English are the frequent neutralization of the feature of voicing in word-final position, the use of non-English intonation patterns, and the phonetic realization of the phoneme /r/. The latter is a variety of a tap rather than any of the types of standard English /r/ as described in Krapp (1919). This characteristic, however, was not usually imitated by the child, whereas the former two were. She also has a tendency to equate the cluster of /ŋg/ with the phoneme /ŋ/ or vice versa, a common feature of non-standard English.

In addition to his parents, Anthony was also exposed to the language of the live-in help. Almost up to the time of the recordings, from his fifth month, Anthony was partially in the care of a Swedish girl who spoke British English with definite Swedish traces. Four characteristics were particularly pronounced in her speech: she used the English phonemes /y/ and /j/ interchangeably since they do not constitute phonemic contrasts in her native Swedish; her intonation patterns were definitely non-English; her pronunciation of words like *grass* was British English rather than American; she had a definite tendency not to use glides where they otherwise occur typically in standard English. In addition, she always pronounced the child's name with an alveolar stop /t/ rather than with the interdental spirant /θ/.

During the time of the recordings, a Danish visitor with fair skill in English with definite Danish traces lived with the family. In addition to the instability of vowel nuclei, similar to the Swedish girl's speech, two non-native features in her English were particularly noticeable: a Danish realization and hence resulting confusion of the /s/ and /š/ phonemes of English since Danish has no such phonemic contrast, and the neutralization of the feature of voicing in any position, substituting the feature of aspiration as contrastive instead.

Like most children of his age, Anthony rarely played actively or talked at length with his peers. Most of his play was solitary or with the adults in the home, his brother being too young to join. In the company of other children of his age, Anthony would play alongside them, their physical presence being enough to satisfy him.

The physical arrangement in the home consisted of Anthony's own room connected by an intercommunication system with the rest of the house. He spent a good deal of time by himself, in his own room, having been taught that this was his proper domain. He requested and was given some toys at bedtime to keep overnight in his crib. He would usually take a bottle of milk with him to bed. One other habit should perhaps be mentioned since it occasionally interfered with the recordings or became the only audible signal, that of what we called "rocking". He would get on his hands and knees, in a crawling position, and move back and forth for some time rhythmically, shaking the crib and objects around it.

Shortly after the last recording, the family went on a vacation for about three weeks. During that time, Anthony shared a room with his younger brother and the Danish visitor who lived with the family. In this environment, any pre-sleep speech could not be classified as solitary monologues, of course. Interestingly enough, upon returning home, he never resumed his monologues, thus making further gathering of data impossible.

This may be partly due to having been deprived of his privacy in the previous weeks; on the other hand, Köhler (1926), who also briefly mentions a child's pre-sleep monologues in her work, found them at their peak between 2:5 and 2:7, and stopped completely at 2:8 (p. 104).

The family has owned the same dog and cat during the whole of Anthony's life, and they are permitted relative freedom inside the house and in the outside play area. Anthony has commented frequently about them and sometimes talks to them, although more to the dog than to the cat.

For about two years, Anthony has shown a strong attachment to his blankets, taking careful count of them, identifying them by color and by wearing one of them after the fashion of a toga in the house and sometimes outside at play. He continues this form of behavior even now.

While he rarely, if ever, sucked his thumb, Anthony remained dependent upon the bottle almost to his third birthday. He was late in toilet training and could be said to be "trained" at about the time he gave up the bottle.

DESCRIPTION OF RECORDING EQUIPMENT AND PROCEDURE

The basic corpus underlying this study are nine tapes recorded between June and August, 1961. The equipment was an Ampex Universal Tape Recorder/Reproducer, Model 960 for some of the tapes, and a Magnecorder Model PT6A with a PT6J amplifier for recording. The Ampex was used in conjunction with a Dynakit Stereo 70 Amplifier and Dynakit Stereo Preamplifier Model PAS-2. The recording microphone was an Electro-Voice Model 418 used with a 30 foot extension line and placed in an upholstered chair in Anthony's bedroom. Koss Model SP-3 stereophonic earphones were used for the playback in conjunction with the Ampex equipment.

Anthony's bedroom is about 12 feet by 12 feet and has two undraped plasterboard walls and one fully draped glass wall. The floor is vinyl tile, uncarpeted. The ceiling is plywood with exposed wood beams placed at about a 25° angle above horizontal. A similar room adjoins Anthony's room, and is separated by a folding wooden door known by its brand name as a "Pella-wood, folding door". The door was closed, separating the rooms at all times during the recording. A standard door, leading from Anthony's room to the hallway, was usually kept partially open. Since no light was on, either in the child's room or in the hall, and since there is not street light in front of the house, the light level in Anthony's room was very low.

The tapes were Scotch Brand, No. 111, All-Purpose, Plastic running at $7\frac{1}{2}$ inches per second. Some recordings at $3\frac{3}{4}$ inches per second were also made but were not as satisfactory; nevertheless, they were usable.

The tape recorder and all controls were outside the child's room. A thirty foot cable connected the microphone placed on a chair at about two feet from the child's crib. The length of the cable necessarily reduced the fidelity of the recording, but no other satisfactory solution could be found. Additional recording difficulties were encountered: the child would occasionally throw a pillow or blanket at the microphone, thus muffling the recording, sometimes to the point of unintelligibility. Also, the child was in the habit of rocking the crib and making noise which became at times so intense as to drown out any other signal.

He was at the time unfamiliar with the concept of recording. At first, he identified the microphone as a vacuum cleaner, probably due to its shape. Later he called it a microphone, as he heard other members of the family refer to it. Once in a while, he would ask for it when he was being put to bed, but usually this was not necessary, since it was put there regularly. The controls on the tape recorder were started as soon as he began his monologues. This could easily be ascertained without the necessity of the physical presence near him, since his room was connected by an intercommunication system to several other parts of the house.

The phonetic transcriptions made from the recordings serve as a basis for all further analysis. They are reproduced in rough phonetic transcription in the Appendix.

PHONOLOGY

In this description of the phonemic system of a child, it must be borne in mind that we are dealing with the speech of a single child, at a given period of time, under clearly defined circumstances, as described earlier. Therefore, generalizations as to children's phonemic speech development must be considered in this particular context. Some of the observations found in the pertinent literature are confirmed, others are not. This does not mean that some of the statements in the literature are incorrect or that some of our conclusions are doubtful. It must be clear that our treatment is *not* based on a comparison of different stages of his linguistic development but is rather an attempt to describe the child's linguistic system on the basis of data collected over a relatively short period of time. The phonemic and grammatical analyses are to serve as the basis for a further discussion of the various functions of this specialized language.

It seems more convenient to start the phonemic analysis from larger units, and, by breaking them up, to arrive at the minimal functional unit, the phoneme and its constituent features. This is also more consistent with the linguistic development of the child, which does not proceed from using single phonemes or building blocks to arrive at larger units, but starts with a larger unit which then is broken up into phonemic constituents and contrasts (Velten, 1943; Carroll, 1961). Our starting point, therefore, will be the phonologically defined sentence as it appears in the child's speech. That presupposes a discussion of prosody which follows.

PROSODY

Under prosody, we include intonation, pauses, and stress. Although length also occurs in the child's speech, it is not discussed here, but will be taken up together with complex syllabic nuclei since its patterning is in variation with them.

Intonation and Pauses

It is frequently noted in observations on the linguistic development of the child that intonation or sentence melody is one of the earliest linguistic features acquired by a child. In our observations, this is certainly true as far as the purely imitative phonetic

aspect of language acquisition is concerned. If a stimulus word or sentence with a
rising intonation is given to the child for imitation, he will repeat it with just that. If
a falling contour is used, the child will reproduce that just as easily. We have
observed this from the time the child began to use language, from the end of his
first year on.

It seems, however, that previous investigators have not tried to analyze intonation
from a structural point of view. The need for more research on this aspect is pointed
out, for example, by Carroll (1961).

Whether we follow a description of intonation in terms of pitch levels and junctures
following Pike (1947) or Trager (1951), or whether we adopt an analysis by contours
as Bolinger (1955) suggests, it seems impossible for our data to identify the functionally significant units unequivocally. Roughly, there are three pitch levels, but they
are not used contrastively. A fourth level occurs, higher than any others, in calls and
urgent requests. This pitch we can classify best as part of the emotive function of
language. In terms of contours, the most frequent one is falling; next in frequency is a
rising contour; a sustained one is found least frequently. But here again we were
unable to discover a functional relationship among them as we do in standard
English. As a matter of fact, to take an utterance and assign it a certain meaning on
the basis of standard English intonation is most misleading. One of the reasons for
the rather confused picture of intonations is undoubtedly due to the models the child
imitates, that is his mother's and the Swedish girl's non-native intonation which we
have mentioned earlier. However, a certain amount of regularity of occurrence of
sustained contours with what we have later (p. 81 ff.) called break-downs and build-ups

does occur, e.g., *Big bottle* has a sustained contour following *Another big bottle*, as

does *What color* preceding *What color blanket*.

Nevertheless, intonation does perform a certain function, but on a different level:
it serves as a marker of sentence boundaries. The syntactic structures found in the
corpus are varied, but a sentence can most readily be defined by an intonation
contour with either a final fall or final rise, or by a sustained pitch, each followed by
pauses of varying length. The relative length of the pauses becomes particularly
significant in our discourse analysis, and the sentence-final pauses are quite consistent
in length. There are few instances where a very short pause occurs within the sentence
as we have just defined it. The intonation contour is then interrupted by it, and completed after the pause. Some instances of such an occurrence would be:

all through | *all done*

then first lunch | *then office*

not yellow | *red*

Stress

Only two contrastive levels of stress can be identified in the child's linguistic system, phonemically stressed and unstressed. The closest example to a minimal pair distinguishing stress would be [áɪdì] "Idey" (proper name) and [àɪdíə] "idea". The child uses, however, contrastive stress in accordance with standard English consistently and correctly. That is to say, he places his heavy stress in standard English fashion, e.g., [rɛ́dì] "ready" or [tʰúfì:t] "Twofeet", and does not make mistakes. On the other hand, he does have a tendency to overuse the feature of stress, that is, to place it on an additional syllable to the one bearing stress. Thus we have both [šàmpʰú:] and [šǽmpʰú:] "shampoo", the second example having two phonemically stressed syllables, whereas the first example bears the stress only on the syllable where we would expect it. In a longer unit, one in the succession of phonemically unstressed syllables may at times use a stronger variant of the phonetically weak stress: [mámì gǽv sèm mílk] "Mommy gave some milk" where [gǽv] uses this variant. A particularly weak variant, on the other hand, is found chiefly in the child's pronunciation of his own name [ǽntǒnì] "Anthony" which appears in a number of telescoped versions as well. We can then say that the feature of stress as opposed to no stress, has been well learned by the child, whereas the more complex contrastive use of various levels of stress has not.

In our phonemic transcription, only stressed syllables are marked with /´/, the syllables without marking being unstressed. Occurrences of overloud stress will be discussed as part of the emotive function of language.

ARTICULATORY FEATURES

In order to arrive at a more revealing picture of the child's structure of vowel and non-vowel phonemes, it is essential to view these phonemes as being constituted of bundles of articulatory features. Articulatory rather than acoustic features were chosen as the means for description. It should be pointed out, however, that no attempt will be made to identify distinctive features as such, the aim of this feature analysis being merely a description of articulatory sound features which the child uses well, of those which are still unstable in his system, and to observe which ones have not assumed as yet a contrastive function. The selection of the features dealt with is based on standard English.

With vowel phonemes, the following independent articulatory movements will be considered: tongue height, with three positions in relation to the oral cavity, called *high*, *mid* and *low* respectively; tongue position, named *front* closest to the lips, and moving backward, *central* and *back*; relative tautness of the organs of speech, *tense* or *lax* respectively; position of the lips during vowel production, the lips pursed or *rounded*, or spread *unrounded*; the relative duration of the vowel produced, or its *length*.

Non-vowels fall into two classes: glides and consonants. The glides are neither vowels nor consonants, but they pattern primarily as consonants, and can be described in terms of tongue position as *front*, *central*, or *back*. In regard to consonants, a general classification is *front* and *back*, that is, consonants produced between the lips and the beginning of the hard palate on the one hand, and from the hard palate on backward on the other. More specifically, the place of articulation will be determined as *bilabial*, *labiodental*, *interdental*, *alveolar*, *palatal*, or *velar*. The way a consonant is produced or the manner of articulation may be a *stop*, *spirant*, *affricate*, *liquid*, or *nasal*. Three accompanying features will be distinguished in addition: *voicing* or the presence or absence of the vibration of the vocal cords, *aspiration* or the noticeable puff of breath accompanying the articulation of a consonant, and the *release* or plosion of stop consonants.

VOWELS

The vowel sounds in this corpus fall into five classes which can properly be called phonemes for this idiolect, although they are not identical with the phonemes of any variety of standard adult English known to the author. We have called the phonetic realizations of the child's phonemes *variants*, and we will look at the features which are utilized in the production of these variants.

Phonetically, a relatively large number of variants can be found in a number of positions. For example, there are high front tense as well as high front lax vowels – for example, in [fikst⌐] and [wɪθ]; mid front tense and lax vowels, as in [bed⌐] and [gɛt]; low front and central vowels, as in [hæt⌐] and [tʰap⌐]; high central tense and lax vowels, as in [mɪlk⌐] and [wɪš]; a mid central vowel as in [bərd]; high back tense and lax vowels, as in [gud⌐] and [bʊk⌐]; and mid back open and close vowels, as in [go] and [dɔt⌐].

Functionally, both under stress and unstressed, contrasts are greatly reduced. The feature of rounding is an invariant, as we would expect and is obligatory with the back vowels. The central vowel /A/ is opposed to non-back vowels as well as back vowels, and in the later two, the opposition is high versus non-high. Thus, we have five vowel phonemes at the cardinal points of the vowel triangle, namely /I, E, A, O, U/. The contrasts can be exemplified by the following graphic representation:

$$\begin{array}{cc} I & U \\ E & O \\ & A \end{array}$$

This "reduced" vowel phoneme system, as compared to standard English analysis of vowels, can be expected in view of the findings of other investigations of children's language. Jakobson (1941) points out that the phonemic status of /æ/ is acquired relatively late by the English-speaking child due to the usually earlier acquired contrast of /a/ and /e/ (p. 43). Leopold (1953) states: "…the child learns to distinguish, passively and actively, low vowels from high vowels first, then the mid vowels, and eventually the breakdown of these three major levels into still more refined sub-divisions. It also appears that a twofold distinction between front and back vowels is made sooner than a three fold distinction between front, back and central vowels." Chao (1951) analyzing the Chinese spoken by a twenty-eight-month-old child, says: "The difficulty with the vowel system is that it is in a state of extreme flux, where the various changes from one stage to the next in the approach to adult language are not going on all in step, thus resulting in internal inconsistencies." (p. 32).

In spite of a wealth of material on sound production in young children, analyses in terms of phonemic contrasts and more particularly into the constituting subphonemic features, have been neglected by some investigators. Here we will attempt just such a description of vowels and non-vowels, taking up each phoneme separately.

The following will consist of a description of each phoneme, with its phonetic variants represented graphically, described phonetically, and charted as to frequency and place of occurrence; the variants will also be described with their main fluctua-tions. The number of occurrences are computed from the running text as it was transcribed from the tape recording. Each occurrence is counted, except for echo repetitions, that is, phonetically identical successive repetitions of the word or phrase. The place of occurrence is determined by word boundaries.[1]

In deciding to disregard echo repetitions for statistical purposes, it had to be determined whether they were scattered randomly throughout the corpus, or whether they occurred more often in one segment than in another. Four samples from the corpus were chosen randomly, and analyzed to this end. Including the repetitions, the samples varied in size from thirty-three to fifty-three sentences. A chi-square test was run, under the hypothesis that the proportion of repetitions was the same in each sample. With three degrees of freedom, chi-square was equal to 1.949, which is not significant. Hence, there seems to be no significant tendency for the repetitions to appear in one segment of the corpus rather than in another. The question whether one repetition was more likely than two or three repetitions, was also answered. In the sample used for the preceding test, the frequencies of none, one, two, and three repetitions were 123, 19, 4, and 2, respectively. Hence, it is apparent that the child is much more likely not to repeat a sentence or to repeat it once, rather than two or three times. The probability that he does repeat one or more times was estimated to be 25/148, or .17.

---

[1] In defining a *word*, we refer to Gleason (1961), p. 110: "An English word characteristically consists of a root and a stress morpheme, with or without derivational and inflectional affixes. Rather exceptionally there may be two or more roots, but there may be several derivational affixes. With very few exceptions no word has more than one inflectional suffix. Every word said in isolation normally has one and only one stress morpheme, though in context the stress morphemes may be altered in certain regular ways... The word is one of the most difficult concepts in English morphol-ogy to define, though in the vast majority of cases little question can arise as to whether a given sequence of morphemes is or is not a word." This statement of course relates to standard English, but it is applicable to our data as well.

Although in our analysis of the phonology, as well as the morphology and syntax an attempt will be made to apply formal criteria consistently, the nature of the data, namely, the speech of a very young child in the twilight zone between wakefulness and sleep, presents special problems with unavoidable structural ambiguity.

/I/

This high non-back unrounded phoneme has four main variants occurring both in stressed and unstressed position: two front, the tense [i] and the lax [ɪ], and two centralized, the tense [ɨ] and the lax [ɪ]. The feature of tenseness *versus* laxness hence is not contrastive, nor is the feature of front *versus* central.

The variant [i], a high front tense unrounded vowel, occurs medially, finally, and initially, in this order of frequency. Figure 1 represents the proportions of occurrence. Following are some examples of these occurrences:

    [i-] [in] "in", [ináf] "enough", [iyt][2] "eat"
    [-i-] [kírstɛn] "Kirsten" (proper name), [biháynd] "behind", [slip] "sleep"
    [-i] [bi] "be", [si] "see", [béybi] "baby"

Next in frequency, [ɪ], a high front lax unrounded vowel, also occurs initially, medially, and finally, with similar relative frequency as [i], as is shown in Figure 2 below. Examples of its occurrence are the following:

    [-ɪ-] [ɪn] "in", [ɪt] "it", [ɪz] "is"
    [-ɪ-] [stɪk] "stick", [hɪl] "hill", [kɪs] "kiss"
    [-ɪ] [hɪ] "he", [mámɪ] "Mommy", [smówkɪ] "Smokey"

The high central tense unrounded [ɨ] occurs only infrequently in the corpus, and then only medially. The occurrence is restricted to few lexical items like *polish*, *glasses*, and the most frequent one, *milk*.

The high central lax unrounded [ɪ] does not occur initially either. It has three occurrences finally: two in *pretty* and one in *Sally*. Medially, it occurs about twenty-five times, usually in the following words: *milk*, *pretty*, *Alice*, *Kirsten*, *Mrs. Fischer* (proper name), *wish*.

The relative frequency of these four variants of the high, non-back unrounded phoneme are shown in Figure 3.

The fluctuation of the variants of the phoneme in this still unstable phonemic system are given below with examples:

    [i] ~ [ɪ] [níla] ~ [níla] "Nila" (proper name)
             [pílow] ~ [pílow] "pillow"
    [i] ~ [ɨ] [póliš] ~ [póliš] "polish"
    [i] ~ [ɪ] [ális] ~ [álɪs] "Alice" (proper name)
    [ɪ] ~ [ɪ] [prítɪ] ~ [prítɪ] "pretty"
    [ɨ] ~ [ɪ] [mɨlk] ~ [mɪlk] "milk"

---

[2] For greater reading ease, final release and aspiration of stops, both occurring quite regularly in accordance with standard English, will not be indicated in the phonetic transcription. Also, the non-vocalic [i̯], [ɪ̯], [u], [ʊ̯] are written [y] and [w] respectively, and only the phonemic stress is marked on words of more than one syllable.

VOWELS

POSITIONAL DISTRIBUTION

[i]

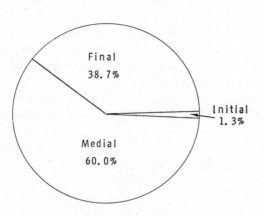

FIGURE 1

VOWELS

POSITIONAL DISTRIBUTION

[I]

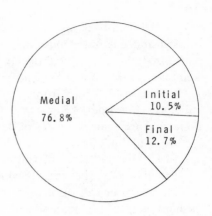

FIGURE 2

VOWELS

/I/

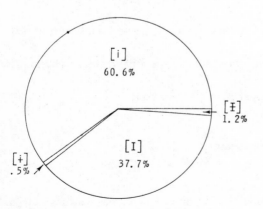

FIGURE 3

VOWELS

POSITIONAL DISTRIBUTION

[ɛ]

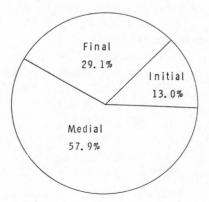

FIGURE 4

/E/

The three variants of this non-high, non-back unrounded phoneme in stressed and unstressed position are the front tense [e] and lax [ɛ], and the low front [æ], thus not utilizing the feature of mid *versus* low, nor tense *versus* lax contrastively. It may seem surprising at first not to find the typical English contrast of mid and low front vowels, but is perhaps less so in view of findings of others on child language, for example, Jakobson (1941), as was mentioned before.

One of the variants of /E/, namely [ə], will be omitted for the moment, and will be discussed separately later.

The mid front lax unrounded variant [ɛ] is by far the most widely distributed one in initial, medial and final positions. The positions of occurrence are charted in Figure 4. Some examples of occurrence are the following:

[ɛ-]　[ɛbáwt] "about", [ébɛlowp] "envelope", [ɛgéyn] "again"

[-ɛ-]　[wɛnt] "went", [dɛt] "that", [lɛft] "left"

[-ɛ]　[ówvɛ] "over", [péypɛ] "paper", [mÍstɛ] "Mr."

The mid front tense unrounded [e] and the low front tense unrounded [æ] are found with about equal frequency, except in initial position. (See Figures 5 and 6.) This is due primarily to the child's frequent use of his own name, *Anthony*, and to the many occurrences of the word *and*, where the [æ] occurs frequently. What is striking about the [e] is the fact that it occurs often as a simple syllable nucleus, contrary to standard English. A partial explanation of this could be the non-native English of the household help where this phenomenon was frequent.

Examples of occurrences of [e]:

[e-]　[eyt] "eight", [eyg] "egg"

[-e-]　[bétsɪ] "Betsy" (proper name), [stend] "stand", [béθrum] "bathroom"

[-e]　[tudé] "today", [owké] "O.K."

Examples of occurrences of [æ]:

[æ-]　[ænd] "and", [ǽntəni] "Anthony" [ænádər] "another"

[-æ-]　[hænd] "hand", [dæt] "that", [bæk] "back"

[-æ]　[bæ] – the only place of final [-æ] in working on the acceptable pronunciation of the word "berry"

The fluctuations of variants of the phoneme /E/ are shown next with examples.

VOWELS

POSITIONAL DISTRIBUTION

[e]

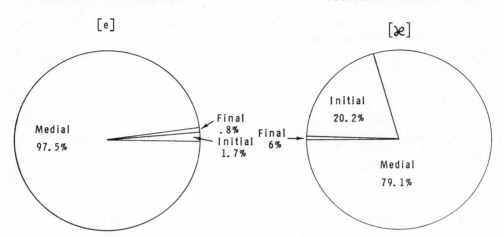

FIGURE 5

VOWELS

POSITIONAL DISTRIBUTION

[æ]

FIGURE 6

VOWELS

/E/

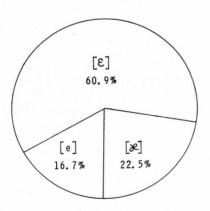

FIGURE 7

VOWELS

POSITIONAL DISTRIBUTION

[u]

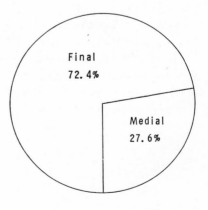

FIGURE 8

VOWELS

POSITIONAL DISTRIBUTION

[ʊ]

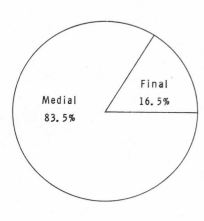

FIGURE 9

VOWELS

/U/

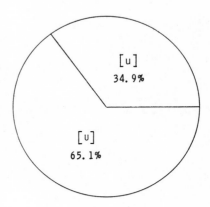

FIGURE 10

[e] ~ [ɛ]   [stend] ~ [stɛnd] "stand"
[e] ~ [æ]   [béθrum] ~ [bǽθrum] "bathroom"
[ɛ] ~ [æ]   [blɛk] ~ [blæk] "black"

Figure 7 shows the proportionate occurrences of the three variants of the phoneme /E/.

/U/

The high back rounded phoneme has only two main variants: the high back tense rounded [u] and the high back lax rounded [ʊ], reflecting again the non-contrastiveness of the tense *versus* lax feature. Both occur in medial and final positions. The only few initial occurrences, disregarded here, are those in interjections or non-standard words, e.g., [u:::].

Figure 8 shows the proportions of medial and final occurrences of [u], Figure 9 those of [ʊ].

Examples of these occurrences follow. The interesting fact here is again the frequent non-glided [u], analogous to the findings of [e], that is the absence of the contrastive use of the feature of simple *versus* complex vowel nucleus.

[-u-]   [kuk] "cook", [muv] "move", [ǰus] "juice"
[-u]   [hu] "who", [tu] "two", [nu] "new"
[-ʊ-]   [bʊk] "book", [pʊt] "put", [rʊm] "room"
[-ʊ]   [tʊ] "to", [yʊ] "you"

VOWELS

POSITIONAL DISTRIBUTION

[o]

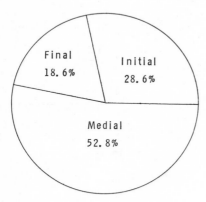

FIGURE 11

VOWELS

POSITIONAL DISTRIBUTION

[ɔ]

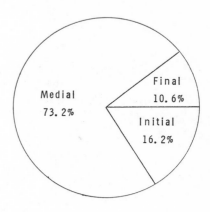

FIGURE 12

Fluctuation occurs frequently between these variants, as is the case with the other phonemes.

[u] ~ [ʊ]   [gud] ~ [gʊd] "good"

[šu] ~ [šʊ] "shoe"

The proportionate occurrences of the two variants [u] and [ʊ] are interesting, the latter occurring about twice as often as the former. This is charted in Figure 10.

/O/

Like the high back phoneme, this non-high back rounded phoneme has only two variants: the mid back tense rounded [o] and the mid back lax unrounded [ə], again disregarding the functional use of this feature. Both occur in initial, medial, and final positions, the proportions of which are shown in Figures 11 and 12. Examples of their occurrence are as follows:

[o-]   [óvər] "over", [ówpɛn] "open", [ównli] "only"

[-o-]   [dor] "door", [gows] "goes", [bóbo] "Bobo" (proper name)

[-o]   [go] "go", [bówbo] "Bobo", [tʊmóro] "tomorrow"

[ə-]   [əf] "off", [əl] "all", [ən] "on"

[-ə-]   [dət] "dot", [fər] "four", [pətétə] "potato"

[-ə]   [pətétə] "potato", [nə] "no"

Again fluctuation is found here, as exemplified by

[o] ~ [ə]   [go] ~ [gə] "go"

[boks] ~ [bəks] "box"

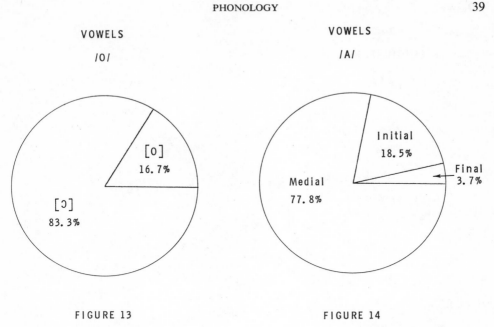

VOWELS

/O/

[o]
16.7%

[ɔ]
83.3%

VOWELS

/A/

Initial
18.5%

Final
3.7%

Medial
77.8%

FIGURE 13   FIGURE 14

However, the most frequent fluctuation is between [ow] ~ [ə], e.g., [ównli] ~ [ɔ́nli] "only", probably again due to imitation of both native and non-native models, showing the instability in the use of the simple and complex syllabic nuclei.

The proportionate occurrences of the two variants [o] and [ə] within the phoneme show a striking predominance of [ə], as shown in Figure 13. This can partially be attributed to the imitation of the Boston dialect in words like "dot".

/A/

This central vowel phoneme is realized most frequently by the low central [a], occasionally slightly fronted, again repeating the non-contrastive function of front *versus* central. [ə], another phonetic variant, will be discussed separately.

By far the greater number of occurrences of this central phoneme are medial, followed by initial and final positions. Figure 14 gives the proportions of occurrences in the running text.

Examples of occurrences:

    [a-]   [ádə] "other", [ápəl] "apple", [ándər] "under"
    [-a-]   [kam] "come", [yamp] "jump", [sam] "some"
    [-a]   [níla] "Nila" (proper name), [máma] "Mamma"

[ə]

This mid central unrounded vowel occurs about six hundred times in the running text, that is, not as frequently as, for example, [a] or [i] (about fourteen hundred times

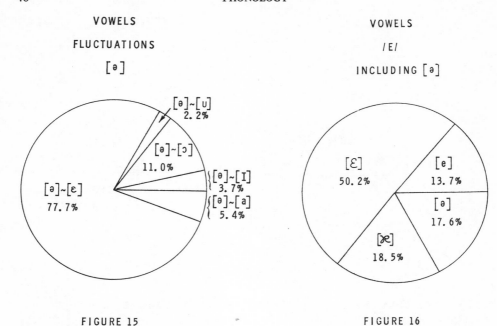

FIGURE 15   FIGURE 16

each), but more frequently than [e] (about three hundred fifty times) or [o] (about two hundred times). However, its occurrence is limited in the following way:

(1) [ə] ~ [a]   [kəm] ~ [kam] "come"

[ə] ~ [ɛ]   [péypə] ~ [péypɛ] "paper"

[ə] ~ [ə]   [ǽntənɪ] ~ [ǽntənɪ] "Anthony"

[ə] ~ [ʊ]   [tədéy] ~ [tʊdéy] "today"

[ə] ~ [ɪ]   [kə́dɪ] ~ [kídɪ] "Kitty"

It should be noted that the feature of front *versus* central is again not contrasted both under stress and unstressed, whereas the feature of back *versus* non-back is not contrasted only in unstressed syllables.

(2) [ə] occurs in fluctuation with zero in stop plus liquid sequences, e.g., [bəlǽŋkɛt] ~ [blǽŋkɛt] "blanket"

(3) [ə] shows fluctuation with length and/or with zero, again showing the instability of simple *versus* complex vowel nuclei, in addition to the feature of length, e.g.:
[dɛər] ~ [dɛːr] ~ [dɛr] "there"
[pʊəš] ~ [pʊš] "push"

(4) [ə] occurs preceding [r] in words like *bird, burn, dirty, early, first, girl, her, hurry, hurt, turn, work*, a total of some fifty running occurrences.

[ə] will therefore be treated as a non-contrastive variant of the phonemes to which the variants listed belong, the occurrences under (4) being included under the phoneme /E/.

Indicated in Figure 15 are the proportions of the fluctuations as described in (1).

The relatively large number for [ə], non-front *versus* back, perhaps requires an explanation: the large majority of them are due to the child's pronunciation of his own name, *Anthony*, as shown in the example, and is an imitation of the Scandinavian girls' pronunciation of the child's name with the back vowel. The occurrences of [ə] in fluctuation with the respective phonemic variant will be included in the total number of occurrences of that phoneme.

Since the assignment of [ə] to the five phonemes materially affects only the proportions of variants of /E/, Figure 16 represents a revised chart for that phoneme, showing again the non-contrastiveness of the feature front *versus* central.

To summarize the role of articulatory features in the child's vowel system, we can say that the feature of rounding has been well learned. In regard to tongue position, the contrasts are basically high *versus* non-high and back *versus* non-back, with small exception, disregarding the intermediary positions of mid and central. This pattern will become even clearer after our discussion of phonemic fluctuation below. The feature of tense *versus* lax is very unstable in the child's system, and is not used contrastively. Length, and simple *versus* complex vowel nuclei are also imperfectly learned features.

Next, the proportions of the total vowel phonemes are shown in Figure 17, as they relate to each other, including the [ə] variant. Figure 18 shows the occurrence of the vowel phonemes in their order of frequency.

To compare our statistical findings with some relevant studies of standard English, we have consulted the work of French, Carter, and Koenig (1930), Hayden's frequency count (1950), and a recent unpublished doctoral dissertation of Roberts (1961). Due to the widely differing analyses used in establishing vowel phonemes and their resulting frequencies in these studies, the data for vowels are not truly comparable. Comparisons of consonant occurrences are feasible and will be discussed. Perhaps the only thing which could be said with some validity in regard to vowels is that our /E/ and /I/, the non-back vowels, are by far the most frequent ones, as are the phonemes /ə, ɪ, æ/ for Hayden and /ə, i, e/ for Roberts, all having approximately similar areas of articulation.

Phonemic Fluctuation of Vowels

A residue of data on vowels remains after this phonemic grouping. It can be accounted for, however, by fluctuation between phonemes. As was indicated earlier (p. 25) several different dialects were spoken by the adults in the child's home environment. It is not surprising, therefore, to find dialectal variation in the child's idiolect. The most striking instability is his fluctuation between /A/ and /O/, as in /dÁŋkI/ ~ /dÓŋkI/ "donkey", /hAt/ ~ /hOt/ "hot", /tAp/ ~ /tOp/ "top", etc. Observation shows that /O/ is used in these words by the child's father, a fact consistent with his New England dialect. /A/, on the other hand, is used consistently in his mother's dialect who has adopted this type of standard English.

Less widespread but still considerable, is the fluctuation of /A/ and /E/, phonetically

VOWELS

PHONEME PROPORTIONS

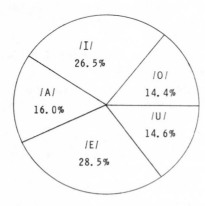

FIGURE 17

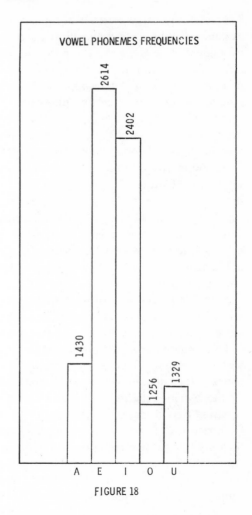

FIGURE 18

[a] ∼ [æ], e.g., /sÁlI/ ∼ /sÉlI/ "Sally", /ÁlIs/ ∼ /ÉlIs/ "Alice", /šAmpÚ/ ∼ /šEmpÚ/ "shampoo", etc. This again can be explained by imitating different dialects at home, in this case, the /A/ was used in these words by the Scandinavian girls living with the family. It is pertinent to note that this particular fluctuation is most frequent in the proper name *Alice*, the name of one of the girls.

Five instances of /I/ ∼ /E/ were found in separate lexical items: /blÉŋkEt/ ∼ /blÉŋkIt/ "blanket", /yÉlOw/ ∼ /yÍlOw/ "yellow", /It/ ∼ /Et/ (unstressed) "it", /dE/ ∼ /dI/ "the", /dEr/ ∼ /dIr/ "there". This fluctuation, however, is also quite frequent in the phonemic make-up of the -ing verb suffix which can appear as /In/ as well as /En/, e.g., /wÓčIn/ "watching" together with /kAwntEn/.

One example of /E/ ∼ /O/, phonetically [ɛ] and [ə] ∼ [ə], occurs in the text:

/rÉkEt/ ~ /rÉkOt/ "record". This is probably due to over-careful pronunciation of the word on occasion by adults, in order to "teach" the word.

In summary then, the original five point vowel triangle can still be reduced further to a three point triangle with the single exception of /E/ ~ /O/ by fusing /O/ with /A/ and /I/ with /E/, with the resulting

A

U   I

the same as given by Jakobson and Halle (1956) as the first vocalic split, opposing the single compact /A/ to the diffuse and grave /U/ and the diffuse and acute /I/, or in our articulatory terminology, the preservation of only two features: high *versus* low, and front *versus* back.

NON-VOWELS

Glides

Since the glides in the child's speech also pattern as consonants, we partially accept the Trager-Smith analysis of standard English (1951). That is, the front glides [i̯] and [i̯] and the back glides [u̯] and [u̯] are analyzed as the non-vowels /y/ and /w/ respectively. In their strictly consonantal function, they are well established and reflect the dichotomy of vowels *versus* non-vowels; there is some initial fluctuation of /y/ and /ǰ/; the single fluctuation of /w/ and /r/ will be taken up together with the liquid. Thus, we have /yEt/ "yet", /wEt/ "wet" and many other examples of the prevocalic occurrence of /y/ and /w/ followed by a simple vowel where they pattern like any other consonant in pre-vocalic position. This positional variant is by far the most frequent one for both glides; it accounts for 84.4% of occurrences of /y/ and 69.4% of occurrences of /w/.

As the second member of a complex vowel nucleus, however, they are much less stable. As a matter of fact, only three complex nuclei are quite stable: /Ay/, /Aw/, and /Oy/, that is the low vowel with either /y/ and /w/, and the non-high back vowel with /y/. For example, /lAyt/ "light", /Awt/ "out", /bOy/ "boy". In all other cases, /y/ and /w/ fluctuate with either length, or nothing, or both. We find [bówbow] ~ [bówbo] ~ [bóbo] "Bobo" (name of toy); [rum] ~ [ru:m] "room"; [dor] ~ [dowr] ~ [dɔ:r] "door"; [geyv] ~ [gæv] "gave"; [ɛ:g] ~ [eyg] "egg"; [lɪv] ~ [li:v] ~ [liyv] "to leave", showing great instability of the feature of simple *versus* complex vowel nucleus.

The phonemic status of length is also highly dubious. It occurs either in fluctuation with a front or back glide, or it occasionally fluctuates with a central off-glide, or most frequently with nothing. For example, [de:r] ~ [deər] ~ [der] "there", [hi:r] ~ [hiər] ~ [hir] "here", [dǽ:dɪ] ~ [dǽ:di] ~ [dǽdi:] ~ [dǽdɪ] "Daddy".

In terms of a phonemic analysis, we can say, therefore, that the feature of length is imperfectly learned, and is not used contrastively. We will consider it as non-functional and disregard it for phonemic purposes, confirming the unstable nature of vowel nuclei as was the case in connection with the glides /y/ and /w/.

The third glide, /h/, also shows great stability in its consonantal function pre-

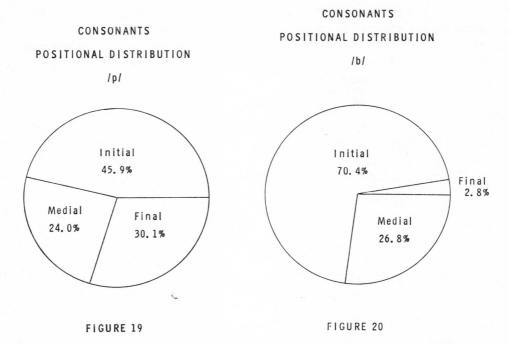

CONSONANTS

POSITIONAL DISTRIBUTION

/p/

CONSONANTS

POSITIONAL DISTRIBUTION

/b/

FIGURE 19   FIGURE 20

vocalically. As expected on the basis of standard English, it occurs only initially and medially, the latter in interjections like /ÁhÁ/. Occasional fluctuation with zero occurs pre-vocalically, e.g., /hImsÉlf/ ~ /ImsÉlf/ "himself", but post-vocalic fluctuation is much more predominant as was shown in the examples of the central off-glide. Again the lack of phonemic distinction between simple and complex vowel nuclei is demonstrated.

Consonants

The system of consonant phonemes presents a much simplified picture in terms of variants than did that of the vowels. Bearing the consonant phonemes of standard English in mind, the findings here parallel those of a standard dialect to a considerable extent, although some of the standard phonemes are found only as variants in the child's system. Since the phonemic analyses of standard English consonants show considerable agreement, a comparison of our findings with those of standard English becomes feasible.

Stops and Nasals. There are a voiceless and voiced stop phoneme at the bilabial, alveolar, and velar points of articulation, /p, b, t, d, k, g/. The voiceless stops are usually highly aspirate and often finally released. All the stops occur initially, medially, and finally, and the proportions of the positional variants are charted in Figures 19–24.

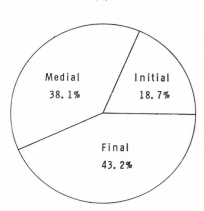

CONSONANTS

POSITIONAL DISTRIBUTION

/t/

FIGURE 21

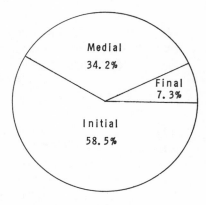

CONSONANTS

POSITIONAL DISTRIBUTION

/d/

FIGURE 22

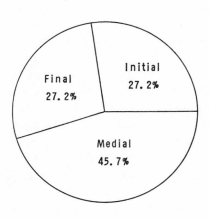

CONSONANTS

POSITIONAL DISTRIBUTION

/k/

FIGURE 23

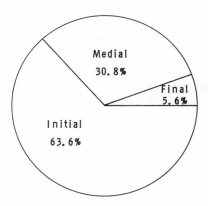

CONSONANTS

POSITIONAL DISTRIBUTION

/g/

FIGURE 24

Following are examples of occurrences of the stop phonemes in initial, medial, and final positions:

/p-/   /pIŋk/ "pink", /plEy/ "play"

/-p-/   /pÉypEr/ "paper", /dÁypEr/ "diaper"

/-p/   [jAmp/ "jump", /Ap/ "up"

/b-/   [blÉŋkEt/ "blanket", /bEθ/ "bath"

/-b-/   /bÓwbO/ "Bobo" (name of toy), /bÉybI/ "baby"

/-b/   [rOwb/ "robe", /bOb/ "Bob" (proper name)

/t-/   /tAč/ "touch", /tUk/ "took"

/-t-/   /prÍtI/ "pretty", /bÁtEn/ "button"

/-t/   /blÉŋkEt/ "blanket", /It/ "it"

/d-/   /dEns/ "dance", /dÉyvId/ "David" (proper name)

/-d-/   /rÉdI/ "ready", /ÁndEr/ "under"

/-d/   /rEd/ "red", /dId/ "did"

/k-/   /kÁlEr/ "color", /kIs/ "kiss"

/-k-/   /bÁkEt/ "bucket", /blÉŋkEt/ "blanket"

/-k/   /klOk/ "clock", /bUk/ "book"

/g-/   /gO/ "go", /gEt/ "get"

/-g-/   /sÍgErEt/ "cigarette", /tÁygEr/ "tiger"

/-g/   /bIg/ "big", /lEg/ "leg"

It is interesting to note that the occurrences of these six stop phonemes account for almost half of all consonant occurrences in the text. That is, 6,155 occurrences of stops and 6,540 occurrences of all other non-vowels combined, 48.5% for the stops, and 51.5% for other consonants. This is at great variance with Hayden's and Roberts' data where the stops account for only slightly more than 18% and 25% respectively of all consonants. Two possible explanations can be offered for our findings, one excluding the other. Either Anthony chose his favorite vocabulary like *blanket*, *color*, *Bobo*, *Daddy*, and others, all of which contain at least one stop, in order to practise or to play with these sounds. Or his choice and repetition of a limited vocabulary produced the mass of stop phonemes. We will deal with this matter in the paragraph analysis.

A further break-down shows the proportions of bilabial stops as compared to alveolar and velar ones (Fig. 25). It is interesting to note that the velar stops are somewhat more frequent than the labials, a fact true only of the oral stops, but not of the nasals. In view of the fact that dentals (alveolars in our case) are retained longest by aphasics (Goldstein, 1948) it is perhaps not surprising that almost fifty percent of the child's stops are alveolar. A similar correlation is found in the nasals (see Fig. 28) where /n/ occurs most frequently, followed by /m/, another consonant lost late by aphasics.

In terms of features, the stop articulation has been well learned by the child, which is consistent with all the findings on child language. This applies also to the feature of frontness *versus* backness where the child shows a greater predilection for the front

STOPS

LABIAL VERSUS ALVEOLAR VERSUS VELAR

STOPS

VOICELESS VERSUS VOICED

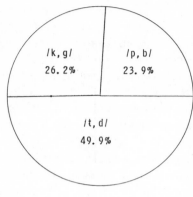

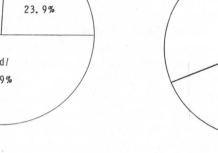

/k, g/
26. 2%

/p, b/
23. 9%

/t, d/
49. 9%

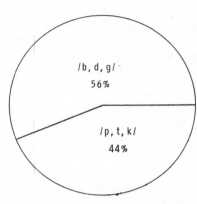

/b, d, g/
56%

/p, t, k/
44%

FIGURE 25   FIGURE 26

stops as compared to the back ones. The points of articulation are also clearly established, with minor exceptions. Aspiration and release are two other well-learned features. It is the feature of voicing which shows greatest instability and is therefore of interest. In Figure 26 we have compared the voiceless and voiced stops occurring only initially and medially, omitting final position because of frequent neutralization of the feature there.

There are also a few phonetic occurrences of the glottal stop, in positions similar to those of standard English occurrences, that is, preceding initial vowels, and as a variant of the alveolar stop in words like *little, button*, etc. For example, [?ɛpəls] "apples", [lɪʔəl] "little", the latter also fluctuating with [lɪdəl].

Templin's (1957) findings on sound discrimination ability and articulation ability in three-year old children show that 90% or more could articulate the stop phonemes. This is consistent with our own findings, with two exceptions.

In a few instances, the alveolar and velar points of articulation become confused and the feature front *versus* back is neutralized but self-correction usually follows immediately. For example, /krEy/ appears for /trEy/ "tray", /wEyk/ for /wEyt/ "wait", /strIyk/ for /strIyt/ "street". Once the velar stop in substitution for /t/ is followed by /y/ in /kyU/ "to", bringing it closer to a front articulation.

The other, much more widespread characteristic of the stop phonemes is the loss of the feature of voicing as we have already mentioned. This fluctuation of voiced and voiceless stop is confined to final position with very few exceptions. Thus, we have /bIg/ ~ /bIk/ "big", /rEd/ ~ /rEt/ "red", /rOwb/ ~ /rOwp/ "robe", and others, and in one instance /dÁypEr/ ~ /tÁypEr/ "diaper". There is also one occurrence of /kOlÁb/ followed immediately by a self-correction /Ap/. In the word "letter" /t/ and /d/ are used indiscriminately, probably due to the different dialects surrounding the child.

The neutralization of the feature of voice also extends to the sibilants. Since this particular linguistic characteristic, word-finally, is typical of German and Czech, the child's mother's native languages, she does use this neutralization in her English frequently; the child has probably imitated her speech in this regard. Confusion between voiced and voiceless consonants has also been noticed among others by Ohnesorg (1948), whose subjects were children speaking Czech. As for the other two examples quoted above, they are probably due to Anthony's imitation of the Danish pronunciation of English which often neutralizes voicing in any position due to the Danish contrastive system.

The preponderance of stop phonemes is perhaps to be expected in light of Jakobson's (1941) theory on the development of the phonemic system in the child. He establishes as the first dichotomy learned (p. 54) that of consonant *versus* vowel, the consonant there being a stop. Next, following Jakobson's observations, the consonantal sphere is broken up into oral *versus* nasal, and here again we find confirmation in our data in the large number of nasals occurring in the text and the feature of nasality well established. Nasals constitute 17.6% of all the consonants, and 34.2% of all consonants excluding the stops. Thus, if we classify nasals with the stops, they make up about two thirds or 66.1% of all consonant occurrences. Figure 27 shows the proportionate occurrences of stops, nasals and other consonants in the total consonant inventory.

The nasals occur at the bilabial, alveolar, and velar points of articulation. The first two in initial, medial, and final positions, the latter only medially and finally. By far, the most frequently found nasal is /n/, which is about twice as frequent as /m/. Again we are confronted with the question whether the vocabulary selection accounts for this, or whether the vocabulary was selected in order to use these nasals frequently. The least frequent nasal is /ŋ/, as shown in Figure 28.

Templin shows /ŋ/ correctly articulated by 70–80% of the children aged 3. However, it seems that in our particular case, the phonemic status of /ŋ/ is just beginning to be developed, that is to say the simultaneous use of the features of velarity and nasality as opposed to the consecutive occurrences of velarity and nasality. The small number of occurrences (about 240 in the total text) is one indication of this, but that may be due to chance. More indicative is the /n/ ~ /ŋ/ ~ /ŋk/ fluctuation in final position, particularly in the -ing participial forms of verbs. This cannot be explained on the basis of a dialect the child imitates, since all the adults in the home use the velar nasal consistently in these verb forms. Nevertheless, /ŋ/ is considered a separate phoneme, albeit with a low functional yield, since it does occur in several words medially, for example, /fÍŋEr/ "finger", /hÉŋEr/ "hanger", where it contrasts with /n/.

CONSONANTS

PROPORTIONATE OCCURRENCES OF
STOPS
NASALS
OTHERS

CONSONANTS

NASALS-PROPORTIONS

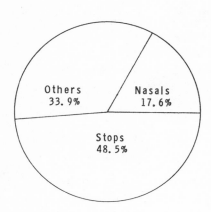

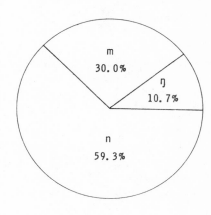

FIGURE 27   FIGURE 28

Following are examples of occurrences of the three nasals:

/m-/ /mIlk/ "milk", /mEč/ "match"
/-m-/ /mÁmI/ "Mommy", /tÓmI/ "Tommy" (proper name)
/-m/ /kAm/ "come", /sAm/ "some"
/n-/ /nOt/ "not", /nEk/ "neck"
/-n-/ /fÁnI/ "funny", /lAnč/ "lunch"
/-n/ /mEn/ "man", /hÉpEn/ "happen"
/-ŋ-/ /fÍŋEr/ "finger", /hÉŋEr/ "hanger"
/-ŋ/ /brIŋ/ "bring", /lÚkIŋ/ "looking"

Liquids. In view of the findings of other investigators, for example, Leopold (1953) or Grégoire (1937), it is surprising to find relatively great stability of /l/ and /r/. Liquids are also lost early by aphasics, supporting a probable late acquisition by the child. On the other hand, Ohnesorg (1948) finds /l/ acquired early, but /r/ late. Templin groups /l/ with the 70–80% correctly articulated sounds, /r/ with the 50–69% group. In our corpus, no fluctuation of /l/ with any other phoneme was found, and only a single fluctuation of /r/ and /w/ in /rÉdI/ ~ /wÉdI/ "ready".

It is also interesting to note the relatively frequent occurrences of /l/ and /r/ – more than one thousand or 8.5% for the former, and over eight hundred or 6.4% for the

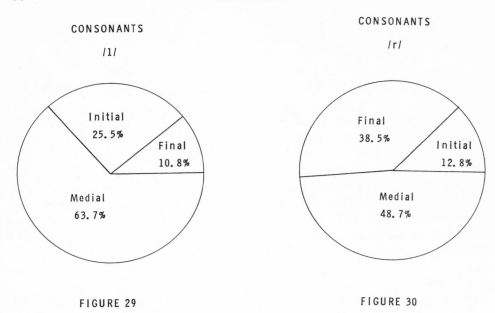

FIGURE 29   FIGURE 30

latter of the consonantal phonemes, a reverse of proportions as compared to standard English.

A partial explanation may again be the child's vocabulary selection. For example, his favorite object, a blanket, is talked about a good deal. Hence, /l/ occurs frequently in this corpus. However, frequent occurrences alone do not account for the stability of a certain phoneme, as was shown in the analysis of vowels. It must be assumed that the distinctive features of /l/ and /r/ had been well learned at the time of the recordings.

Figures 29 and 30 show the proportion of initial, medial, and final occurrences of the two phonemes. Following are examples of their occurrences:

    /l-/   /lAyt/ "light", /lEft/ "left"
    /-l-/   /lÓlIpOp/ "lollipop", /blAk/ "block"
    /-l/   /bOl/ "ball", /hIl/ "hill"
    /r-/   /rAyt/ "right", /rUm/ "room"
    /-r-/   /brIŋ/ "bring", /fErst/ "first"
    /-r/   /kAr/ "car", /čEr/ "chair"

As was mentioned earlier, post-vocalic /r/ occurs regularly in the dialects of English which the child imitates, and he has also selected the phonetic realization of an American English /r/ rather than his mother's non-native type.

Spirants and Affricates. Both the voiceless and voiced labiodental spirants occur, presenting a very interesting picture. /f/, the voiceless labiodental spirant, occurs 341 times and constitutes 2.7 % of the total consonant occurrences. 311 of these occurrences are the labiodental variant, and the remaining thirty are interdental, [θ]. We find free variation of [fɪŋ] ∼ [θɪŋ] "thing", [námfɪŋ] ∼ [námθɪŋ] "nothing", [wɪf] ∼ [wɪθ] "with", etc., showing instability of the feature of interdentality.

Since the voiceless interdental spirant [θ] never occurs in contrast, but only as a variant, it cannot be considered a separate phoneme in the child's speech. This bears out Jakobson (1941) in his statement that relatively rare distinctive features in the languages of the world are learned late by the children in their mother tongue. Templin also puts both the voiceless and voiced interdentals into her last group, which has been mastered only by 10% to 49% of the children at age 3. Jespersen (1922) considers interdentals "difficult" in the linguistic development of the child, and Goldstein (1948) has found them absent early in the speech of aphasics.

The voiced labiodental spirant /v/ Templin classifies as belonging to group three, articulated correctly by 50% to 60% of the children. In our data, we find only 73 occurrences of this spirant, or 0.6% of occurrences which may be quite accidental. It must be considered a separate phoneme in the child's speech since it is consistently used contrastively in the minimal pair [vérɪ] "very" : [bérɪ] "berry". Its functional yield is extremely low, and, therefore, we assume that it is just being learned as a distinctive unit. This is confirmed by a great deal of fluctuation between /v/ and /b/, as for example, in /šÁvEl/ ∼ /šÁbEl/ "shovel", /ÓlIv/ ∼ /ÓlIb/ "olive", /dÉyvId/ ∼ /dÉybId/ "David" (proper name), which fluctuation, however, does not occur initially where /v/ is used frequently in /vÉkyUm/ "vacuum" (cleaner), one of the child's names for the often-present microphone. In terms of features, it should be pointed out that we are confronted with a confusion of point of articulation – bilabial *versus* labiodental, as well as of manner of articulation – stop *versus* spirant. This occurs only when the feature of voicing is present also, hence it does not apply to /p/ and /f/. Grégoire (1947) finds the /b/ *versus* /v/ contrast still lacking in the child's third year, supporting our observation.

Both interdental spirants, the voiceless [θ] and the voiced [ð] occur, but quite rarely. There are a total of 38 occurrences of [θ], and fewer of [ð] in the total corpus. The fluctuation between [θ] and [f] has been discussed above, and accounts for thirty occurrences; in the remaining eight [θ] ∼ [t], hence can be classified as a variant of /t/ and not as a separate phoneme. This variation again occurs initially and finally, for example [θrow] ∼ [trow] "throw", [θam] ∼ [tam] "thumb", [wɪθ] ∼ [wɪt] "with". The voiced [ð] occurs, e.g., in [ðɛ] ∼ [dɛ] "the", in [ðɛr] ∼ [dɛr] "there", and in [áðər] ∼ [ádər] "other", and is therefore a variant of the phoneme /d/. The above three lexical items are among the most frequent ones in the data, so that no lack of opportunity to practice [ð] would exist. Yet, it certainly is not a phoneme, and even as a variant it is conspicuous by its absence. Again, we must return to Jakobson's observation mentioned above as the most plausible explanation. It is also interesting to note that the *voiced* [ð] is less frequent than the *voiceless* [θ], the reverse of standard English. Could the features of voicing have any relevance here? An analogous situation is presented by the labiodental spirants discussed above, where the voiced

CONSONANTS

/s/

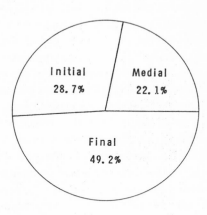

FIGURE 31

member is by far less stable. On the other hand, the functional yield of /ð/ is very low in English in general, and perhaps therefore its development is quite late.

Coming back to the articulatory features, it should be pointed out that, contrary to most of the data, the feature of voicing is fairly stable with the substitutes for standard English /θ/ and /ð/. It is the feature of interdentality which is unstable, substituting labiodentality for the voiceless, and the alveolar point of articulation for both the voiceless and voiced members. Concomitantly, labiodentality preserves the fricative articulation, whereas the alveolar point requires a stop.

The voiceless alveolar groove sibilant phoneme /s/ has more than eight hundred occurrences or 6.5% of the total consonants. The proportions of its initial, medial and final occurrences are shown in Figure 31. By far, the most frequent variant is the groove alveolar sibilant of standard English. However, there are a few instances of a slightly different sibilant similar to the realization of the Danish /s/, easily confused with our /š/. This is no doubt due to the child's imitation of the Danish member of the household in whose native tongue the /s/ *versus* /š/ contrast does not exist. Anthony occasionally substitutes the English /š/ for /s/, as for example in [šwétər] "sweater", a confusion of points of articulation.

Examples of occurrences of /s/:

    /s-/   /sAm/ "some", /spIld/ "spilled"
    /-s-/   /jAst/ "just", /lÍsEn/ "listen"
    /-s/   /dIs/ "this", /dEns/ "dance"

The voiced alveolar groove sibilant phoneme /z/ is listed by Templin in the last acquisition group, together with the interdentals. In our data, we find a parallel situation. There are fewer than two hundred occurrences: none initially, thirteen medially, and 176 finally. The phonemic status of /z/, in the corpus of monologues only, seems dubious. However, we know that the child does have the contrast /klowz/ "to close" and /klows/ "near" in his day speech, a factor which weighed in our considering /z/ a phoneme here. Its medial occurrences are confined to a few words like /prÉzEnt/ "gift", /wÉnzdEy/ "wednesday", /myÚzIk/ "music". Most of its final occurrences are found in plurals, possessive endings, and third person singular verbs. However, there is frequent fluctuation in final position with /s/, for example /flÁwErz/ ~ /flÁwErs/ "flowers", /gOwz/ ~ /gOws/ "goes". This can probably be explained in the same manner as the final voiced – voiceless fluctuation of stops, that is, the child imitates his mother's speech where at times the feature of voicing is neutralized in final position. In one instance, however, the /z/ ~ /s/ fluctuation occurs medially: /myÚzIk/ ~ /myÚsIk/ "music" probably due to the imitation of Danish speech.

There are less than fifty occurrences of the voiceless palatal sibilant phoneme /š/, 28 initially, 8 medially, and 11 finally. For example: /šUr/ "sure", /fÍšEr/ "Fischer" (proper name), /pÓlIš/ "polish". In spite of the relatively few occurrences, /s/ clearly contrasts with /š/, with the only fluctuations between the phonemes as were mentioned above.

The voiced palatal sibilant [ž] occurs only in the example [žämp] "jump", and is clearly a variant of /ǰ/. Both Ohnesorg and Grégoire have parallel findings on sibilants, that is, their relative later development and the instability of /š/ and /ž/ contrasts.

The two English affricates /č/ and /ǰ/ are phonemes in our data. The voiceless /č/ occurs 36 times: 15 occurrences are initial, 6 medial, and 15 final, e.g., /čÍkEn/ "chicken", /wÓčIn/ "watching", /mAč/ "much". Several times we find /č/ ~ /ǰ/ fluctuation as, for example, in /čEynč/ ~ /čEynǰ/ "change". This fluctuation is always final and can again be explained by the neutralization of voicing in final position. With the voiceless /č/, the affricate characteristic is stable.

The voiced palatal affricate /ǰ/ with a total of 43 or 0.3% occurrences has four variants, namely [ǰ], [ž], [d^z] and [d^y]. For example, the word "jump" appears in all these phonetic shapes: [ǰamp], [žamp], [d^{z}amp], [d^{y}amp]. Similarly, "juice" is found as [ǰus] and [d^{z}us]. In addition, /ǰ/ fluctuates with the glide /y/ in these and other words, hence /ǰUs/ ~ /yUs/. This fact is not at all surprising in view of the Swedish member of the houshold who constantly confused the English phonemes /ǰ/ and /y/ in her speech, and realized them either with the affricate feature or the palatal feature present, but rarely both. The child obviously imitated her in these instances, particularly in vocabulary occurring frequently in conversations with her. However, Goldstein's observation on the early loss of affricates by aphasics probably points also to their late acquisition by the child.

To summarize the status of articulatory features of the consonant phonemes, the instability of the feature of voicing is striking. It is only fairly stable in the case of an even greater instability of another feature, namely, that of interdentality. With few exceptions, the place and manner of articulation are quite stable, as are release and aspiration.

Before leaving the description of consonants, it may be worthwhile to study further their proportions and relative occurrences and then compare them with standard English. In the discussion of the oral stops, we showed their proportionate occurrences as to point of articulation (see Fig. 25). We shall now show the proportionate occurrences of all consonant phonemes as to point of articulation in Figure 32. The striking preponderance of consonants produced in the front of the mouth suggests a further representation of the relationship of bilabials, labiodentals and alveolars as opposed to palatals and velars in Figure 33.

In regard to manner of articulation, we have already mentioned that oral stops account for 48.5% of all consonant occurrences, and with the addition of the nasals (17.6%) occlusives constitute 66.1% of the consonants found. Figure 27 shows these proportions. We will now give a more detailed breakdown in Figure 34 as to oral stops, nasals, liquids, spirants, and affricates.

Voiced and voiceless stops were compared in Figure 26. To carry this analysis further, we now compare all consonants in all positions occurring in pairs of voiceless/voiced (including /š/, although it has no phonemic voiced counterpart) in Figure 35. This is the only time that voiceless consonants predominate, due to the loss of the feature of voicing of the marked member of the pair. If, however, we take all non-vowel phonemes, that is, include the nasals, liquids, /y, w, h/ which occur only voiced, then voiced consonants are by far more frequent than voiceless ones, as shown in Figure 36.

Finally, in Figure 37 all of the child's non-vowel phonemes are listed, arranged in order of frequency of occurrence.

To summarize, we show all phonemes found in the data in order of frequency of occurrence in Figure 38, and the proportions of consonants, glides, and vowels in Figure 39.

A comparison of the non-vowel phonemes of the child's idiolect with the studies of standard English, mentioned previously, can be made because of greater comparability of analyses than was the case with vowels. It is a striking fact that the first three most frequent phonemes of Roberts coincide with our findings, taking into account the child's own phonemic system. Roberts lists /ə, i, t/ where we have /E, I, t/. /t/ is also the most frequent phoneme finally, and second in rank order initially in French's study and second in Haynes'. However, the total alveolars, with the addition of /ð/ in Roberts' and Haynes' data account only for less than 30% and 37% respectively of consonantal occurrences as compared with our findings of more than 60%. The relative ranking of /n/ is sixth in Roberts' and our studies, but first in Haynes'. The precedence of alveolars and /k/ over the bilabials /b, p/ in that order, followed by /g/ is common to all findings. Comparing the manner of articulation, where in our data stops accounted for slightly less than 50% of occurrences, we are at sharp dis-

CONSONANT PHONEMES

POINTS OF ARTICULATION

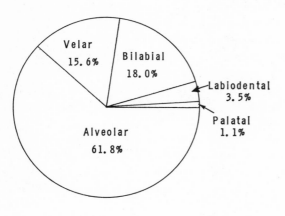

FIGURE 32

CONSONANT PHONEMES

FRONT VERSUS BACK POINTS OF ARTICULATION

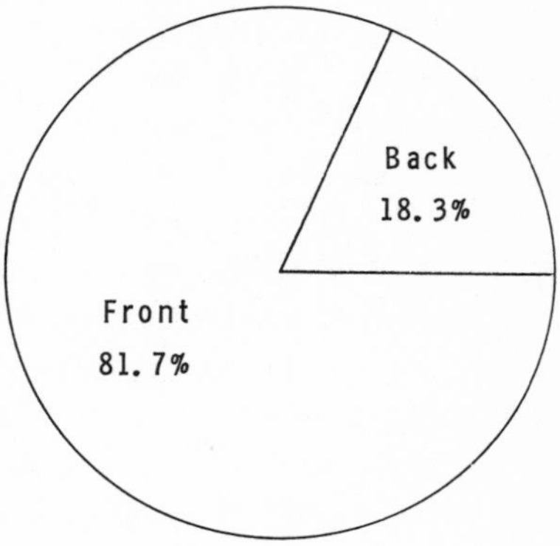

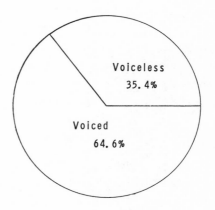

FIGURE 33

CONSONANT PAIRS

(INCLUDING /š/)

VOICELESS VERSUS VOICED PROPORTIONS

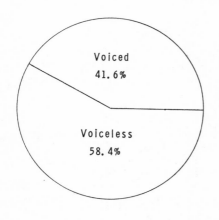

FIGURE 34

NON-VOWELS

VOICELESS VERSUS VOICED

FIGURE 35

CONSONANT PHONEMES

MANNER OF ARTICULATION

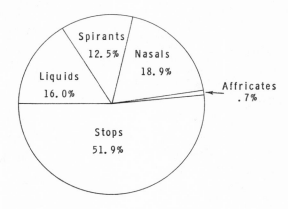

FIGURE 36

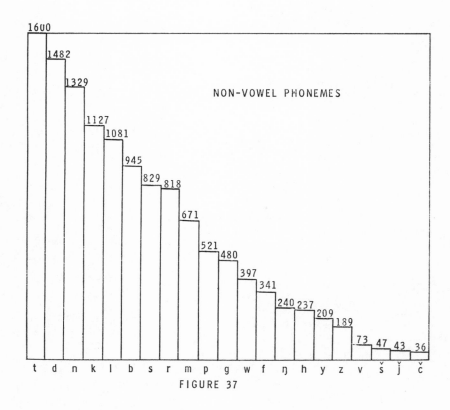

FIGURE 37

CONSONANTS, GLIDES, VOWELS

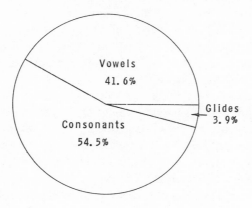

FIGURE 38

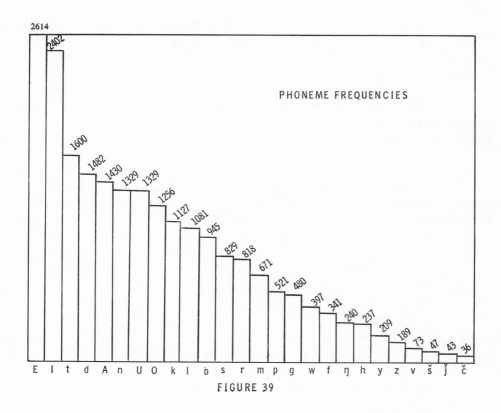

FIGURE 39

agreement with French and Roberts whose findings are very similar, differing only by one percent, their stops accounting for 28.4% and 29.4% respectively. (We have again included /ð/ here to make our data more comparable.) In regard to liquids, our total of over 15% parallels the totals of Roberts (over 15%) and French (over 14%), but our proportions of /l/ and /r/ are just the reverse of theirs, /l/ being more frequent in our data than /r/. Although the proportion of both liquids is smaller in Haynes' work (10.75%), his relative order of /r/ and /l/ agrees with the other two standard English studies. In the case of spirants, nasals, and affricates our data parallel those for standard English quite closely. Due to the child's frequent devoicing of consonants paired by the voiceless *versus* voiced feature, it is not surprising that our proportion of occurrence of the voiceless member of the pair is about 20% higher than standard English occurrences. However, in comparing all voiceless with all voiced consonants, our findings again parallel closely the proportions of standard English. Due to Anthony's peculiar system of glides it is to be expected that their proportion will be considerably smaller in his speech than it is in standard English. In terms of absolute frequency, the palatals /š, č, ǰ/ appear low on French's and Haynes' list and last on Roberts' as they do on ours.

Clusters

Two, three, and four consonant and glide combinations are discussed here according to position where they occur in the word. In addition, the child uses certain phoneme sequences always in close transition, e.g., /sfOr/ "is for" or /OldE/ "all the", hence these consonant sequences are included in our lists of clusters. On the other hand, instances where open transition regularly occurs are excluded from the data here. Also, some fluctuation occurs of clusters consisting of stop plus /l/, with the phonetic [ə] appearing between the two consonants, thus constituting a separate syllable with the vowel phoneme /E/.

Two-Consonant Clusters: *Initial*. All six stops combine with /r/, the bilabials and velars with /l/, and /t/ and /k/ with /w/. The bilabial nasal /m/ is found as the first member in the cluster /my-/, and as the second member in /sm-/. The spirant /b/ combines with the liquids /r/ and /l/, and the glide /y/. /s/ is found with the three voiceless stops, with /m/ as mentioned above, with /n/, and with /b/, /l/, and /w/; /š/ also occurs with /p/ and /w/. The only other initial clusters are /hw-/ and /gw-/ which occur rarely. Thus, we have 27 types of initial clusters. Examples follow:

pr-	/prÍtI/	"pretty"
br-	/brIŋ/	"bring"
tr-	/trAy/	"try"
dr-	/drAyv/	"drive"
kr-	/krOs/	"cross"
gr-	/grEy/	"grey"
pl-	/plIs/	"please"

bl- /blOw/ "blow"
kl- /klOk/ "clock"
gl- /glEs/ "glass"
my- /myÚzik/ "music"
sm- /smÓwkI/ "Smokey" (name of toy)
sn- /snOt/ "is not"
fr- /frOm/ "from"
fl- /flAy/ "fly" (insect)
fy- /fyUks/ "Fuchs" (proper name)
sp- /spIld/ "spilled"
st- /stEnd/ "stand"
sk- /skUl/ "school"
sf- /sfOr/ "is for"
sl- /slIp/ "sleep"
sw- /swIč/ "switch"
šp- /špÓrtkAr/ "sportscar"
šw- /šwÉtEr/ "sweater"
hw- /hwAy/ "why"
gw- /gwAyn/ "whine"

The last four clusters require comment. The two clusters starting with /š/ are certainly attempts at imitating the Danish speaker who was particularly interested in sportscars and used to point them out to the child. "Sweater" was a frequent subject of discussion between the Danish girl and Anthony as well. The /hw-/ cluster of "why" is often used by the child's mother in that particular word. /gw-/ in /gwAyn/ occurs only once immediately following /wAyn/, both meaning "whine".

Two-Consonant Clusters: Medial. As we would expect, more medial than initial clusters occur; we have a total of thirty-seven types. Arranged according to the first member of the cluster, the stop /p/ combines with /t/, /d/, and /s/; /t/ with /s/; /k/ with /t/, /r/, /l/, /y/. The bilabial nasal with /p/, /t/, /s/; the alveolar with /t/, /d/, /s/, /č/, /l/; and the velar with /k/ and /g/. The only initial spirant found is /f/ combined with /t/ and /r/. The affricate /č/ clusters with /m/. Most combinations occur with /r/, namely /b/, /t/, /d/, /k/, /n/, /b/, /s/, /z/, and /l/. The lateral /l/ is found with /d/, /k/, /g/, /m/, /s/, /r/, /w/.

Following are examples of medial two-consonant clusters:
-pt- /dÁptI/ "Dumpty" (name of toy)
-pd- /ApdÉr/ "up there"
-ps- /ÁpsAyd/ "upside"
-ts- /bÉtsI/ "Betsy" (proper name)
-kt- /dÓktEr/ "doctor"
-kr- /mÁykrOfOwn/ "microphone"
-kl- /tÍklIš/ "ticklish"
-ky- /vÉkyUm/ "vacuum" (cleaner)

-mp-   /šÉmpU/ "shampoo"
-mt-   /sÁmtIŋ/ "something"
-ms-   /hÍmsElf/ "himself"
-nt-   /hÁntI/ "Humpty" (name of toy)
-nd-   /stÉndIŋ/ "standing"
-ns-   /InsÁyd/ "inside"
-nč-   /čÉynčIn/ "changing"
-nl-   /ÓnlI/ "only"
-ŋk-   /blÉŋkEt/ "blanket"
-ŋg-   /bÉyŋgE/ "banging"
-ft-   /hÉftU/ "have to"
-fr-   /bÓyfrEnd/ "boyfriend"
-čm-   /gÁrbIčmEn/ "garbage man"
-rb-   /bÁrbArA/ "Barbara" (proper name)
-rt-   /stÁrtEd/ "started"
-rd-   /gÁrdEn/ "garden"
-rk-   /bÁrkIn/ "barking"
-rn-   /kÓrnEr/ "corner"
-rf-   /kÉrfUl/ "careful"
-rs-   /hÓrsI/ "horsie"
-rz-   /hÍrzE/ "here's a"
-rl-   /ÉrlI/ "early"
-ld-   /OldE/ "all the"
-lk-   /wÉlkAm/ "welcome"
-lg-   /ÓlgÓn/ "all gone"
-lm-   /ÓlmOwst/ "almost"
-ls-   /ÁpElsOs/ "apple sauce"
-lr-   /ÓlrAyt/ "all right"
-lw-   /ÓlwEys/ "always"

The forms /hÁntI/, /dÁntI/, and /dÁptI/ with cluster simplification occur as does the standard three-consonant cluster /hÁmptI/ and /dÁmptI/, the names for the toy "Humpty Dumpty". In the simplification, we probably have a representation of an earlier linguistic stage. It should be pointed out, however, that in /hÁntI/ and /dÁntI/ the nasal and the alveolar stop are preserved, whereas in /dÁptI/ both stops appear without the nasal, due perhaps to the initial stop /d/ so that only stop consonants used so frequently by the child, occur in the word.

It should also be mentioned that in /čÉynčIn/ "changing" we have /č/ rather than the standard /ǰ/ which could be due to two reasons: either the decomposition of the word into /čEynč/ with the -ing ending and the use of the finally devoiced form here, or an imitation of lack of voicing in any position after the Danish speaker.

The example cited of the medial cluster /ŋg/ is one of the few occurrences of this cluster in any position throughout the corpus. This could be due to the child's imitation of his mother's inconsistent use of this cluster, or, more probably, it could also point to his not yet having learned the rather complex morphophonemic rules of English for the use of this cluster.

Two-Consonant Clusters: *Final.* There are 38 final consonant clusters; many of those having a sibilant as the second member are due to plurals, possessives, and third person singular verb forms. Those ending in an alveolar stop are frequently past forms of verbs. Specifically, the following combinations occur, listed by the first member. The clusters containing the same final consonant except for the feature of voicing, occurring in the same word, are not surprising in view of the child's imperfect learning of this feature.

The stops /p/ and /k/ combine with /t/, /s/, /l/; /b/ with /l/; /t/ with /s/; and /d/ and /g/ with /z/. The nasals /m/ and /n/ are both found with /s/ and /z/; in addition, /n/ clusters with /t/, /d/, /č/, /ǰ/. The velar /ŋ/ occurs with /k/ and /g/. One cluster is found with /f/, namely /-ft/, one with /č/ – /-čt/, two with /s/ – /-st/ and /-sk/, and one with /z/ – /-zd/. Most final clusters occur with the liquids: /r/ combines with /t/, /d/, /k/, /m/, /n/, /s/, /z/, and /l/; /l/ clusters with /d/, /k/, /b/, /s/, and /z/. Here are examples of occurrences:

-pt /drOpt/ "dropped"
-ps /kAps/ "Cobbers" (telescoped form of dog's name)
-pl /Apl/ "apple"
-bl /šAbl/ "shovel"
-ts /dOts/ "dots"
-dz /wIdz/ "weeds"
-kt /kIkt/ "kicked"
-ks /stIks/ "sticks" (noun)
-kl /mÓwtOsÁykl/ "motorcycle"
-gz /dOgz/ "dogs"
-ms /kAms/ "comes"
-mz /kAmz/ "comes"
-nt /Ent/ "and"
-nd /stEnd/ "stand"
-ns /dEns/ "dance"
-nz /ÍndyEnz/ "Indians"
-nč /lAnč/ "lunch"
-nǰ /čEynǰ/ "change"
-ŋk /bEŋk/ "bank"
-ŋg /strOŋg/ "strong"
-ft /lEft/ "left"
-čt /skrEčt/ "scratched"
-st /krOst/ "crossed"
-sk /dEsk/ "desk"

-zd	/klOwzd/ "closed"
-rt	/kArt/ "cart"
-rd	/bErd/ "bird"
-rk	/bArk/ "bark"
-rm	/wOrm/ "warm"
-rn	/bErn/ "burn"
-rs	/čErs/ "chairs"
-rz	/flÁwErz/ "flowers"
-rl	/gErl/ "girl"
-ld	/spIld/ "spilled"
-lk	/mIlk/ "milk"
-lf	/hImsÉlf/ "himself"
-ls	/bÓtEls/ "bottles"
-lz	/bÁbElz/ "bubbles"

It should be noted that final clusters consisting of a stop plus /l/ particularly fluctuate with the sequence stop plus /E/ plus /l/, for example, /bOtl/ ~ /bÓtEl/, the variant of /E/ being realized there either as [ɛ] or as [ə].

Three-Consonant Clusters. Perhaps by chance, in the pre-sleep monologues only /s/ plus /t/ or /k/ plus /r/ occur initially, although in the child's day speech the third voiceless stop also occurs in the three-consonant initial cluster, as does the cluster /spl-/. This is probably due to the selection of vocabulary and subject matter of the monologues.

Medially, some clusters are listed which occur in two-word sequences of standard English, but are considered one word by the child. Thus, we have /p/ and /r/ + /s/ + /t/; /m/ + /p/ + /t/; /n/ + /d/ + /y/ and /n/ + /z/ + /d/; /ŋ/ + /k/ + /y/; /s/ + /t/ + /m/; /r/ + /t/ + /k/ and /r/ + /g/ + /r/.

Finally, all clusters but one in these groups have as their final members either the sibilants /s/ and /z/, or the stop /t/ since they occur mostly in plurals, possessives, third person verbs, or in the past tense. It should be noted that stop plus /l/ clusters again fluctuate with the syllable /-El/, as they do elsewhere.

Examples of three-consonant clusters, found in the monologues only, follow:

Initial

str-	/strIt/ "street"
skr-	/skrEčt/ "scratched"

Medial

-pst-	/lÍpstIk/ "lipstick"
-mpt-	/hÁmptI/ "Humpty" (name of toy)
-ndy-	/ÁndyEn/ "onion"
-nzd-	/wÉnzdEy/ "Wednesday"
-ŋky-	/tÉŋkyU/ "thank you"
-stm-	/pÓwstmEn/ "postman"

-rtk-	/špÓrtkAr/ "sportscar"
-rgr-	/mÁrgrEt/ "Margaret" (proper name)
-rst-	/kÍrstEn/ "Kirsten" (proper name)

Final

-pls	/Epls/ "apples"
-tls	/bOtls/ "bottles"
-kst	/fIkst/ "fixed"
-nts	/pEnts/ "pants"
-ŋks	/fIŋks/ "things"
-znt	/dAznt/ "doesn't"
-rdz	/bErdz/ "birds"
-rst	/fErst/ "first"
-rlz	/gErlz/ "girls"

The form /ÁndyEn/ "onion", which adds a consonant as compared to standard English, is formed in analogy with /ÍndyEnz/ "Indians".

Four-Consonant Clusters. Only one occurrence of such a cluster is found in the data, namely, medially -ksky- in the word /ÉkskyÚz/ "excuse".

As is apparent from the description of clusters, the child has a considerable number of them occurring where we would expect them on the basis of standard English. He does not use the much greater number of mathematically possible combinations that Velten (1943) has described. It may be profitable, however, to examine some lexical items with cluster simplification within Anthony's own speech as compared to standard English. Cluster simplification is also mentioned as a characteristic of children's speech by investigations of Grégoire (1947), Jespersen (1922), and Ohnesorg (1948), to mention a few. However, the last two observed that the stop members of the cluster normally remain as the simple consonants, a fact borne out by our findings with some exceptions. For example, "sportscar" appears both as /špÓrṭkAr/ and /fÓrṭkAr/, in other words the initial /šp-/ cluster fluctuates with the single consonant /f/, a fricative, thus the approximate point of articulation of the stop /p/ is preserved, but the manner of articulation of /š/ is the predominant one.

Although the sequence of consonant plus /l/ plus vowel occurs frequently, it also appears occasionally as just a simple consonant plus vowel sequence. Thus, we have /sl-/ ~ /l-/, /kl-/ ~ /k-/, /-nl-/ ~ /-l-/, for example, /slÍpIŋ/ ~ /lÍpIŋ/ "sleeping", /klÍnEr/ ~ /kÍnEr/ "(vacuum) cleaner", /ÓnlI/ ~ /ÓnI/ "only". On the other hand, the /bl-/ in /blÉŋkEt/ also fluctuates with [bəl] hence /bElÉŋkEt/. The homorganic alveolar cluster /nd/ or /dn/ fluctuates with the nasal /n/, for example /wÍndOw/ ~ /wÍnOw/ "window", /stEnd/ ~ /stEn/ "stand", /gUdnÁyt/ ~ /gUnÁyt/ "good night", another loss of the stop feature.

Although post-vocalic /r/ occurs in the dialect of both parents, the /rk/ cluster of "market" is simplified to only /k/ in /mÁkEt/. Similarly, "New York" appears as /nUyÓk/. Both the standard cluster and the child's simplification occur in the forms

/slÍpErs/ and /slÍpEs/ "slippers". Only the simplified cluster occurs in /bAč/ "bunch" although the full cluster appears in another word /lAnč/ "lunch". Both /čEynč/ and /čEyn/ "change" occur, with the nasal rather than the affricate preserved her in the simplified version. Since clusters are a later linguistic development in child language, and since we find clusters and cluster simplifications side by side, we must assume that we are dealing with two linguistic strata: an older one, without clusters, and a newer one, where clusters already occur. The same conclusion would apply to vowels where the newer stage of complex vowel nuclei, however, is much less developed than the clustering of consonants is.

Two more simplifications should be mentioned. /ÁŋkI/ "uncle" is the only instance found of a vocalization of the standard consonant /l/. In our recordings, it occurs only in the father's presence, which does not seem relevant since the same phonetic form occurs frequently in Anthony's day speech. An interesting fluctuation takes place with the proper name "Fuchs": both /fyUk/ and /fyUks/ occur. An explanation of this example could be Anthony's mistaken assumption that the /s/ is a sign of the plural, a morpheme known to him, but omitted frequently.

With three-consonant clusters, we again find fluctuation within the same lexical items. Thus, the "Humpty Dumpty" example quoted earlier, or, e.g., /-kst/ ~ /-st/ in /fIkst/ ~ /fIst/ "fixed".

Two consonant clusters called for by the lexical items do not appear, the words being "envelope" and "belt". In the first instance, Anthony solved the problem of his unstable /v/ by simply substituting /b/, his frequent substitution for /v/, for the whole cluster, hence /ÉbElOwp/. In the second word, since /-lt/ is absent in his speech, he uses an epenthetic vowel, thus, /bÉlEt/. One more comment: /spÓrtkAr/ appears regularly with a three consonant sequence rather than the standard "sports-car" with four consonants due to the pronunciation of the word by the Scandinavian members of the household.

PHONEMIC SHAPES OF WORDS

In terms of their length, words in the corpus can be divided roughly into three groups: monosyllabic, dissyllabic, and trisyllabic words. As we would expect, monosyllabic words constitute by far the largest proportion, followed by the dissyllabic and tri-syllabic ones. Figures 40 and 41 show their number of occurrences and their proportions. This fact, however, does not seem to be characteristic of children's language alone, but of English in general, as shown by Roberts, who has found the same relative order of syllabic word length. In counting words, we have followed the same principles as were used for determining phoneme frequencies.

As for the shapes of words, we have analyzed their consonant and vowel sequences in Figures 42, 43 and 44. In regard to the glides /y/ and /w/ and /h/, if their function is not purely consonantal they are indicated in parentheses if they do occur in some

PHONEMIC LENGTH OF WORDS

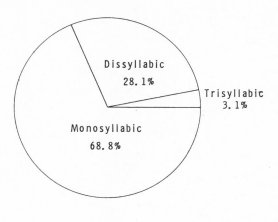

FIGURE 40

instances. It should be remembered that in postvocalic position they are still unstable in the child's idiolect, and hence we have word shapes ending in simple vowels, unusual for standard English, which may fluctuate with the sequence of vowel plus glide.

The most frequent shape is CV(G)C, accounting for 3.59% of the monosyllabics, and for 24.7% of the total words. Next in frequency is the CV(G) shape, due to occurrences of the definite article, and the words *do, go, to, too*; in terms of percentages, CV(G) makes up 21.5% of the monosyllabics and 14.8% of all the words. V(G)C is the next frequent shape, 18.1% of the monsyllabics and 12.5% of the total. This is of course due to words like *up, on, it*, and others like it. The indefinite article *a* accounts for fifty-four out of fifty-eight occurrences of V(G) shaped words, a much smaller number of occurrences than the definite article. *And* occurs over one hundred times which is almost all the occurrences of the V(G)CC shape. It should perhaps be pointed out that the relatively large number of VCCVCV sequences, as compared to other similar sequences, is due to occurrences of the child's name, *Anthony*. (The only other word of that shape, occurring twice, is *already*.) Furthermore, the VCCVCVC shape consists entirely of occurrences of the possessive *Anthony's*.

The CV(G)CV(G) shape is fourth in order of frequency due to common usage of words like *Bobo, Daddy, Mommy*; the CV(G)CC, CV(G)CV(G)C, and CCV(G)C. shapes are also quite common, as might be expected on the basis of standard English.

Several occurrences of telescoping were found, some side by side with longer forms as /ÉntI/ and /ÉnI/ together with the much more usual /ÉntOnI/ "Anthony", or /nÁdEr/ side by side with /EnÁdEr/ "another", others only in the shorter form, as

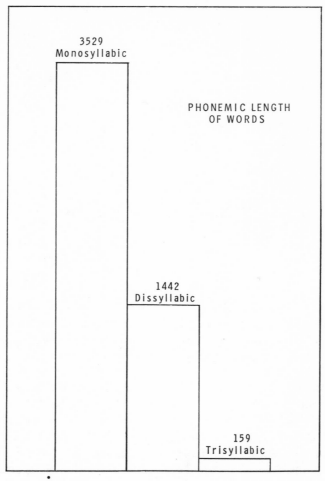

3529
Monosyllabic

PHONEMIC LENGTH
OF WORDS

1442
Dissyllabic

159
Trisyllabic

FIGURE 41

/bÉkAs/ and /frÍkAs/ for the standard *Rebecca's* and *Frederica's*. Grégoire has made similar observations on omission of syllables in polysyllabic words. On the other hand, an addition of a syllable to a word also appears e.g., /wÍkI/ together with /wIk/ "weak", and /wÓlE/ for "wall", a form also current in the child's day speech, although /l/ occurs finally elsewhere.

In describing the canonical forms of words, Roberts has also found the CVC pattern to be most frequent. In listing the types of phonetic syllables, French's 33.5% for CVC is closely parallel to our 35.9%, as is his CV of 21.8% as compared to our 21.5%. French also lists VC as the next frequent shape at 20.3% comparable to our 18.1%, the third in frequency as well.

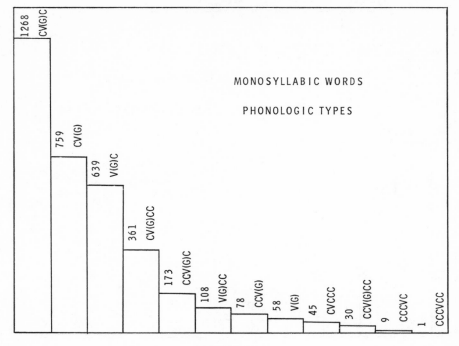

FIGURE 42

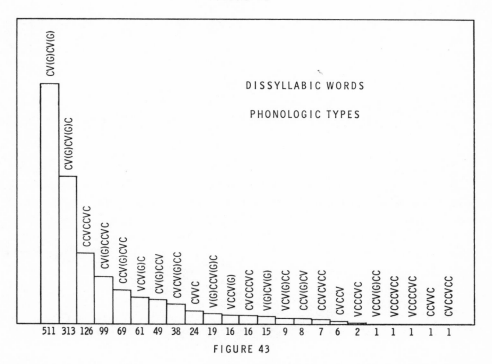

FIGURE 43

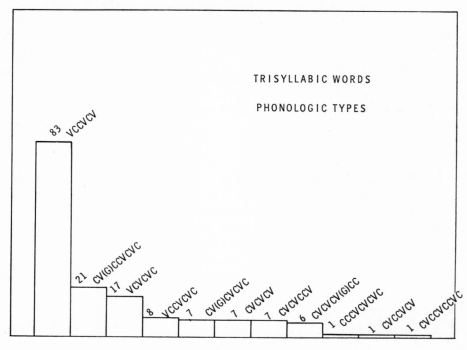

FIGURE 44

GRAMMAR

The question has been raised by investigators of child language whether the development of morphology, that is, the formation of elementary units containing both form and meaning (morphemes) and their combinations into words, precedes that of syntax, the make-up of sentences from words, or vice versa. Leopold (1949) arrived at the conclusion that syntax had reached a more mature stage than had morphology in his daughter's speech by the age of two. This would not be surprising with a monolingual child learning English in view of the fact that syntactic arrangements play such an important role in English grammar. However, Leopold's daughter was bilingual and German, her other language, has a rather complex system of inflection. Gvozdev's investigation (1949) of monolingual children learning a highly inflected language, in this case Russian, confirms Leopold's conclusions. Evidence that the syntactic relationships are mastered earlier than morphologic inflection is borne out by cases where endings are used correctly syntactically, but belonging to the wrong paradigm of the standard language. Thus, for example, an instrumental is used properly, but a masculine instrumental ending is attached to a feminine stem, distinguishing clearly between imperfect morphologic and good syntactic learning of the language.

Anthony's monologues present an analogous situation. Although rapid morphologic and syntactic development has been observed between the 27th and 30th month in the child's life, for example, by Velten (1934), no significant differences have been observed in these recordings which cover roughly the same period of time. The child's syntax appears more mature than his morphology in the recordings, and even more so in his day speech; this is probably to be expected in an English-speaking monolingual child due to the grammatical structure of English with its morphologic paucity. It is particularly interesting, therefore, to have the findings corroborated from investigations of children learning highly inflected languages, a fact perhaps pointing to the greater universality of syntax over morphology suggestive of Jakobson's (1941) phonemic acquisition theory. Since contrastive word order is one of the most distinctive aspects of English grammar, it is the best learned feature in the child's syntax, and we can illustrate with it what is meant. There are only few instances in Anthony's speech where his word order does not conform to standard English patterns, although there are a number of instances of elliptical constructions. However, the relative order remains and is quite stable. On the other hand, he may or may not use an ending where it properly belongs. We have, for example, the sequence: *Three bottle. Four bottles. And two bottle.* It could be argued that he considered the numeral alone a sufficient signal for the plural, and the plural morpheme of the noun an unnecessary redundant feature used only with the highest number in the context, but this does not hold true when we compare the phrases *All the bird* and *All the birds*, both of which occur, *all the* being the highest numerical concept for the child. It seems clear that he knows that there is a plural morpheme, but he uses it at will, showing its instability in his speech. The syntactic pattern remains the same and is often the standard one. Another example would be the haphazard use of the past tense morpheme. Both the forms *happen* and *happened* occur, but so does the sentence *What happen to man* where open transition after the nasal /n/ and before the alveolar stop /t/ clearly indicates the lack of a past tense morpheme. (The third person singular morpheme could occur in the same position, but context precludes it.)

For greater convenience and ease, standard orthography is used in discussing Anthony's speech in this and the following sections. However, when the phonetic make-up of an item or items appears relevant to our discussion, phonetic or phonemic transcriptions will be used or referred to.

MORPHOLOGY

Morphology is traditionally divided into two parts: inflection and derivation. For the purposes of this study, such a division will be maintained.

The recent experiments of Berko (1958) with pre-school and first-grade children present some conclusions which correlate rather closely with our findings. Similarly, the rather limited morphology which Leopold (1949) found at the end of the second year in the speech of his daughter shows an analogous pattern. Since Anthony falls chronologically between the age of the children in Berko's experiment on the one hand and Leopold's daughter on the other, it will be of interest to see how far-reaching Anthony's morphological patterns are. It should be kept in mind, however, that the sample of speech studied here is confined to the recorded pre-sleep monologues, although the morphologic system of the monologues, like the phonemic system, differs little from his day speech. This is not true of units larger than morphemes.

Inflection

In regard to inflection in the immature morphologic system of a child, the question must be raised whether a paradigm of the language has been learned, or whether different forms of the paradigm still function as separate lexical items, unrelated grammatically. Some of the latter instances do occur, but the most common English morphologic patterns have been learned quite well.

Nouns. The two English noun inflections, plural and possessive, are phonemically identical in Anthony's speech. However, they can readily be distinguished by context. Furthermore, the possessive forms are limited to proper names, or names of personalized toys: *Anthony's, Becca's, Betsy's, Daddy's, Frica's, Kitty's* (this is the proper name of the cat in the household), *Mommy's, Bobo's, Smokey's.* All except *Becca, Betsy, Frica* occur as well in non-possessive forms, and they are the names of people, animals, and toys of greatest importance to the child. The only one missing which could be expected is *Cobbers*, the name of the dog in the house, but there, because of the phonemic shape of the word, the possessive does not have a special marker. This implies a classification of nouns into personalized and non-personalized nouns which is also supported by the pattern of pronominal substitution. An analogous classification was arrived at by Kaper (1959) on the basis of the use or non-use of the article with nouns.

Fewer than fifty instances of the possessive were found in the corpus. Nevertheless, it seems to be a learned pattern in the child's speech, and not mere quotations of separate lexical forms, although constructions do occur which would require a possessive suffix where it is missing.

Similarly, in regard to plural inflection, a pattern has been established, but it has not yet been learned perfectly. Over one hundred instances in the running text are plural formations, confined to some forty different lexical items, a relatively small proportion. A few occur only in the plural, for example, *slippers, weeds, woods,* and others. Most of them have both singular and plural forms. One "irregular" plural form occurs, *mice*, without a singular counterpart, and it is probably a citation form from the nursery rhyme "Three Blind Mice" with which the child was familiar, without his awareness that this was actually a plural form. Few of the English "irregular" plurals occur together with a singular form, although the child's lexicon includes a number of nouns falling into this category. The forms *man* and *men* are found several times, both in their simple forms as well as in compounds like *mailman*, but the phonemic pattern of the child which does not include the standard English phoneme /æ/ makes it impossible to distinguish the singular from the plural in this case. On the other hand, the regular plural has not yet been learned sufficiently well to extend it to an analogous new formation **mans* by the child, something which did occur a few months later. *Foot* occurs, as does the plural form *feet*, separately and in the proper name *Twofeet*, and the child seems aware of the relationship of the singular and plural forms of this particular word.

As to the morphemic variants used both with the possessive and plural morphemes, both /-z/ and /-s/ occur as expected on the basis of standard English, but the voiceless variant frequently fluctuates with the voiced, a common pattern in Anthony's phonology. He encounters no difficulty in plural or possessive formations of words ending in a vowel; one /-Ez/ plural occurs, *glasses*, as well as the singular *glass*, but it is questionable that the /-Ez/ is an active plural formation in his language. Two different stem morphemes seem to be present here: the singular *glass* refers to a drinking glass, and the plural *glasses* to spectacles, hence true plural formation seems dubious. In Berko's experiment, the pre-school children found little or no difficulty in the use of /-z/ or /-s/. They responded very well to the plural formation in *glasses* (75% of the pre-school children formed the plural correctly) but the majority were unable to use the /-əz/ plural in new situations.

Adjectives. Adjectival inflection does not exist in Anthony's speech. The word *better* occurs once, obviously a separate lexical item, unrelated paradigmatically to *good* which also occurs. There is an example of *those* in adjectival function, also apparently unrelated to the singular *that* in the child's mind. Leopold arrives at a similar conclusion for his daughter's speech and in Berko's study only one out of eighty children, including first graders, was able to supply a comparative and superlative in a standard English paradigmatic fashion. This, in spite of the fact that the adults, tested along with the children, were unanimous in their response of inflection. Gvozdev (1949) also reports that the meaning of comparisons is learned by a child only at about three and a half years of age; deviations of forms from the standard occur frequently until the age of seven. Apparently adjective inflection, although an active pattern in adult speech, is acquired quite late by the child, perhaps an indication that it is not a common pattern in the languages of the world.

The possessive adjectives *her*, *my*, *your* are found rarely; they are used syntactically correctly, but it is apparent that the category of gender has not yet been learned, as the example *Bobo took off her blanket* shows.

Verbs. Turning next to verb inflections, our findings again show some parallel to those of Berko. The best learning of marked forms is found with the progressive forms which occur with more than thirty different verbs (it should be noted that "two-word verbs" like *get up* are considered separate verb entries, different from the simple verb *get*), most of which also exist unmarked in the corpus. This is a well-learned paradigm which has been in the child's morphologic system for some time, although its phonemic shape is unstable. Nevertheless, it is perhaps the most firmly established morphologic pattern and a favorite verb form, although used in sentences quite often elliptically without a form of the verb "be". Interestingly enough, Leopold finds the *-ing* form poorly established before the end of the second year.

Next in frequency of marked forms is the past inflection. Out of the pattern forms occurring, only few do not have an unmarked counterpart in the corpus. The different verb forms include relatively few regularly formed past morphemes, most of them being strong verb forms. No analogic new-formations with the past suffix are found. In view of the relatively great number of strong verbs with past forms, and the past ending of *started* (a late development in Berko's data) it seems that the past paradigm as a morphemic feature has really not yet found a foothold (which is not true of the *-ing* formations), but the past and non-past forms of individual verbs have been generalized in the child's system.

A few verbs exhibit both the -*ing* and, in addition to the unmarked form, the past forms. Again, several are not "regular" verbs which seems to strengthen our conclusions, namely, the weakness of the past as a paradigm, as compared to the relative strength of active -*ing* formations. Still, a paradigm it is for individual verbs, as its contrastive use shows, for example, in these two successive sentences: *Bobo, go take off the hat. Bobo took off the hat.*

The third person singular morpheme exhibits the only analogic new-formation – *brokes*, although it is found only in two verbs with the unmarked stem occurring as well, *plays* and *wants*, and in three more verb forms with both the unmarked and the -*ing* forms, *comes, looks, puts.* The status of this particular morpheme is similar to that of the past marker: it has been generalized only for several individual verbs, fewer in number than those using the past. Otherwise it is characterized by its frequent omission and only its occasional use. The -*ing* form takes the place of a marked non-past, and the great number of unmarked forms make it quite difficult to distinguish between imperative and non-imperative constructions.

The few verbs which remain to be discussed are the following: *broke*, with analogic formations of *brokes*, as well as *broken.* The standard English "break" does not occur, and *broke* is the unmarked form in this paradigm. *Have* occurs in its unmarked form, as well as *has* and *had. Go* includes *goes, going, went,* and *gone,* the latter used adjectivally in *all gone* most frequently. The paradigm of *be* in addition to the infinitive includes *am, is, are,* and *was.* It is our belief that the above forms do represent fragmental paradigms in the child's language, not used with complete consistency by any means, but still showing some awareness of their paradigmatic relationships. The discussion of modal auxiliaries is included in the section on the Verb Phrase.

Pronouns. Analyses of standard English pronouns vary in their interpretations of the various pronominal forms as variants of a single morpheme, or as separate morphemes. This problem is not at issue here since we are primarily interested in the forms which occur, and in how well they are established. Of the personal pronouns, the form *it* has by far the widest occurrence (over one hundred), and is firmly established in the child's speech pattern. Occasionally it is over-used as a substitute for a plural noun at the expense of *them.* The frequent use of *it* confirms the child's classification of nouns into personalized and non-personalized classes as was pointed out. The non-personalized nouns permit substitution by the pronoun *it* rather frequently, whereas the personalized nouns (including names of persons, favorite toys, and animals) rarely are substituted for by pronouns.

In speaking of himself, the child uses *Anthony* much more frequently than *I*, the use of which is restricted to special situations. The instances where *I* does occur are either instances of complete quotations from adult speech, like *I don't hear you* where the use of *do* in a negative indicative sentence also points to a non-internalized structural pattern; or *I* occurs in the child's attempts at adult speech as apparent from the context surrounding the sentence, e.g., *Door. I'm fixing the door. Door's open*;

or *I* appears when the rest of the sentence contains no particularly bothersome structural consideration for the child, as in *I have a blanket like a lipstick* where *blanket like a lipstick* is one of the child's "set" expressions as it were. However, the pronoun is also consciously practised, as the two consecutive sentences show: *I'm taking the yellow blanket, I gave the yellow blanket.*

Of about the same order of frequency is *you*, also about twenty-five times, and its usage shows similarity to that of *I*. They are also practised together, for example, in this question-answer interchange: *Where are you going. I am going.* The other personal pronouns occurring are *she*, *her*, *he*, *him*, *me*, *we* and *them*, all with a frequency ranging from one to fewer than ten occurrences. All these pronouns appear in the correct syntactic slots as compared to standard English, but the category of gender has not yet been learned, similar to the case of possessive adjectives. There is one occurrence of *himself* in the corpus, and we have no additional information on the reflexive paradigm except perhaps for the sentence *I told me*, conspicuous by the non-use of the reflexive. It is certainly not surprising to find pronominal substitution with the child's class of personalized pronouns so poorly learned in that it involves viewing the speech event not only from the point of view of the addresser and addressee, but also from the point of view of the person or thing discussed.

Interrogative pronouns show an interesting distribution. *Why* occurs only very few times, which certainly would not be true a few months later in the child's development. At the time of the recordings, he had not yet reached the "why" stage in his day speech either. *How*, *which*, and *who* also are quite rare. *What* has the widest occurrence (more than fifty) due to his preoccupation with colors and his favorite question *What color*. Asking for location, *where*, has about half the distribution of *what*, and it is a firmly established question pattern.

Derivation

New-formations of words by derivation or compounding as active linguistic patterns are neither strong in the monologues nor in the day speech at the time, but they do begin to appear strongly about two months later in Anthony's day speech.

In the monologues, there are *pig* and *piggie*, *horse* and *horsie*, *dog* and *doggie*, but the two items of the pair are used interchangeably without any awareness of *-ie* as a diminutive suffix. Both *tickle* and *ticklish* occur, the only example of adjectival derivation. The child is certainly aware of the semantic relationship of the two words, but it is doubtful that he could use this grammatical device in a new situation. Subsequent to the recordings, however, neologisms were quite frequent. For example, the child owned a whistle and apparently did not like to use the same phonetic sequence for noun and verb, and the action of whistling he termed [wɪs]. The same apocopation was performed on *measure* where the verb became [mɛž]. Sentences like [wɪs də wɪsɛl] and [ɛ́ntə̀ní wɔ́nts tʊ̀ mɛ́ž] were not uncommon. Could he have become aware of the English agentative suffix with which the ending of *measure* could easily be confused, and his conclusion was extended by analogy to *whistle*? The answer must be yes because this seems the only possible explanation of these new-formations. Two more original compounds were also found: one, *bathing room*, is used in addition to the standard *bathroom*. The new-formation was probably coined by analogy with "bathing suit", a word well known to the child. The other neologism is *phone call book*, a coinage due to the child's greater familiarity with *phone call* than merely "phone".

A number of standard English compound forms occur, for example *lipstick*, *necktie*, *applesauce*, and others. Both *mailman* and *postman* are found due to different linguistic background of the speakers in the home. The single morphemes *mail* and *man* are also used, and it is quite possible that the child is aware of the separate morphemes in *mailman*. The same would hold true for *Twofeet* (proper name in a story), and *two* and *feet*, kept apart by the child by different stress patterns, two morphemes he plays with as will be shown later, showing his awareness of more than one morpheme in the name. *Cider, applecider, cider* follow each other in this order during the monologues, another indication of his awareness of compounding. One truly "creative" effort in new formations is shown in his word /nÁmfIŋ/ "nothing", for which he obviously had to decompose *something*, also occurring, into *some* plus *thing*, and replace the first part by the negative of his own, /nÁm/.

The use of the same phonetic sequence for two different morphemes did not bother him in the monologues, however, e.g., *dance* is used both as a verb and as a noun. As a matter of fact he can perform this transformation of form classes on the same sound sequence quite readily, as the two consecutive sentences in the text, *Bite the mailman* and *Mailman have a bite* clearly show. *Bite* in the first sentence is an un-ambiguous imperative of the verb, whereas in the second sentence the preceding indefinite article as well as its position in the pattern identify *bite* as a noun.

Statistical Findings

In presenting some statistical information on the types of words which occur in the monologues, we are confronted by a difficulty inherent in the material, which will be even greater in our syntactic analysis, namely, the use of strictly formal criteria with the sentence as the highest unit for the analysis of the language of a very young child who is about to fall asleep. We had to make some arbitrary decisions as to what was a "word" in the child's language particularly in those instances that we have grouped under the heading of *interjections*. Specifically, this category is made up of greetings, the expression *OK* which occurs about ten times, and those phonemic sequences other than those included in the remaining classes which occur as part of a paragraph. Their phonemic shapes are varied; some are different phonetic realizations, analogous to standard English *oh* or *ah* or *yeah*, others may have the phonemic shape or a reasonable approximation of a standard English word but do not contain its referential meaning, e.g., [bɪŋk], and still others may just be part of the paragraph for a number of reasons, like [bɪš], without standard English analogy.

Applying also these criteria, we can distinguish in the corpus about 5,500 running

CONTENT AND FUNCTION WORDS

WORD EVENTS

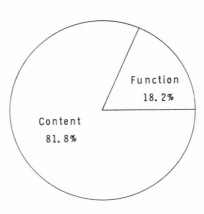

FIGURE 45

words. These in turn are made up of about 4,500 "content" words, that is, nouns, pronouns, verbs, adjectives, adverbs, and numerals. The rest can be grouped into a general category of "function" words of which there are about 1,000 consisting of prepositions, articles, conjunctions, and interjections. As Figure 45 indicates, the relationship of these two large subgroups is better than four to one, content words making up more than 80% and function words less than 20% of the running text. The relatively small number of semantically empty words is to be expected in the language of a young child, those words with a primarily grammatical function being secondary in importance to him to symbols relating to the world of experience. Articles, consisting mainly of the definite article, constitute almost 50% of function words, an indication that this grammatical feature of English has been quite well learned. A more detailed analysis of the content words shows roughly 3% for the numerals (the ordinals from one to ten occur, and *all* is included since it functions as the highest numeral in the child's language), 8% are adjectives, 9% pronouns, 15% adverbs, 27% verbs, and 38% nouns. The following Figures 45, 46, 47, 48, 49, give detailed representations of the number of occurrences and their proportions.

It is important to distinguish, however, between running words, or word events on the one hand, and different words or word designs, on the other. Particularly in regard to content words, the question of word design is important (see Figures 50, 51) and we have therefore compared these events and designs. The ratio of verb events and designs remains basically unchanged, the difference being about one percent. Adjectives and numerals do not differ appreciably either, showing similar ratios. In

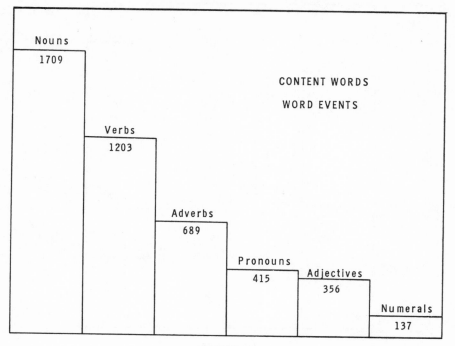

FIGURE 46

CONTENT WORDS

WORD EVENTS

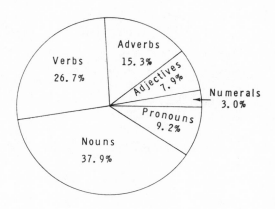

FIGURE 47

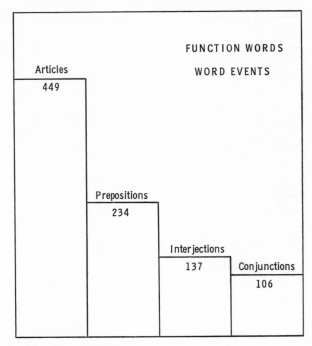

FIGURE 48

FUNCTION WORDS
WORD EVENTS

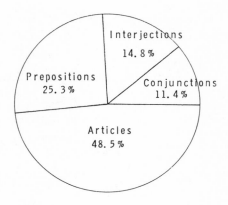

FIGURE 49

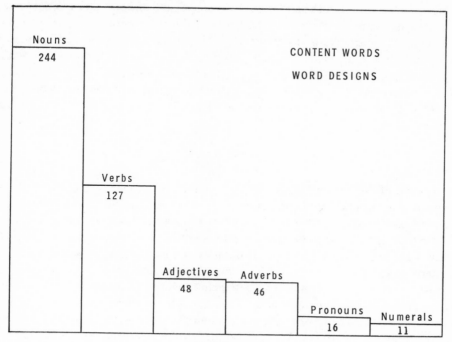

FIGURE 50

CONTENT WORDS

NUMBER OF OCCURRENCES OF WORD DESIGNS

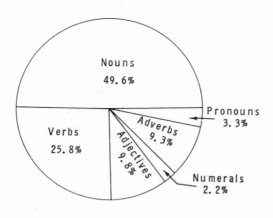

FIGURE 51

regard to nouns, pronouns, and adverbs a significant difference can be observed:
noun designs jump to almost 50% with a reduction of pronoun designs to slightly
more than 3% and adverbs to about 9%. Nouns have the highest ratios both in
events and designs, an expected finding on the basis of other investigations on child
language, but they also offer a far greater design than verbs do, almost twice as many.
Pronouns show just the opposite, their designs having a considerably smaller ratio
than their events, pointing to a limited repertoire of pronouns with quite frequent
syntactic use.

SYNTAX

The analysis of Anthony's syntax presents a number of problems in terms of formal
descriptive techniques. Some phonologic criteria for delineating units of speech were
discussed previously (p. 29) but, as mentioned, their functional role is still unstable
in the child's speech. Various levels of pitch and contours certainly accompany his
speech, but their structural role seems dubious at best. Wherever we can recognize
a pattern, it will be used in the analysis, often in a supplementary fashion. A rising
intonation contour, for example, can only help to identify at times a question, if it is
also supported by other features pointing to the same conclusion. It cannot be used
by itself, however. The most consistent phonologic criterion for delimited sentences
in the monologues are pauses. We have adopted this as our basic phonologic criterion,
with accompanying pitch distributions as described earlier. Still, phonologic criteria
alone are unsatisfactory, as are morphemic ones. The corpus must be viewed in terms
of larger units than sentences, and the analysis proceeds from these larger units on
down, until we get to the word, the smallest unit in our syntax.

Categories

The largest unit or the constituent of the corpus is what we are going to label a
PARAGRAPH. In relation to the corpus, a paragraph can be defined in terms of a
number of language functions, a classification which will be dealt with more fully in
the section on Discourse Analysis. Suffice it to say here that a paragraph is a
linguistically defineable unit in terms of the various hierarchical orderings of its
functions. Following is an example of a paragraph, with each line numbered to
facilitate further discussion.

(1) *Daddy*
(2) *Daddy bucket please*
(3) *Another other book please*
(4) *Donkey*
(5) *Fix the donkey*
(6) *And the blue box and the big box*

Our next unit, smaller than the paragraph, is the SEQUENCE. In our example, there
are four sequences: lines (1) and (2), line (3), lines (4) and (5), and line (6) are separate

sequences. In delimiting the unit of speech by pauses, our most consistent criterion, we often encounter instances where the child's capacity for language is exceeded in the attempt to produce an intended unit of speech and he has to proceed in a step-by-step fashion. In our example, *Daddy* in line (1), followed by a pause, is the first essential step for the child in order to produce line (2), *Daddy bucket please*, just as *Donkey* in line (4) constitutes a necessary prerequisite for the child to come up with line (5), *Fix the donkey*. This linguistic characteristic of his "idiolect" is not confined to the pre-sleep monologues, but is all-pervasive. It is on this level that we define the sequence, a rather mechanical operation by the child which permits him to produce longer units otherwise not possible. The important linguistic feature is purely combinatory and not also selective as it is in the case of the next unit, the sentence.

The make-up of the speech unit within the pauses is varied: (*a*) it can be a complete grammatical sentence, as in line (5), *Fix the donkey*, or (*b*) it can be an elliptic sentence easily completed by us so that its meaning is unambiguous, like telegraphic style, e.g., line (2), *Daddy bucket please*. Without resorting to the context we know that a vocative is present, followed by the object of an imperative with the verb omitted. Another type of ellipsis (*c*) occurs in line (6), *And the blue box and the big box* which is a non-elliptic phrase, but an elliptic sentence. We have no information whether the noun phrase with the copula *and* is subject or object or what syntactic function, other than that of the phrase, it is to perform. Still another problem (*d*) is posed by line (3), *Another other book please* which is obviously also elliptic, but also non-grammatical in terms of English syntax. Another example from the corpus of a non-grammatical utterance would be, for example, *What the take the blanket*. It would be futile to attempt to perform a syntactic analysis on non-grammatical utterances in order to describe the child's operative linguistic system. These utterances are syntactic mistakes, by no means haphazard, but at the same time not reflecting what has been internalized by the child. For the purposes of sentence analysis we disregard them and deal only with grammatical sentences as defined under (a) and (b), describing their constituent phrase make-up. This will include perforce the description of units under (*c*) phrases, with possible additional comments about those not encountered under (*a*) and (*b*).

Sequences

There are three basic types of sequences which we will call *build-ups*, *break-downs*, and *completions*, all consisting of more than one unit of speech delimited by pauses; there are usually two, and sometimes three such units. In the case of build-ups and completions, as the names imply, the resulting or last unit is the longest and may be a sentence; the reverse is true of break-downs. An analogy could be drawn to Jones' *breath groups* or *sense groups* (1940), or to Jakobson's *speech measures* as being the beginning of a build-up or combination, and a result of a break-down.

Build-ups. This is the most frequent sequence type in the corpus. Examples appear in the paragraph on p. 80, and here is another one of the same type of build-up:

Thumb	*Sit down*
or	
That's a thumb	*Sit down on the blanket*

The characteristic feature of the build-up sequence is that the original phonemic shape of the initial speech measure is contained in the subsequently constructed longer combinations of words, as our examples show. Increasing length is important. Semantic content of the first speech measure as relating to the resulting unit is secondary, as shown by the example: /yUs/, *You sleep and rest*, where both lines contain the same initial phonemes, but /yUs/ is the actualization of "juice", bearing no semantic relation to *You sleep and rest*.

The build-up can contain more than two parts, usually three, where an additional step is interposed between the first speech measure and the resulting unit, e.g.:

Block
Yellow block
Look at all the yellow block

Here the process is very orderly, starting with a simple noun and adding only more relevant context to it. A somewhat less orderly example would be:

Light
See yellow blanket
Up there in yellow light

where the original *light* also appears as the last member of the resulting unit, as *block* did in the previous example, but from the second unit only *yellow* has been included in the third.

Break-downs. Break-downs work in a similar fashion in the opposite direction, e.g.:

Anthony jump out again	*Another big bottle*
or	
Anthony jump	*Big bottle*

In the first case, the beginning two words are echoed, in the other, the last two. Decrease in unit length is important. A somewhat different example would be a three-step break-down, as in:

Clock off
Clock
Off

where each word of the first unit is repeated separately, or where the original unit is broken down into two longer units as in:

Was that from that
Was that
That from that

the final *that* in the second speech measure and the initial *that* of the third being repetitious.

Build-ups and break-downs can alternate with each other, thus forming a chain with essentially the same vocabulary. For example:

Call up Mommy
Call up Mommy's all gone
All gone

where the first part of the longer unit appears as a build-up, the second part as a break-down; only "is", phonemically a single sibilant phoneme is omitted.

A slightly more complex example of the same combinatory process would be:

Mommy
Mommy went bye-bye
Mommy
Mommy went

Here *Mommy* just serves as a build-up for the longest unit, then as its smallest break-down and together with *went* as a longer break-down.

Completions. Completion is similar to the build-up in that its characteristic is the construction of longer units from shorter ones, but it differs in two important ways: one, comparative length of the units is irrelevant, and two, the child does not produce the longer combination himself and is satisfied with the intervening pause. Examples of completion sequences are:

Look at those pineapple		*And put it*
	or	
In a pretty box		*Up there*

where no repetition of identical phonemic shapes occurs, the length of each unit within the sequence is not important, and yet the second part is obviously inteded as part of the first sentence. Sometimes a partial repetition of phonemic shapes occurs here, however, like with, e.g.:

Anthony take the
Take the book

where there is little doubt that the second part is a completion of the first. A completion sequence consisting of three units is also possible:

Bobo's goes
To the bathroom
Clean off

translated would be the grammatical sentence "Bobo is going to the bathroom to clean off", the *-ing* being implied in the first line by a variant of "is", and the word "to" is omitted in the third line probably because the child felt that its presence in the second line was sufficient.

Sentences

In describing and analyzing sentences in the speech of children, some investigators have found the mechanical length of each sentence to be the most convenient starting point. Leopold (1949), for example, has done just that, beginning with one-word sentences, describing all types in this category, then going to two-word sentences and doing the same, and so forth. His sentences were determined by pauses which is also our main phonologic criterion in isolating sentences as well as non-grammatical utterances, but, because of the nature of the data, we have not chosen to use sentence length as our descriptive mold; instead, we view the sentence as made up of various layers which can be described in terms of immediate constituents. However, since some statistical information is relevant to our analysis of the corpus, we give it here as well, and then proceed with the description. For statistical purposes, no distinction was made between sentences and non-grammatical utterances, and the term *sentence* here includes both.

As is evident from Figures 52 and 53, two- and three-word sentences are the most frequent ones. There are somewhat fewer one-word sentences. This can be partially explained by the fact that the child's vocabulary includes a number of two-word verbs like *stand up*, *put on*, and others, which, when delimited by pauses, are two-word sentences. Also the child has clearly reached a higher step of linguistic development than that characterized by the predominance of one-word sentences. Four- and five-word sentences are still quite common, and the drop to six-word sentences is considerable. Longer sentences are quite rare. However, as we have shown in our discussion of sequences, the construction of longer sentences often exceeds the child's linguistic capacity, and he resorts to a step-by-step procedure in working them out. Many of his six- and seven-word sentences also appear to be repetitions or close approximations of sentences heard, e.g., *Anthony wants to talk to Daddy* or *And then put this one right there*. Another source of longer sentences are small syntactic additions to "set" expressions like *I got a blanket like a lipstick* where *I got a* is added to one of his pet phrases. Longer sentences often result in non-grammatical utterances like *That's Mommy put on Anthony's slippers* which is an example of the child's exceeding his combinatory ability and of his inability to use a relative pronoun. Of the three eight-word sentences one appears a quotation, the other two are enumerations. The one nine-word sentence is the chain of counting from one to nine, and the ten-word sentence came into being by the omission of a pause in a negative transformation, *There's the doggie not yet there's the doggie*.

As was mentioned, the analysis of sentences will not include the description of non-grammatical utterances, but only non-elliptic and elliptic sentences as defined on p. 81.

Three basic sentence types can be distinguished, using Fries' (1952) definitions: the imperative, the declarative, and the interrogative, to be discussed in this order.

Imperatives. The interpretation of the imperative as a wish, request, or command is of secondary concern to us in this section. What we are interested in here is the formal structure of this sentence type. Following Fries' statement on the basic contrastive patterns for the three kinds of sentences, the definition of the imperative is: "Class 2

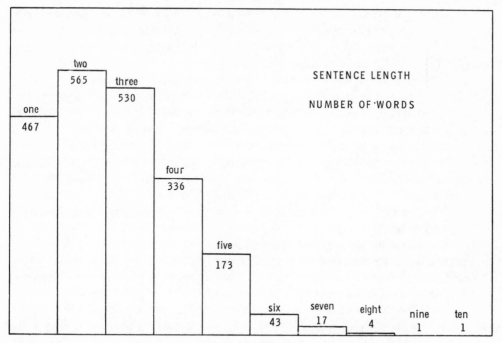

FIGURE 52

SENTENCE LENGTH

NUMBER OF WORDS

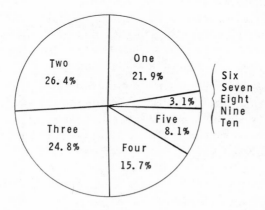

FIGURE 53

[verb] (in the simple unchanging form of this part of speech; alone, or) followed by a Class 1 word [noun] *not* "tied" by a correspondence or correlation of forms, signals a *request*." Instead of Class 2 and Class 1, we use the rough equivalents of *verb* and *noun* as we indicated in brackets above.

In our corpus, there are a number of imperatives which are verbs alone, either simple verbs or two-part verbs, e.g., *Come, look, lie down, turn around*. A purely verbal imperative can also occur expanded, as *Go lie down* or *Go to sleep, Go drive* or *Let's wait*, the last probably being a quotation form. Another possible expansion is with a negation, e.g., *Don't jump* or *No, go*, the second type being less frequent. We shall call the expanded or non-expanded verb a verbal phrase (VP), and this type of imperative will schematically be represented as VP. There is one more shape of VP which is elliptic although it occurs by itself only rarely; it is the non-verbal part of the two-part verb, in one example *Up*. This type of VP is more usual in longer imperatives as in *Up, Bobo*.

In addition to the VP imperative, several other constructions occur. A frequent imperative is the VP followed by a noun phrase (NP). As Fries has pointed out, in the imperative Class 2 and Class 1 are not "tied", that is, they do not exhibit correspondence or correlation of forms, and we, therefore, represent this sentence type VP $\leftarrow/\rightarrow$ NP. The shape of the VP here can be any of the ones already described in the VP, except the "up" type: single verb, two-word verb, two verbs, or a negative verb, e.g., *Take the book, Take the book off, Put on the blanket, Go get Smokey, Don't take the glasses off*. The NP can also have a number of shapes. In *Go get Smokey, Get shampoo, Take off slippers*, it is a singular or plural noun alone. More frequently, it consists of article plus noun, *Get the pillow* or *Open the window*. In a few elliptic imperatives, only the article constitutes the NP, e.g., *Open the*. *Some* can occur in the same position as the article, *Get some powder*. Preceding the article itself can be *all*, the highest numerical concept for the child, e.g., *Look at all the birds*.

Another modification within the NP is the possessive, occurring in the same slot as the article does, e.g., *Change Anthony's diaper*, or *Look at Kitty's feet*. Further expanding the NP, we find article + adjective + noun, *Move the yellow blanket*, or *Look at all the yellow block*, or *Put on a black robe*. The indefinite article does not occur without an additional modifier, either an adjective as in the last example, or an explanatory prepositional construction following the NP as in *Put on a record for you*, a possible quotation from adult speech. Postnominal modification occurs only infrequently and is usually non-grammatical, e.g., *Look at the lady standing orange*.

Instead of a noun and modifier, the NP can also consist of a pronoun: *Give it, Put it on, Look at it, Don't take it off*. The position of the pronoun in the sentence is usually correct in accordance with standard English, even in instances with a complex VP, e.g., *Get them fixed*. A complex sentence like *Put it on and put on record* by its sheer length indicates the lack of the usual pause in a substitution exercise (p. 110). Besides *it*, *that* and *this* also occur as in *Catch that* and *Now open this*.

After a VP with an intransitive verb, the following NP has a prepositional construction: *Lie down on the pillow* or *Go off to school*. Elliptic constructions also occur here, e.g., *Go to sleep in the*.

The next layer in the make-up of imperatives are adverbs or adverbial phrases (AP). If they occur with the VP alone, they follow it: *Stay there* or *Come here*. If, however, a NP is present as well, the AP can either precede or follow the VP: *Now put on the belt* or *Take off the block now* or *Look at the doggie again* or *Take the bottle then too* or *Put it there* or *Then lock it*, to give a few examples.

The last layer in the structure of imperatives is the vocative. It can be defined syntactically as well as morphologically and phonologically. In terms of syntax, it is the outer-most layer of the immediate constituents in imperative constructions. That is to say, it appears either at the beginning of the sentence or at the end. For example, *Put on the record, Daddy* or *Donkey, hold the door open*. It is either an unmodified noun as in the above examples, or the pronoun *you* as in *You stay*, or with a complex VP in *You stay and rest*; the pronoun only precedes the VP. Morphologically as to nouns, the same class of nouns which takes the possessive and which rarely permits pronominal substitution appears in the vocative. There are a few additions to the list given which represent additional personalized toys and objects, but the basic characteristic of this class of pseudo-animate nouns remains the same.

Two phonologic criteria can also be applied to distinguish the vocative, although neither is mandatory. One is a break in the intonation contour following or preceding a vocative, wherever it occurs. Thus, we have *Bobo stand on the blanket* or *Stop donkey*. The second phonologic characteristic is a pause, for example, *Bobo / come off*, either following or preceding the vocative. The duration of the pause is shorter than that of the pause delimiting sentences. It is crucial to apply as many of these vocative criteria as possible in order to arrive at unambiguous imperatives since a NP preceding an elliptic or unmarked VP is often ambiguous as to imperative or declarative interpretation.

Most imperatives are within the five-word, and occasionally, the six-word sentence pattern. However, there are a few which belong to the longer types. *Get him up at nine o'clock, Fifi* occurs in the corpus, but is somewhat different from most imperatives in that it uses the pronoun *him* and specifies a time the concept of which the child has not yet learned, in addition to being quite long. We suspect this to be mainly a quotation form, taken over as a unit from adult speech, in spite of the vocative *Fifi* which is the name of the child's toy poodle and which was the only part added independently by the child. Most other longer sentences of which there are only few, contain the conjunction *and* which takes the place of the usual delimiting pause, e.g., *Take the phone and get Smokey there*, simply a construction of two consecutive imperatives as were already described. *Say hello to Mrs. Fischer* is obviously an exact echo of a sentence heard. *See the blanket that I found* is a rare example of a sentence with a relative clause which could possibly be interpreted as an imperative, but it is without doubt a quotation form. Although *Let Daddy have it* is not unusually long, this construction is not within the child's linguistic capacity and must be considered a quotation as well. The most complex imperative structure handled quite well by the child is of the type *Look what Bobo did* where *look* and *Bobo* can be substituted for by other verbs and nouns respectively, thus showing an active pattern in the child's language rather than a mere quotation from adult speech.

Declaratives. Turning now to declarative sentences, we will again use Fries' definition as our starting point: "Class 1 ↔ Class 2 ("tied" by a certain correspondence or concordance of forms) signals a statement." (p. 145) The crucial word here, of course, is "tied", meaning the exhibit of some agreement of form as far as standard English utilizes this device. In terms of the imperative, where "not tied" was the characteristic feature, our task was easier because markers were not required. As we have discussed in our Section on Morphology, inflections have by no means been perfectly learned by the child, and hence "correspondence or concordance" is at times difficult to determine. The great number of elliptic constructions compounds the difficulties.

Leopold (1949) encountered similar problems, witness his statement that he could not find clear-cut formal criteria for wish, emotion, statement, etc., and that his classification is primarily determined by context. He considers as true imperatives only those followed by a vocative. However, he does find word order of significance since its pattern had already been learned quite well by his daughter. He also concludes that the character of a statement is clearest if the verb is non-present.

Leopold's formal criteria apply to our data as well, and since we are dealing with a child about two-and-a-half years of age, additional formal criteria can also be established. Nevertheless, a number of sentences remain ambiguous. The attempt will be made to use only formal criteria in this section and to refrain from interpretations although a number of sentences will remain unclassified for the time being. Meaning is at times also in conflict with formal criteria, as e.g., *Anthony wants the belt please* is clearly a request rather than a statement, but formally Fries' formula applies, the noun *Anthony* being "tied" with the verb *wants*, exhibiting concordance of form.

Throughout our discussion of the imperative, we have assumed word order in the child's language to be the same as in standard English, since we have found very few non-grammatical utterances attributable to word order alone, thus showing this feature of English grammar to have been well learned and even used contrastively to signal a question. Therefore, for the purposes of the description of declarative sentences, word order will not be discussed further.

As Leopold stated, one of the unambiguous declarative sentence types is that with the verb in the past, that is, containing a marked verb form, e.g., *He took it* or *Mommy gave some milk*. In addition, in our data, other marked forms of the verb serve the same purpose. Thus, the *-ing* form as in *Bobo waiting* or *I'm going* signals a declarative sentence as does the third person singular morpheme, for example, *Daddy goes on the train*, or *Cobbers has it*. In some instances, the modals perform the same function, as in *Will close it* or *We'll close it*, whichever it may be, a fact which cannot be determined. Much more frequent are constructions with *can* as in *Anthony can* *look* or the elliptic *Can smile. Only Daddy can* is a favorite construction permitting noun substitution in the pattern, and it is also the only frame where *could* occurs, *Only Nancy could.* Verb phrases with *have to* and *want to* are just being learned as shown by the fact that most sentences containing them seem to be quotations, but some, because of their elliptic character or vocabulary selection have already been constructed by the child: *I want to go Mommy's house* and *Had to close the door* on the one hand, and *Anthony want take it* and *Piggie had to* on the other. The same applies to the negative declarative constructions. We find *I don't hear you*, a quotation, as well as the still non-grammatical *Sally don't see.* It is by no means surprising that *do* constructions of negative commands have been learned so much better than declarative and interrogative *do* constructions; the child has certainly heard the former much more often with meanings important to him.

Unambiguously declarative are equational sentences beginning with *Here is* or *That is* and the relatively fewer *There is*, as in *Here is another hat* or *That's the tiger* or *There's the light.* Similarly, if the verb form has a grammatical marker and is inflected, Class 1 and Class 2 are "tied" in Fries' sense, and we have a declarative sentence structure, e.g., *Anthony wants the box.*

However, since inflection is often omitted, "tied" cannot be strictly applied to our corpus. Still, some instances are unambiguous without the presence of grammatical markers, e.g., *Anthony want the blue one* or *She go up there.* These are clearly declarative sentences; in the first example, except for the particular selection of *Anthony*, none of the vocative markers are present, and the berb *want* further points to a declarative structure. In the second example, the pronoun *she* makes the structure unambiguous, in spite of the absence of the third person singular morpheme. *Anthony take all the candies* is similarly interpreted as a declarative sentence. Nevertheless, a number of sentences still remain which are ambiguous as to declarative or imperative.

The simplest declarative sentence consists of a NP + VP, non-elliptic or elliptic, e.g., *Fifi standing* or *Sun is shining* or *I'm going* or *I have to read* or *Bobo can throw* or *I can* or *Shoe fixed* or *Bobo started sleeping*, or *Bobo's going to sleeping.* In all these constructions, the NP consists of an unmodified noun or pronoun. The favorite VP here are the *-ing* or past forms, with or without the appropriate form of "be". The omission of *is*, in particular, is a common feature throughout, and occasionally an unmarked verb form follows *is*, e.g., *Blanket is jump.* A further ellipsis of this pattern is the omission of the NP, leaving only a marked VP as in *Is sleeping* or just *Sleeping.* This simple declarative sentence occurs also in the negative, e.g., *I cannot* or *Bobo is not staying.*

A vocative, as defined phonologically and morphologically, also may occur with this sentence pattern as in *I'm looking, Bobo* or *Mommy, Bobo's not get off* showing clearly that the vocative is not confined only to imperatives.

A more complex sentence pattern is NP + VP + NP, the first NP usually equivalent to what is traditionally called "subject", the NP following the VP includes the traditional "object" as well as other NPs occurring in the same position. An example of this pattern would be *Donkey is closing the door* or *I have the yellow blanket*. As in the simpler sentence pattern, the NP preceding the VP is either an unmodified noun or a pronoun. In unambiguous constructions, the VP is usually "tied", that is, it exhibits some concordance or is a marked form or is made up of a modal with a verb, e.g., *I am fixing the door* or *Anthony found it* or *Doggie can bite the mailman*. Only once is the NP preceding the VP modified by an adjective in the elliptic sentence *Dirty Cobbers in the car*. We also find an example of a vocative used with this construction, *Alice, we have it*. We will return to ambiguous constructions after describing the make-up of the NP following the VP.

This NP, in contradistinction to the NP preceding the VP, exhibits a number of different shapes. It can be an unmodified noun or a pronoun, as in *Anthony got on Bobo* or *Bobo can throw it*. It can be also a modified noun, the modification being either the article, *Bobo took off the hat*, or a possessive adjective or noun occupying the same slot as the article, *Bobo took off her blanket* or *Going to get Mommy's skirt*, or the expanded construction of article + adjective, *I have the yellow blanket*, or the article or demonstrative preceded by *all*, *Anthony taking all the papers* or *Doggie's making all that noise*. The NP can also consist of two coordinate nouns as in *Anthony's watching ladies and man/men*. Modification by another NP occurs in the child's favorite saying *I got a blanket like a lipstick*.

This sentence pattern also occurs negatively, *I do not see the Kitty* or *I don't hear you* but we suspect those to be quotation forms.

After the verb "be" and the intransitive "go", "stand", "talk" a prepositional NP occurs: *Bobo's in Anthony's pillow* or *Daddy goes on the train* or *Bobo is standing on his ears* or *Anthony wants to talk to Daddy*. Only one instance of two NPs following the VP occurs: *Anthony puts his feet on Bobo*, possibly a quotation form except for the last word *Bobo* substituted by the child.

A number of elliptic constructions occur in this pattern. Leaving aside the NP preceding the VP for the moment, the elliptic VP again frequently omits a "be" form, e.g., *Baking a cake* or the VP disappears completely as in *Kitty in bed*. The NP following the VP can consist only of the article, *I got a*, or of a preposition + article, *Pig in the*, or of an unmodified noun, *Bobo's taking hat* or *Bobo sitting on pillow*.

We have already mentioned equational sentence as being declarative, and the shape of the NP is similar to the constructions just described, e.g., *This is light* or *That's a big book* or *That is it* or *There's a hat* or *There is the light* or *This is light on it*. Elliptic constructions also occur, as in *Here yellow spoon* or *Here's hat* or *That's lollipop* or *That's your* or *Is for Nila* or the negative *Is not for Anthony*. Negation preceding the sentence also occurs: *No, that's little book*.

The equational sentence can also contain an adjective phrase: *Mommy's too weak* or *The lady's all clean* with modified adjectives, or in elliptic constructions simple adjectives: *Alice strong* or *Is not black*. The NP preceding the verb in this construction is either an unmodified noun, or article + noun, or a pronoun. One instance of a NP following the adjective also occurs: *Cobbers all dirty in the car*.

The declarative sentence pattern which remains to be described is the pattern containing adverbial phrases (AP). NP + VP + AP is a frequent pattern, for example, *I am here* or *Anthony comb too much* or *All the hats going down* or *One pillow up there*. The NP in this pattern exhibits similar characteristics as the NP following the VP in the previous pattern. It can be a pronoun, a modified or unmodified noun. The pattern may be elliptic or non-elliptic. Negative sentences also occur, e.g., *Betsy's Mommy is not home*.

However, the AP belongs to an outer layer, and if an NP follows the VP, the place of the AP is either before or after the NP preceding the VP, or after the NP following the VP. For example, *Now it is fixed* or *Cobbers always cross the street* or *Anthony wants another box too* or *Anthony wants the belt please*.

Other than simple declarative sentences, that is, sentences consisting of two or more clauses, are very rare. The only copula well-learned is *and*, occurring frequently in the corpus, but it is usually not used as a conjunction for the construction of complex sentences but as a device for connection. *But* occurs only in *But Twofeet had no horsie*, a direct quotation from a favorite story, and in *But had a horsie*, an elliptic quotation of the same origin. One declarative sentence with a relative clause appears, *One that Sally made*, probably also a quotation, and two more sentences can be interpreted as having elliptic relative clauses, omitting the relative pronoun: *That is Mommy put on her shoes* and *That is Mommy put on Anthony's slippers*.

Returning to the question of ambiguity, we find that omission of the NP preceding the VP poses the greatest problems. If the VP contains a marked verb form, the ambiguity is resolved, and the sentence is classified as declarative, e.g., *Broke the Bobo* or *No, took it off* or *Looking for the blanket*. However, the question remains of how to classify sentences like *Make too much noise* or *Jump on yellow blanket*. From a purely formal point of view, in terms of construction and ellipsis, these sentences must remain unclassified. Other criteria have to be employed to analyze sentences like these, and there are many such sentences. This is reserved for the following Section, but suffice it to say here that because of the nature of the corpus, that is, vocalized inner speech, we generally tend to view structurally ambiguous instances as imperative rather than declarative because of the nature of inner speech. Hence *Jump on yellow blanket* is probably an imperative. On the other hand, *Make too much noise* could, because of its content, probably be declarative, but it can really be classified only in relation to its larger context.

Interrogatives. The remaining sentence type to be described is the interrogative. It is a much smaller class than that of imperative or declarative sentences, a fact which is not surprising in view of the solitary nature of the corpus, and also partially due to the child's age. The "why" questions started to be prominent only some six months after the recordings had been made. Nevertheless, the occurrence of questions, frequently with answers supplied by the child, in the monologues, points again to the dialogue of inner speech.

Lewis' (1951) and Leopold's (1949) dichotomy of distinguishing between questions for information on the one hand, and confirmation on the other is not relevant here since outside of the child himself there is no live interlocutor present to provide new information. The child asks the question addressed to himself.

As for the structure of interrogative sentences, Fries' statement "Class 2 ←→ Class 1 ("tied") signals a *question*" will serve as the basis of our discussion. In Fries' as well as in our discussion, word order is the fundamental criterion for the identification of interrogative sentences. Together with word order, "question words" or interrogative pronouns serve as question markers. For the purposes of a formal description of question patterns, the phonologic criteria of contours cannot be utilized as an unambiguous marker of questions. We have, however, used it as a possible signal within the larger unit of the paragraph as will be shown later.

The standard English "do" constructions of sentences have not yet been learned by the child. Although negative imperatives using "do" are quite common in the corpus and some declarative constructions are used as well, there is only a single example of a "do" construction in an interrogative without a question word, non-grammatical at that: *Did Penny wants water*. This interrogative pattern is being learned very slowly by the child, and even eight months after the recordings were made, his ability to use this construction was very limited.

Inversion without a question word occurs only in a few examples: *Is that Bobo*, *Is this a pillow in the back*, *Is that right*, *Is he sleeping*. This transformation is being practised, but it is still a poorly learned structure.

In describing the interrogative pattern with question words, we can speak of a true pattern only in regard to *what* and *where*. *Why* occurs only by itself, without syntactic context; *which* is found rarely, both used grammatically and non-grammatically: *Which one* and *Which side go*, hardly enough to establish a pattern of occurrence. *Who* is also infrequent, as in *Who is coming*, perhaps a quotation. One of the favorite uses of *What* is in the phrase *What color* followed by one or two unmodified nouns: *What color blanket* or *What color pillow*, or just the phrase *What color* usually with rising intonation by itself. Only rarely the attempt is made to produce this construction non-elliptically in *What color are this room* and *What color is Bobo*. Post-nominal modification also is occasionally found as in *What color chair for the egg*. Following the same pattern, *What kind* or *What kind lady* or *What time occur*. A somewhat different pattern is *What is that* or *What is this* or *What is the matter* or *What is the matter with it*, conforming to standard usage, possibly quotation forms, particularly the last two examples.

What Daddy got or *What clock is that* with rising intonations occur, as does the elliptical *What a*, apparently elliptic interrogative constructions since the pattern has not yet been learned.

Another pattern which the child probably could not use productively is *What happened* or *What is up there* or *What is crying* or *What will happen*.

The *where* constructions are mostly of the pattern *Where + is + NP* as in *Where is*

Bobo or *Where is the yellow blanket*. *Where* also precedes some "do" constructions, a poorly learned pattern as was mentioned. A few non-elliptical sentences using this construction such as *Where did Anthony go* or *Where did it go*, occur, probably quotations, but most are elliptical as *Where the white one go*.

The pattern *where* + infinitive + NP occurs once, *Where to put the blanket* and we suspect this to be a quotation form, as is the probably interrogative *See the blanket that I found*. Some unsuccessful attempts are made with *how about*, but the results are non-grammatical, as in *How about the Daddy*.

Phrases

As defined under (*c*) on p. 81, one type of ellipsis is the use of phrases which are not sentences. Their construction is essentially the same as that of their respective counterparts included in sentences. There is one addition to the substitution list for *the* in noun phrases, *another*, e.g., *Another big bottle*, and a greater repertoire of prepositions occurs as well. Adjectival modification is expanded by an adjective modifier, as in *light grey*. In adverbial phrases, there is also greater variety, particularly the phrases common to child language like *all through*, *all gone* are found frequently.

VOCABULARY

Following is a frequency list of the vocabulary occurring in the corpus, arranged alphabetically. The number following each entry indicates how many times it was found. All inflected forms are listed as separate entries. Form classes are indicated wherever such clarity seemed desirable. In some instances, e.g., in the case of *dance* or *bite* it is clear from the corpus that the child uses the identical phonemic shape both as noun and verb. Some cases are ambiguous, and we have made the decisions of classification on what was felt to be best in accord with the data. E.g., we classified *jump* in the construction *the jump* as a noun, and followed the same principle in classifying *the broke*. The form class of *like* is sometimes not apparent from the data, and there again we have used whatever seemed in accordance with the context, e.g., we consider *like* in *like music* as a verb because immediately afterwards the negative *don't like music* occurs.

A	54	almost	1	Anthony	81
an	1	alone	1	Anthony's	8
about	3	already	2	apple	2
again	12	also	2	apples	2
ah	13	always	2	are	10
Alice	26	am	8	around	6
all	84	and	105	at	20
all right	1	another	16	ate	1

away	5	Bobbies	3	cart	1
aw	8	Bobo	132	catch	6
		Bobo's	3	chair	2
Babette	1	bologna	1	chairs	1
baby	14	book	37	change	7
back	10	books	7	changing	1
bag	2	bottle	26	chicken	1
baking	1	box	20	china	1
ball	8	boy	18	cider	3
bang	1	boyfriend	1	cigarettes	4
banging	3	bring	5	clean	1
Barbara	3	brought	1	clean off	1
bark	1	broke (n.)	1	clean out	1
barking	3	broke (v.)	13	clean up	1
bath	1	broken	2	cleaner (vacuum)	15
bathing	1	brokes	1	clock	3
bathroom	4	brown	1	clocks	1
be	4	bubble	1	close	12
beach	4	bucket	3	closed	2
Becca's	1	bunch	1	closing	1
bed	7	bunny	4	Cobbers	26
behind	2	but	1	coffee	6
belt	12	burn	1	color	21
berry	2	button	2	come	10
berries	10	buy	4	came	1
Betsy's	2	bought	1	comes	5
better	1	by	2	coming	8
bit	24	bye-bye	7	come off	1
bird	4			come on	4
birds	10	cactus	1	cook	1
bite (n.)	2	cake	1	cookie	1
bite (v.)	5	cakes	1	cool	1
black	4	call	4	corner	5
blanket	125	call up	5	correct	2
blind	1	can	12	count	8
block	17	could	5	counting	1
blocks	2	candy	4	cracker	1
blouse	1	candies	1	cross	3
blow	2	car	6	crossed	1
blue	23	cars	1	crossing	1
Bob	11	careful	6	cry	3
Bobby	6	carry	1	crying	1

Daddy	68	egg	3	get on	3
Daddy's	7	eight	2	get out	1
dance (v.)	7	enough	1	get up	5
dance (n.)	2	envelope	1	getting up	9
dancing	1	excuse	1	got	13
dark	8			girls	2
David	3	face	2	give	6
day	1	feet	7	gave	2
Dennis	1	Fifi	25	glass	2
diaper	3	find	1	glasses	1
dinner	3	found	1	go	93
dirty	4	fine	2	goes	9
do	7	finger	4	going	20
doing	2	fingers	3	gone	18
did	9	fire	4	go back	1
don't	16	first	6	go off	1
doesn't	1	Fischer	6	go out	2
doctor	4	five	2	go up	1
dog	1	fix	3	good	18
dogs	1	fixed	10	grass	2
doggie	16	fixing	1	green	5
doggies	1	floor	2	grey	7
donkey	10	flower	1	grow	1
door	13	flowers	2		
dot	3	fly	2	hair	3
dots	4	for	30	hand	1
double yu	1	forgot	1	hands	1
down	44	four	10	hanger	1
drawer	1	Frica's	1	hanging	1
drink	3	Friday	2	happen	3
drinking	1	friend	1	happened	1
drive	1	from	4	happy	2
drop	1	fruit	2	hat	21
dropped	1	Fuchs	2	hats	3
dry	1	funny	3	have	10
duckey	1	funnies	1	has	5
Dumpty	6			had	8
		garbage	3	he	5
early	2	garden	8	head	1
ears	1	get	20	hear	2
eat	2	get away	2	heavy	2
edge	1	get off	14	hello	4

her	3	jumps	1	lock	4
here	36	jump out	6	locking	1
hey	6			locked	1
hi	17	keep	1	look	19
hiding	6	kick	2	looks	1
hill	2	kicked	1	looking	4
him	3	kicking	1	look at	32
himself	1	kind (adj.)	1	look out	6
his	1	kind (n.)	3	lollipop	1
hit	1	king	1	luck	1
hold	1	Kirsten	6	lunch	2
hole	2	kiss	1		
holes	1	Kitty	45	machine	2
home	4	Kitty's	3	mail (v.)	2
honey	6	know	1	mailman	4
hook	1			make	7
hope (v.)	1	lady	14	making	2
horse	3	ladies	1	made	5
horsie	5	last	1	man	10
hot	2	late	1	many	1
hot dog	1	leaf	2	Margaret	1
house	9	leave	3	market	1
how	3	leaving	1	mat	1
Humpty	5	left	7	match	4
hurry up	1	left on	1	matter	5
		leg	2	maybe	1
I	24	legs	3	me	6
idea	1	let	2	meat	1
Idey	1	lets	3	mess	2
in	64	letter	2	messing	1
Indian	1	letters	4	Meyer	2
Indians	1	lie down	9	mice	4
inside	1	lying down	1	microphone	23
is	167	lift	2	milk	23
it	103	lift up	1	mirror	1
		light (n.)	33	Miss	1
jacket	1	light (adj.)	2	Mommy	61
Jonny	1	like (v.)	5	Mommy's	18
juice	7	like	28	Mama	11
jump (n.)	3	lipstick	12	Monday	2
jump (v.)	31	listen	16	monkey	6
jumping	2	little	13	monkeys	2

mop	1	once	1	possible	2
more	22	one	58	potato	1
morning	5	onion	1	powder	4
motorcycle	2	only	12	present	2
mountain	2	open	12	pretty	2
move	3	orange	1	pull	1
moving	1	other	10	pulling	1
mow	1	out	34	push	2
Mr.	1	outside	6	put	37
Mrs.	6	over	9	puts	1
much	9	ow	43	putting	18
music	12			put on	12
my	9	pajamas	4	put up	1
		pants	3		
nail (n.)	3	paper	7	quick	2
nail (v.)	1	papers	6		
naked	1	party	2	reach	3
Nancy	8	Paul	1	read	1
Nan	3	pen	2	reading	11
necktie	1	pencil	1	ready	4
need	3	Penny	8	record	16
net	1	phone	5	records	4
next	1	Phyllis	1	red	18
new	7	pick up	3	rest	2
New York	1	pig	2	right	25
nice	5	piggie	6	robe	5
night-night	6	pillow	8	rock	3
Nila	3	pillows	2	rocking	3
nine	2	pineapple	1	room	1
no	18	pink	5	Ruth	2
noise	2	plane	1	"s"	1
not	47	play	4	sauce	1
notice	1	plays	1	Sally	3
now	65	player	2	Sam	2
		please	50	same	2
o'clock	1	plug out	1	Saturday	7
off	33	pocket	1	say	2
office	11	polish (n.)	4	school	1
OK	14	pool	1	screen	3
old	2	pony	1	scratched	1
olive	1	poor	3	see	37
on	30	postman	1	saw	1

set	1	sticks	1	thumb	6
seven	1	stomach	2	tickle	5
sewing	1	stop	17	ticklish	1
shampoo	2	store	1	tiger	5
she	2	strawberries	1	time	1
sheet	8	street	5	tired	1
shining	1	strong	1	to	1
shoe	7	sweater	1	today	7
shoes	2	swimming	1	toilet	4
shovel	2	switch	1	Tommy	1
side	9	sun	1	tomorrow	5
sign	1	sure	1	too	18
sing	1			top	11
sit down	4	take (n.)	1	towels	1
sit up	1	take (v.)	32	toy	4
sitting	1	taking	8	toys	2
six	2	took	6	train	8
size	1	taken	1	tray	1
skirt	1	take away	1	truck	5
sleep	11	take back	1	trunk	1
sleeping	15	take off	14	try	2
slippers	3	took off	8	trying	2
smile	1	talk	2	turn	2
Smokey	6	talking	1	turn around	6
Smokey's	1	teddybear	1	turn of	3
so	2	tell	1	turn on	1
soap	2	ten	1	turn out	1
some	15	today	1	T.V.	3
something	2	told	1	twice	2
Sophie	2	thank	1	two	28
spoon	1	that	121	Twofeet	5
sportscar	3	the	394		
stairs	1	them	11	uncle	1
stand	2	then	9	under	1
standing	3	there	67	up	47
stand up	3	things	2		
start	1	this	33	vacuum	15
started	1	those	1	very	2
stay	7	three	24	wait	6
staying	2	through	6	waiting	3
step	3	throw	4	wake	1
stick	7	throwing	1	woke	1

walk	1	welcome	1	window	3
wall	1	Wendy	2	wire	1
want	10	went	2	wish	3
wants	9	wet	2	with	29
warm	2	what	54	wonderful	1
was	2	wheel	1	woods	1
watching	2	where	26	work	3
water	3	which	2	writing	2
way	13	whine	1	wrong	1
we	5	whining	1		
weak	5	white	17	yellow	54
wear	1	who	1	yet	1
Wednesday	1	why	3	you	25
weeds	1	will	3		

Compared to the child's repertoire during the day, the poverty of vocabulary and of topics in his monologues is striking. Within this limited selection, however, some items show much greater frequency of occurrence than others. *Blanket* is by far the most frequent non-personalized noun with 125 occurrences, reflecting Anthony's great attachment to his blankets. All other nouns in this class which occur quite often are either toys he has in the crib with him or which are near him in the room; or they are the nouns *door, light, microphone, vacuum cleaner*, both of the latter meaning "microphone" which stands on the chair near him, the former two referring to his not being alone: that is, the *door* should be kept open so that he has some *light*; or they are *bottle* and *milk*, both of which he likes to request. Of the personalized nouns, the name of his toy, *Bobo* occurs by far most frequently, 135 times. Next in frequency is *Mommy* and *Mama*, but its most frequent use is in calls, not included in larger syntactic units. This is in contrast with the two names next in frequency, *Anthony* and *Daddy* which occur more often in sentences. *Kitty* and *Cobbers*, the names of the cat and dog in the household, and *Alice*, the name of the girl living with the family, are also found often. This is not true of *David*, Anthony's younger brother.

One other non-personalized noun is quite frequent, namely *color*, which is consistent with the adjectives found. Color adjectives outnumber by far any other descriptive adjectives, with *yellow*, Anthony's favorite color, occurring most often. This is in spite of the fact that the level of light in the child's room during the monologues is too low to distinguish colors.

With regard to numerals, the higher they are, the fewer times they occur. This is true of the numerals from one to ten. However, *all*, the child's highest numerical concept, occurs most frequently.

The verb *go* with all its marked forms is by far the most used verb. *Jump* follows, with *get* and the two-part verbs using *get* third.

The fifty occurrences of *please* are peculiar to this particular step of the child's development. Its use then was also frequent in his day-speech, a habit abandoned later on.

One reason for the limited repertoire and the recurrence of the same topics might be the constancy of his environment during the monologues. The fact that a certain physical location often evokes a repetition of former thoughts whenever it is visited has been suggested to the writer by George Miller. An analogy could be drawn from Abernathy's experiment on "the effect of changed environmental conditions upon the results of college examination" (1940), where he shows convincingly that the constancy of the environment produces most efficient recall. We could then say that for the monologues the constancy of the crib and the child's room had an effect on the type of speech which occurred in this unchanging environment. Unfortunately, to the writer's knowledge, this hypothesis has not been explored further in psychological literature.

Another question concerns the particular selection of this limited vocabulary. As the matter of combinations has been of importance in the sequences and sentences, so is the problem of selection at issue here. We could argue that the numerous occurrences of *Bobo* in the monologues was due to the child's great attachment to the toy. Inadvertently, we tested this by forgetting to take the toy along on the vacation immediately following the recordings, something which was not intended since we had assumed from monitoring the recordings that Bobo meant a good deal to the child. Surprisingly, the child did not particularly miss the toy. We could ask further why other toys did not play a more prominent role in the monologues, toys which during the day seemed as important to the child as did the ones constantly appearing in the soliloquies. Also naming articles of clothing seemed to preoccupy the child during the day, be it his own or those of other members of the family, something which is not of prominence in the monologues. Shopping trips with his mother, and the naming of a great variety of foods were some of the activities the child particularly enjoyed, as he did "helping" his father on weekends with do-it-yourself chores. These pleasurable experiences do not seem to affect his monologues particularly. There are probably psychological explanations available, but our concern is that of overt linguistic symbolization.

It seems clear that the role of Bobo is primarily that of an interlocutor making the dialogue of thought more realistic for the child. We can begin to understand better the make-up of the speech by viewing it as dialogue in Vygotsky's sense of vocalized inner speech which is essentially social. But linguistically we can understand it only from the perspective of learning linguistic combinations and selections. Having dealt with combinations on the phonemic level with its circumscribed selection, with combinations of phonemes into morphemes and words, and in turn combinations of words into phrases, sentences, and sequences, we now deal with paradigmatic and sequential selection in its widest sense which is not only grammatical, but semantic as well.

DISCOURSE ANALYSIS

In the analysis of syntax, we have established as the largest linguistic unit of discourse the *paragraph*. This section is devoted to analysis of the paragraph.

The linguistic material contained in the child's monologues could not be presented satisfactorily if it were confined to sentence analysis, or even to the *sequence* as established in our syntax. Although we have applied only the mechanically formal criteria of build-up, break-down, and completion in describing this unit of syntax, parallels can be drawn with other descriptions of the child's mental processes. Wallon (1945) suggested as primary in immature thought the matter of pairing of ideas, preceding the state of isolated thoughts. Our sequences are already suggestive of such pairs, by uniting most often the linguistically delimited units into a new whole. But even if we were satisfied with our analysis thus far, the selection of sentences or non-grammatical utterances outside of the sequence would remain uninterpreted. We have to look further for more adequate means for analysis.

If we assume denotation to be the primary function of Anthony's monologues, we are at a loss to understand much of it. In distinction to his language during the day when the requirements of situations demand referential language in order to be understood and to communicate efficiently with his interlocutors, his monologues do not have the same requirements and they do not follow the same path. As Wallon has pointed out, the young child's thought is dominated mainly by paired association of contrasts, by assonance, by identifications or pseudo-identifications. We would venture to say that the soliloquies are characterized by the small role played by denotation. There are too many instances which do not "mean" anything or where the child does not seem to "say" anything. True, the referential function is present, but it serves as a spring-board for other functions most of the time. In his day speech, the referential is explicit as was observed by a number of people in calling him "verbal"; in his monologues it is elliptic, inverting the pyramid of Sapir's "supreme reign of ideation" (1921) as the usual communicative function of language.

Coming back to the unit of the paragraph and its description, we do not have to resort to purely subjective criteria or wholly speculative interpretations, but we do have to apply a linguistic analysis in a less restricted sense as was suggested in Jakobson's statement on "Linguistics and Poetics" (1960). There he analyzed verbal communication as consisting of six factors, with six language functions accompanying each factor. In addition to Bühler's three functions, the emotive, conative and referential functions in relation to the addresser, the addressee, and the context of the verbal communication respectively, Jakobson added the phatic, poetic, and metalingual functions corresponding in turn to the contact (channel), message, and code of the speech event. In applying these six language functions operating in different hierarchical orders at various times to our data, the unit of the paragraph becomes well defined and the linguistic analysis of the monologues proves much more satisfactory.

Before proceeding with our analysis, we want to touch briefly on the question of the child's imitation of adult speech. Obviously, the child has learned his rules of linguistic selections and combinations by imitation, and he is still very much in the process of learning to refine these rules further, so that his communication becomes increasingly more efficient, and finally his language will be indistinguishable from the one used in his surroundings, except for personal characteristics. However, we are here concerned with imitation in a narrower sense, namely that of taking over words, phrases, or sentences, said by an adult, in parrot-like fashion, without really having deduced the grammatical rules underlying a particular linguistic unit. This type of imitation is somewhat removed in the monologues since no adult interlocutor is present, and we assume that most of the recorded language follows internalized rules, some applied more consistently than others. We base this on the recordings themselves as well as on our observation of the language spoken by the child during the day. That does not mean, however, that the child does not use many sentences which he has heard, but in most cases he knows the grammatical rules underlying them. Some sentences do not fall into this category, they are complete echoes of a sentence spoken by an adult which the child repeats as a unit. We have called such speech events *quotations*. Some examples of quotations would be *I hope so* or *You are welcome* which could be considered as having the same syntactic structure for the child as one-word sentences, that is to say, none. At times part of a sentence identifies it as a quotation, for example, the conjunction *but* is devoid of grammatical meaning in the child's language and occurs in a sentence, *But Twofeet had no horse* which is a quotation from a favorite story. Sentence length may at times serve as a sign for quotations, as the imperative *Get him up at nine o'clock Fifi* which is outside the child's usual combinatory ability.

LANGUAGE FUNCTIONS

We often encounter reference to linguistic play in the literature on child language. Thus Chao (1951) says: "There is occasional intentional playing with language... The resulting syllables are usually not expected to make sense" (p. 40). Or Kaper (1959) talks of the use of words for pleasure by the young child (p. 22). Ohnesorg (1947) also confirms the play with words, as do Jespersen (1922) and Stern (1928).

The latter two, however, go further when they mention the child's prediliction for rhythm, rhyme, and alliteration. Scupin (1907) discusses "Klangassoziationen", association based on recurring sounds. In our recordings, a great deal of play with the sounds of words and with the words themselves is found. Coming back to Jakobson's outline of the functions of language, we have in such instances as the primary function what he calls the POETIC function of language. That is not to say that the child is creating poetry, just as the political slogan "I like Ike" analyzed by Jakobson (p. 357) is not a poem, but a poetic exploitation of the function of language with the referential function being only secondary, so there are a great number of instances in the child's monologues where play with the sounds of the language is basic in the hierarchy of language functions with other functions, be they referential or conative or metalingual, subordinated to it.

Let us look at this, at first glance perhaps, meaningless paragraph:

(1) *Look at those pineaple*
(2) *In a pretty box*
(3) *And cakes*
(4) *What a sticks for cakes*
(5) *For the click*

As to a possible referential function, *pineapple* was a rather usual fruit for the child and he developed a great fondness for it. He could have heard a close approximation of *look at those pineapples* during supper when he was given some in his dish. The conative function of the imperative is probably the primary one in this line, but it does not continue. However, the *pineapple* never came *in a pretty box* (the second part of a completion sequence) but usually out of a can onto his plate. *Cakes* or cake were usually not given to the child because he was not fond of them at the time. As for the next two lines, we are at a loss to infer any denotative function. Looking at the message, however, from the point of view of sound play, let us analyze its shape. A certain symmetry characterizes the lines: the first line contains five syllables (*pineapple* containing two syllables in this instance with a weak non-syllabic /l/) as does the second, the third only has two, the fourth five again, and the fifth three, so that lines three and five together again add up to five. The stresses show a pattern as well: if only one stress occurs, it is on the last syllable in the line, in the example in lines (2), (3), and (5). Only line (1) has three stresses, and line (4) has two. In regard to consonants, the first line begins and ends in /l/ which is not repeated until the last line at the paragraph, and, moreover, the /l-k/ of *look*, the first word in line (1) appears as /kl-k/ in *click*, the last word of line (5). We have serious doubts that the child knows either the meaning of "click" or "clique", and we are sure that sound play is the only function of this particular word. The bilabial /p/ is found twice in the first line, the bilabial stop is repeated voiceless and voiced in the second line only. The second line introduces a final /-ks/, repeated once in line three and twice in line four, and the vowels preceding it are also played with: /O/ in line (3) with all other vowels being non-back unrounded; in the two syllables of line (3) the same vowel is repeated, and the reverse of line (2) occurs in the longer lines (4) and (5) where the vowels preceding /-ks/ and /-k/ are non-back unrounded in distinction to /O/ occurring elsewhere except in the article *a* and *the*. The *a* of line (4), phonetically [ɛ], is a repetition of the same vowel of line (2), in an exactly parallel position following a back rounded vowel.

We have to explain the history of our next example before analyzing it. Anthony was particularly fond of his blankets, and they seemed to mean a good deal to him. He was rarely seen without carrying one around with him or being near one. He also liked to watch his mother grooming herself and he knew all the necessary items for it. The lipstick left a very definite impression on him, and he decided that a certain corner of a certain blanket was like a lipstick. He knew exactly which corner it was, and he never made a mistake. He asked for or identified spontaneously the *blanket like a lipstick* during the day, a sentence which occurs frequently in the monologues as well, without apparent connection with preceding or following context. To assign this a primarily referential function would be a mistake. That this expression is sound play becomes apparent upon closer examination. Breaking the longer sentence down into three units each starting with a strong stress, we arrive at a striking picture of interplay of stops and /l/, diagrammed as follows:

blanket	b l	ŋ	k t		
like a	l		k		
lipstick	l p	s t	k		

The occurrence of /l/ and /k/, in this order, is central to this sentence occurring in every one of its parts, and it is what ties the shorter phrase. The longer one is tied even more intricately in that in the first part the bilabial /b/ precedes the /l/ and the alveolar /t/ follows the /k/, whereas in the third part the bilabial /p/ follows the /l/ and the alveolar /t/ precedes the /k/, reversing the order. The feature of voicing in the bilabial is lacking here due to its neutralization before the voiceless /s/. Two identical vowel phonemes also occur in /blÉnkEt/ and /lÍpstIk/, giving the sentence even more internal unity.

A great number of examples of the child's play with sound can be found throughout the corpus. We will quote a few more simple examples.

The paragraph:

Like a piggy bank (2×)	k p g		b ŋ k			
Had a pink sheet on			p ŋ k			
The grey pig out	g p g					

is another such instance. The phonemes /p, b/ and the phonemes /g, k, ŋ/ are obviously played with, a velar and labial exercise as diagrammed above. The first line contains /k/ in *like* and *bank*, in addition to /p/ and /g/ in *piggy*, and /b/ and /ŋ/ in *bank*. Line (2) repeats the /p/, /ŋ/ and /k/ in *pink* which bears strong resemblance to *bank* except for the feature of voicing of the labial. Line (3) omits the /k/, but uses /g/ twice instead, in addition to repeating the /p/. The phoneme following /p/ is always /I/.

/E/ is the last phoneme of the word preceding the noun or its modifier. Also, liquids occur only in lines one and three, once /l/, once /r/.

A paragraph related by sound play only, devoid of any other function that we can discern, is:

Babette
Back here
Wet

Babette is the name of an acquaintance whom the child has seen only very few times, and it is unlikely that she had made any particular deep impression on the child. However, for phonologic reasons, the name probably has appeal to him since the syllables alliterate and have rhythm. *Back* of the next line repeats the alliterating /b/, followed not only by the same phoneme /E/ as in the second syllable of *Babette*, but also by the same phonetic variant [ɛ] which again occurs in the third line, *wet*. The alveolar /t/ of the first line is changed to velar /k/ in the second, but /t/ reappears in the third line where the bilabiality of the preceding two initial /b/'s is again reflected in the glide /w/.

The sentence *Daddy dance*, formally an imperative, expressing a wish which has rarely, if ever been granted, occurs several times non-contiguously in a paragraph, and it is a clear example of sound play where every syllable begins with the same consonant /d/, the first and third also having the same vowel phoneme /E/, giving the sentence rhythm and alliteration.

Perhaps even more interesting is alliteration of initial consonants, produced in the words *shampoo* and *swimming-pool*. Usually, the child's initial phoneme of *swimming* was /s/. However, there was some confusion in his use of /s/ and /š/ due to imitation of the Danish girl living in the household who, not having this contrast in her native language, frequently confused them in English. In this particular instance, /š/ occurs in *swimming*, in order to conform to the initial /š/ of *shampoo*. The repetition of /m/ and /pU/ in both words is also not accidental in their selection. As we can see from this and previous examples, selection is by no means random for the child, sound play being only one of his criteria, however.

In several instances, the child even made up syllables to fit into his scheme of things. We have to resort to phonetics to show it:

[bíŋk]
[lɛt bóu̯bɔ bíŋk]
[bíŋk bɛ́n bíŋk]
[blú kìŋk]

The [ŋk] cluster is quite frequent in the child's speech in contrast to [ŋg] which is rare. *Let* and *Bobo* are the obvious two words with meaning, and perhaps [kìŋk] could be interpreted as "king". However that may be, the four lines are meaningless outside of sound play.

Another type of sound play is what could be called *reduplication*. It is not the type of reduplication of syllables so often mentioned by investigators of child language, like, for example, Lewis (1951), who shows that the earliest words are reduplicated to a great extent, but that words consisting of reduplication are greatly diminished by the end of the second year. The reduplication we are referring to is of a different kind, yet analogous to syllable repetition, but units longer than syllables are selected and it may be better therefore to call it *echo repetition*. It consists of identical repetitions of phrases, or of two or more repetitions of the whole sentence. The redundancy of language is thus also increased.

The CONATIVE function, addressed to the person spoken to, is primarily served by the vocative of the noun, and the imperative of the verb. In the Section on Syntax these constructions have been taken up in detail, and the fact that imperative constructions outweighed all others is good evidence of the importance of this function of language to the child. Anthony's making his toy Bobo the addressee of his commands and calls was a fact completely unknown to the parents until it was discovered in the recordings. No conversations were carried on with Bobo during the day except perhaps for a fleeting greeting of "Hi Bobo" by the child.

The fact of discussing play with the message itself, and orientation to the addressee of the message is not intended to imply that messages having a primary REFERENTIAL function are absent in the monologues. However, they do constitute a minority as was shown also by the relatively few unambiguously declarative sentences and by the even fewer questions in the discussion of syntax, together with a good deal of structural ambiguity because of lack of grammatical markers. Nevertheless, referential function does exist although it is at times questionable whether the primary function is not sound play after all, or linguistic practice to be discussed below. The only complete paragraph which could be justly called narrative consists mostly of quotation forms.

Use of antonyms or metonymy is usually a fairly good guide to the classification of messages with a primarily denotative function. For example, we can take a sequence like

> *Up there*
> *Over here*

and consider it to have a cognitive function because of its contrastive meanings. Or the two phrases following each other:

> *Like the garbage man*
> *A big truck*

seem to be primarily tied by the association of *the garbage man* driving a sizeable *truck*. Garbage collection has made a strong impression on the child due to the barking of all dogs, including his own, in the neighborhood. Since anything automotive interests him and he can usually see from his room the garbage *truck* rather than *the garbage man*, this seems to be a referential association.

Although we have no visual records or observations of the child during the recordings of the monologues, we can occasionally find a paragraph relating something he apparently did. Thus:

> *More milk please*

Here is the bottle

indicates that after having made his request he is holding out the bottle so that his wish would be fulfilled more readily.

Questions and answers sometimes fall into this category although not always, by any means. It should be pointed out that since the questions asked are also answered by the child, this typical dialogue situation further supports the social aspect of this vocalized inner speech. An example of a question paragraph belonging here would be:

What color TV
Red and
Fire

Anthony is intrigued by fire engines, he knows that they are *red*, and he at times mistakenly identifies a red truck as a fire engine. The television set in the house certainly is not *red*, but with the sun shining on the brown finish, it does acquire a reddish cast. *Red* is also a color the child knows very well, brown is not. *Fire* in the third line is a further association with *red*, the fire engine, supporting our conclusion that the function of this sequence is primarily referential.

Another example of a cognitive question paragraph would be:

What's the matter
All is fixed
O.K.

which is perhaps somewhat elliptic, but nevertheless associates a supposed defect with its correction.

At times, negations can also be included here, as for example:

Not yellow
Red

simply a correction of an implied original assumption.

These negative or contradictory utterances Wallon considers typical of child thought which operates in paired associations. A statement is made and immediately contradicted and the contradiction reinforced at times or made negatively to begin with so that a positive alternative can be found. Examples of the first type follow:

That light
No, is vacuum cleaner
Like a vacuum
Cleaner here

belongs to the first type with reinforcement of the contradiction. Without reinforcement is:

Coffee
Get some coffee
No, milk

Of the second type is the original example given, or this one which has also the reinforcement:

Not the yellow blanket

> *The white*
> *White*

Another example of a primarily negative association, but mated with sound play, is the following:

> *Too hot*
> *Not too hot*
> *Not too good*
> *This one*

Interesting enough, both his possible phonemic realizations of *hot* appear in this paragraph, that is /hAt/ as well as /hOt/, and, not unexpectedly, the phoneme /O/ is in the second line where perhaps the preceding *not*, also with /O/, suggested the variant with /O/. The first two lines are obviously related by negative association, but sound play again enters, and is carried further in the third line which probably was intended as a reinforcement of the negative, a common pattern; but the child was again seduced by other considerations, using a new substitution item in the pattern, *good*, no doubt suggested by the immediately preceding word, *too*. The last line is probably intended as an amplification, and since we have no visual records, we do not know if pointing or some other identification accompanies this line.

We can at times clearly distinguish between sound PLAY with its own function as we have discussed it, and sound PRACTICE which properly belongs to another function of language. Following is an example of sound practice; phonetic notation is essential in order to show what is happening.

> [bǽk] *please*
> [bériz]
> *not* [bǽriz]
> [bǽriz] (2×)
> *not* [bǽriz]
> [béri:z]
> [bǽ] (2×)

This type of sound practice is not common in the corpus. The particular sequence just quoted occurs shortly before the child falls asleep. The history preceding the exercise was the child's visit, with his mother, at a neighbor's house where he was given some raspberries which he enjoyed eating. What is happening linguistically is obvious. Anthony is, in general, satisfied with his phonemic contrasts and usually just plays with them without much regard to their phonetic make-up. However, as we have shown, the standard English phoneme /æ/ is one of the variants of Anthony's phoneme /E/. Apparently latent, however – so that it appears just before he will drop off to sleep – is an awareness that his non-high non-back phoneme is not quite all right. This cannot be attributed to adult correction, since except for cases of unintelligibility he was not corrected by his parents or others, and unintelligibility is certainly not present in the case of [bǽriz]. Therefore this paragraph is a clear example of sound practice leading to the acquisition of a larger phonemic inventory.

It is not a play even of phonetic variation, but a conscious exercise of learning a new phonemic contrast. We therefore classify this example differently from the previous ones in that conscious learning of a contrast occurs, its function being metalinguistic.

Second only to the role of sound play is the one assumed by grammatical practice. This can be subsumed under the heading of METALANGUAGE as the logicians have called speaking about language. In the child's monologues, it is often accomplished by the selection of a grammatical pattern where substitution occurs in one slot of the grammatical frame. The words substituted often belong to the same form class, or pronouns are substituted for nouns. The selection within the form class, in turn, can be governed either by sound or meaning associations. The paragraph:

    (1) *What color*
    (2) *What color blanket*
    (3) *What color mop*
    (4) *What color glass*

is an exercise in noun substitution. The first line is merely the frame of the pattern, the full pattern occurring in the second line, with lines three and four repeating the frame with different substitution items of the same form class as in the original pattern sentence. The items are selected phonologically, that is, on the basis of sound. The bilabiality of the initial consonant in *blanket* is repeated in the /m/ and /p/ of *mop*, as is the nasality of the original /n/ in /m/. The phonemic sequence /blE-/ of the first substitute, consisting of voiced stop plus liquid plus /E/, is reflected in the initial phonemes of *glass*, the velar stop there rather than the bilabial being an echo of the velar /k/ of *blanket*. However, the primary function of this paragraph is pattern practice, sound play being relegated only to the selections of items within the form class to be substituted.

The matter of paradigmatic selection is of great importance to the child. Vinogradov (1930) and Chukovsky (1956) in their analysis of the language patterns of children's games, nursery rhymes, and sayings have shown clearly the role played by the paradigmatic axis in this formalized aspect of children's language. The child finds great joy in practising his discovery that linguistic units can be combined freely up to a point, but subject to rules which he is exploring. In our example just given, the tautology of the noun form class is presented. We have no semantic redundancy here, no synonyms, but the characteristic of the paragraph is morphologic redundancy. Anthony is testing a list of substitution items for a particular slot. In the paradigm just given, all items fit, and the pattern is being "overlearned" as it were. But at times the practice of a pattern starts out grammatically incorrectly and reaches grammaticality in the last unit, e.g.:

    Three bottle
    Four bottles

where the plural is practised but the plural morpheme appears with the second occurrence of *bottle* only, not with the first one. The possessive case of the noun also forms a paradigmatic practice pattern, with a minimum of semantic content, as in:

Betsy's Mommy not home
Frica's Mommy not home
Betsy's Mommy not home

The name of the first line reappears in the third so that only the second line contains new information as to the person who is *not home*. The semantic selection is kept at a minimum to work the paradigm.

Pronominal substitution exercises occupy the child a good deal, to be expected in view of the difficulty of tying a pronoun, a general substitute, to a specific noun. The great number of pronominal substitution exercises also point to the fact that these are genuine learning exercises rather than mere repetitions of patterns which have already been well internalized since the use of pronouns is often grammatically incorrect during his day speech. The example:

I go up there (2×)
I go
She go up there

is an exercise of substituting one personal pronoun for another with *I go* occurring as a partial echo repetition between the two pattern sentences. Both pronouns used in this paragraph have not been well learned by the child as yet; the third person singular marker is missing in the verb which also points to the imperfect learning of the pattern.

Pronouns can also be substituted for nouns or vice versa, using *it*, the best learned personal pronoun:

Take the monkey	*Stop it*
Take it	*Stop the ball*
	Stop it

One form class is now substituted for another correctly, and the selection here has proceded along semantic sameness, but grammatical difference. Such transformation exercises occur also with other grammatical structures. Sound play occurs again as well, but the primary function of these paragraphs is substitution exercises.

Verb substitution patterns, although not as frequent as noun substitutions, since verb designs are fewer than noun designs, like

Go get coffee
Go buy some coffee

show an example of a substitution of an unmarked verb form, whereas in

I'm fixing the door
Door's open
I'm locking

marked verb forms are the substitution items. In the next example:

Listen to microphone
Go to microphone

the different functions of *to* are equalized for substitution purposes. Here again we have grammatical sameness and semantic difference, which is also true of adjective substitution patterns which are quite frequent, particularly with color attributes, as the following example shows:

Put on a blanket
White blanket
And yellow blanket
Where's yellow blanket

Other noun modifiers can be substituted as well:

There's a hat
There's another
There's hat
There's another hat
That's a hat

the longest line being the most explicit one. This is also the case with the following expansion exercise:

Look through the window
Look through all the window

where the second line contains the highest numerical concept for the child, *all*, putting the sentences into a hierarchical order, arriving at the highest number gradually.

Equational sentences are also frames for substitution, and the list culminates in the longest unit, perhaps also the most important one to the child.

Monkey (3×)
That's a (2×)
That's a Kitty
That's a Fifi here
That's teddybear and baby

This paragraph also is reminiscent of enumerations, a frequent exercise which serves as a practice of the conjunction *and*, the only conjunction well learned by the child:

You take off all the monkeys
And Kitties
And Phyllis and Humpty Dumpty
And monkey and horsie
And vacuum cleaner
And Fifi
And horsie
No house
And house (2×)
No records
And the blue blanket
This the blue blanket

As before, the selection of various nouns enumerated is based on sound play, but the primary function of the paragraph is grammatical practice.

Enumeration par excellence, counting, is another linguistic practice:

One two three four
One two
One two three four
One two three
Anthony counting
Good boy you
One two three

Here the child even informs us what he is doing, he commends himself for the activity and counts once more for good measure. He not only produces the speech event, but discusses it as well, as if he were citing someone else. It is very doubtful that he fully understands the concept of numbers. He is learning to count as a linguistic activity, and yet usually the numbers appear in ascending order as in the example, with one culminating line.

Negatives are also practiced occasionally as in:

Don't jump   *Like it*
          or
Jump   *Don't like it*
                 Like it Daddy

where in the second example *Daddy* was no doubt evoked by *don't* of the preceding line, but essentially this is another transformation exercise showing the transformation to and from a negative structure.

Don't ticklish
Don't do that

is an example of a somewhat different type where the negative is not contrasted with the affirmative, but occurs in both lines. Identical initial consonant phonemes in all three words also occur in the second line.

Another favorite transformation exercise is the one of question to non-question or vice versa, as exemplified by:

Step on the blanket
Where is Anthony's blanket

Manipulation of imperative and interrogative signals is central to this paragraph. A three step operation can also be performed by the child as in:

There is the light
Where is the light
Here is the light

where he also answers the question, another exemplification of the dialogue of vocalized inner speech.

Other types of transformations occur: one is a form class transformation of a verb to a noun which we will discuss later; another is a transformation of the past to the non-past form of the verb, or vice versa. Here are two examples:

Bobo go take off the hat   *Cobbers crossed the street*
Bobo took off the hat   *Cobbers always cross the street*

In the first example a vocative imperative sentence is transformed to a past indicative;

in the second example the initial verb is in the marked past form, and is transformed into an unmarked non-past although the third person would require a marker. Its absence is probably due to phonologic difficulties because the verb ends in a sibilant.

The beginnings of learning of declarative to interrogative (and vice versa) transformations can also be found:

That's a boy

Is that Bobo

is one such example, the substitution of *Bobo* for *boy* is probably based on phonemic grounds. To one example we could impute an active to passive transformation:

Fix the music

Music is fixed

but the question remains whether a more accurate interpretation would be that *fixed* is considered an adjective by the child rather than part of the paradigm *fix – fixed*.

What Jakobson has called the PHATIC function of language, that is the making of language noises to keep the channel of communication open, occurs also in our data, particularly shortly before the child falls asleep. He does not want to go to sleep, and he keeps himself awake by non-linguistic and linguistic means. The linguistic means are often favorite expressions relating to pet objects, or they are babbling as we have described it earlier. There is an example of a sequence immediately preceding sleep:

Yellow blanket please (2×)

/bÁm bÁm/

/kÍdI kÍdI kÍdI/

/bÁm bÁm/

/kÍdI kÍdI kÍdI/ (3×)

Yellow blanket please

Phonemic transcription was used to indicate the interjectional parts, although they do have the shape of standard English words, but lack their meaning. The last line *Yellow blanket please* was also said by the child with very low volume of voice.

At times, squealing, difficult to reproduce even phonetically, occurs just before sleep begins. Also, naming members of the household, which really cannot be called calling, satisfies the phatic function of language to go on "talking without saying anything".

Calls belong much more frequently to the EMOTIVE function of language. As the child lies or plays and talks in his crib, he sometimes feels like having company. He then calls either one of his parents or the girl living in the household. These calls for one person are often repeated several times and may also carry extra heavy stress. This extra heavy stress functions here frequently as the characteristic feature signalling that the emotive function is the primary one in the message. Thus in

Bíg twó trúcks

Thréé trucks

three with the extra heavy stress carries as its primary meaning "not two", a correction rather than just part of an enumeration. As so often in counting, here again the gradation upward is present, starting with *big two* and going to *three*, the higher numeral.

Occasionally, a word is pronounced in exaggerated staccato fashion, separating each syllable carefully from the next, thus showing greater emphasis and the importance of the word to the child at this particular moment.

Over-long syllables as in [dǽ:::dí:::] are another marker of the emotive function of the word. Of course many interjections like [ɔ:::] or [u:::] serve just this function and are frequently also quite long. Much of the babbling belongs in this category as well.

The function of some imperatives, when addressed to the child himself, are primarily emotive. *Anthony jump*, for example, is a frequent imperative in the corpus. To interpret it as a command by the child to actually jump seems improbable. In the place where he is, physically, as he says it, there is no room to jump very far or high. It should instead be considered an expression of a desire to jump which appears in the most-used syntactic structure, the imperative, with a primarily conative function

A less ambiguous example where the linguistic structure of the speech event signals desire is *want to listen*, a verb phrase the structure of which he is just beginning to learn.

PARAGRAPHS

Having tried to present each one of the language functions in separate examples, we now want to continue with longer and more complex paragraphs where there is usually an interplay of the various functions.

We can come back to our original example of a paragraph (p. 80) and try to analyze it:

(A) (1) *Daddy*
    (2) *Daddy bucket please*
    (3) *Another other book please*
    (4) *Donkey*
    (5) *Fix the donkey*
    (6) *And the blue box and the big box*

Line (1) is a vocative, although the addressee is really not expected to respond. *Daddy* is repeated in line (2), still retaining its conative function but now the imperative is expanded by *bucket please*. This is a time in the child's life when he does use *please* fairly automatically in requests, unfortunately, a passing fancy. *Please* is repeated, but the vocative is omitted in line (3), the substitution item in the slot for *bucket* is now *book*, both containing the phonemes /b-k/, probably not accidentally. The noun phrase is now expanded by modifiers, *another other*, together referentially meaningless, but related to each other by one being included in the other. The "th" is the phoneme /d/, possibly part of the reason for the particular selection of these modifiers, as also reflected in line (5) where *donkey* again starts in /d/, the two consonants of the original *Daddy*. The choice of *donkey* is not accidental in other respects either: the first vowel is /A/, and not the also possible and elsewhere occurring /O/, followed by a nasal, the reverse of /A/ plus nasal of *another*. The second vowel is /I/, just like in *Daddy*. A new imperative, this time with the verb *fix* is in line (5) showing the primarily conative function of this paragraph, although the addressee, probably *Daddy*, is omitted. One more /d/, one of the favored consonants here, is added in *the*, making the line a non-elliptic sentence. Both /d/ and /n/ reappear in line (6) in *and the* twice, also serving as a conjunction exercise. The noun *box* now returns to the initial /b/ of *bucket* and *book*, repeated also in the modifiers *blue* and *big*. The final /ks/ of *fix* is mirrored twice in the same final cluster of *box*.

Let us now take a long sequence from the corpus which occurred in the middle of a tape, that is half-way after the child was put to bed and before he fell asleep. It presents a more complex picture and at the same time shows the various functions of language in different hierarchical arrangements:

(B)   (1) *That's office* (2×)
      (2) *Look Sophie*
      (3) *That Sophie*
      (4) *Come last night*
      (5) *Good boy*
      (6) *Go for glasses*
      (7) *Go for them*
      (8) *Go to the top*
      (9) *Go throw*
    (10) *Go for blouse*
    (11) *Pants*
    (12) *Go for shoes*
    (13) *Powder*
    (14) *S'not dry*
    (15) *Get powder on*
    (16) *Shoe fixed* (2×)
    (17) *And the shoe*
    (18) *Some powder*
    (19) *On the leg*
    (20) *Anthony's leg*
    (21) *Put in Daddy's legs*
    (22) *Put some Mommy's legs*
    (23) *Mommy's legs* (2×)
    (24) *Mommy get some* (2×)
    (25) *Soap*
    (26) *Mommy took a shower*

(27) *Take some soap*

(28) *Down*

There seems to be little question that the first three lines of the sequence are related by sound play. The phonemic sequence /sÓfI/, phonetically [sɔ́fì], is repeated in every one of the first three lines. Except for the final /s/ in line (1), it is identical phonemically with line (3); syntactically they can be considered identical as well since the syntactic difference of *That Sophie* and *That's Sophie* is phonemically obliterated. Line (1) is said twice so that there is balance between the forms /sÓfIs/ and /sÓfI/. Both the first and the last lines begin with *that*. Moreover, if we take only the different sentences in the first three lines, the pattern of thesis, antithesis and synthesis also emerges.

The emotive function is the predominant one in the next three lines which, however, are also tied to the preceding lines. *Sophie*, a family friend living out of town, had come for a visit which apparently had made an impression on the child. *Last night* is not factually correct, it was an afternoon visit, and not on the previous day. The time expression *last night* was a favorite one of the child's, perhaps because of its rhythm with the two vowels /ʌ/ and the final /t/. The reason *Sophie* had made an impression on Anthony was because he was a *good boy* and in turn he was a *good boy* because of *go for glasses*. In addition to the primary emotive function of these lines there is again some sound play present. Lines (4), (5), and (6) begin in a velar, once voiceless, twice voiced; the voiced velar is repeated once more in line (6). Three [ə]'s follow each other in lines (5) and (6), the second word final, the first and third followed by another single phoneme.

The following lines are tied by substitution patterns, the child's practice of selection and substitution, or we can say that the function of metalanguage is the predominant one. Line (7) is a simple pronominal substitution for the noun in line (6). In lines (8) and (9) only the frame *go* remains, different form classes are substituted, but the vocabulary is related in terms of sound: every word in the substitution items begins with an alveolar phoneme, once the voiced /d/, three times the voiceless /t/. Basically, though, this is a transformation exercise. Lines (10) and (12) return to the original longer frame *go for*, also using unmodified nouns as substitutes in the pattern, keeping the grammatical structure the same with paradigmatic substitutions. The particular selection of *blouse* and *shoes* is determined by their final /s/ which is also the last consonant of the original *glasses*. *Blouse*, in addition, has an initial cluster of voiced stop plus /l/, as does *glasses*. *Pants* of line (11) is probably also meant as a substitution item for the pattern, but occurs without the frame. It too ends in /s/ as all other previous substitution items did.

The substitution pattern ceases to be the primary function of the next two lines where in line (13) *powder* alliterates with *pants* of line (11), and the /nts/ sequence of phonemes is repeated as /snt/ in line (14), as is the /dr/ sequence of line (13). The sentence in line (14) is probably one which the child has heard frequently.

The original substitution pattern is now changed in line (15) to *get*, still alliterating with *go*, however, using the last substitute of the previous pattern, *powder*, as the noun, and repeating the phonetic sequence [nə] in reverse as [ən]. *Shoe fixed* of line (16) is another substitute for the frame *get*, repeating one of the nouns of the first substitution pattern, without the final /s/.

Line (17) is a conjunction exercise, a very frequent practice with *and*. Line (18) has the third repetition of *powder*, and *some* can be related to *shoe* in the line above by the child's frequent confusion of /s/ and /š/ as was pointed out earlier. Lines (18) and (19) are a referential statement, part of the daily bathing routine of the child, and the completion sequence of the two lines is probably a quotation of a single adult sentence.

The next lines again present a substitution pattern, the frame being *leg* or *legs*, and the possessive case of nouns the selected grammatical relationship to be practised since it also presents a final /s/ as did the nouns substituted in the former pattern. The first noun substituted, *Anthony's*, echoes the consonantal environment of *leg* of the previous line: /n/ and an alveolar stop. *Daddy's* and *Mommy's* follow since these three people are of greatest importance to the child, an emotive selection. The /t/ and /n/ of *Anthony's* in line (20) are repeated in the frame of line (21), with the addition of /p/ which reappears in line (22), reminiscent of *powder* of lines (13), (15), and (18). Line (22) repeats *some*, containing the same phoneme sequence /Am/ as does the following *Mommy's*. *Mommy's legs* of line (23) is a type of phrase reduplication, a play with a whole phrase, here repeated twice, once with rising, once with falling intonation. Also repeated twice, both with sustained intonation, is line (24), using the pattern frame *get* from line (15) and repeating *Mommy* and *some* from line (22), the last line containing more than one phrase. Together with line (25), a vocative request is formulated, utilizing still a different function of language, the conative. The selection of the object of the sentence is again phonologically determined, alliterating with the immediately preceding *some*, and ending in /p/, the initial consonant of the first word of the preceding pattern. Line (26) is an imaginary statement of fact, evoked by the preceding and following word *soap*. However, relationships of sound are not irrelevant either. *Mommy* is repeated from line (24), and we have already commented on the relationship of /s/ and /š/ in the child's phonemic pattern. Lines (27) and (28) show the exercise of changing the past form of the word *took* to the non-past *take*, a transformation practice, repeating the sequence *some soap*, and ending with *down*, containing the alveolar stop and nasal sequence of phonemes which had been played with in lines (19), (20), and (21).

Now another example which occurred at about the same relative time as the paragraph just discussed:

(C) (1) *Lock the door*
    (2) *Mail all the letter*
    (3) *Mailman*
    (4) *Doggie can bite the mailman*

   (5) *Bite all the letters*
   (6) *Mailman have a bite*
   (7) *Bite the letters*

An explanatory note for a better understanding of the paragraph may be in order. The dog in the household did not care for the mailman and had shown strong evidence of this dislike. If he possibly could, he would bite letters delivered through a slot in the front door – which delivery Anthony called mailing the letters – and he would have liked to accord the mailman the same treatment. The front door was always kept closed around the time the mailman was expected, and in addition secured by a chain so that Anthony would not inadvertently open it. Now back to the paragraph.

   The first two lines are imperatives, hence, their function is primarily conative, but also metalingual, since they have the same grammatical pattern. The consonants are interesting, however. All except /k/ are voiced, and they are only /l/, occurring four times, /d/, occurring also four times (here the pronunciation of "letter" is [lǽdər]), /r/ twice, and /m/ only once. Line (3) repeats the /m/ and adds another nasal, /n/. Line (4) repeats all the preceding consonants except /r/, adds /t/ which then reappears in every succeeding line also, and reinforces the alveolar point of articulation by a voiced alveolar stop as well. Line (4) which is in the middle of the paragraph, is also the longest line, and could also be a quotation of adult speech, although the child has learned the construction of verb phrases with *can*. Line (5) repeats the original imperative pattern by substituting the verb *bite*, or more precisely it is the pattern of line (2), but this substitution exercise results in a misuse of syntactic liberty as a command is given ordering something which is not semantically acceptable. The nasals are reintroduced in line (6), *mailman*, and since the child knows that mailmen do not usually *bite*, the pattern is changed to a vocative imperative, performing also another transformation, that of the same phonemic shape assigned to another form class, here the original verb *bite* now appears as a noun, *a bite*. The end of the sequence, line (7), repeats the originally introduced pattern in line (1), repeating the substitution items of line (5), thus giving the sequence added symmetry.

A sequence using the functions of language somewhat differently, and occurring closer to the onset of sleep, is the following one:

(D) (1) *Hi big Bob*
     (2) *That's Bob* (2×)
     (3) *Big Bob* (3×)
     (4) *Little Bob*
     (5) *Big and little*
     (6) *Little Bobby*
     (7) *Little Nancy*
     (8) *Big Nancy*
     (9) *Big Bob and Nancy and Bobby*
    (10) *And Bob*

(11) *And two, three Bobbys*
(12) *Three Bobbys*
(13) *Four Bobbys*
(14) *Six*
(15) *Tell the night, Bobby*
(16) *Big Bob*
(17) *Big Bob not home*
(18) *Nancy and Wendy*
(19) *Wendy gave Anthony's*
(20) *On Nancy*
(21) *Only Nancy could with the Kitty*
(22) *Mommy go sweep*
(23) *Aw, Nancy again*

It would perhaps be better to first comment on the cast of characters. The names are those of close family friends, the father's name is *Bob*, sometimes called "big Bob" by Anthony, an added redundancy to distinguish him even more clearly from his son *Bobby*; the mother's name is *Nancy*, and the children are named *Bobby* or *little Bobby* and *Wendy*.

The first line is simply a greeting intended for a real person who is not present, but whom the child sees rather frequently. *Big Bob* is preferred by Anthony to *Bob* alone, probably because of alliteration. Line (2), repeated twice, identifies the person, and two of the repetitions of line (3) serve to clarify who it is, returning to the alliteration. In the third repetition the intonation is changed to a rising contour, showing the adjectives in still another function as they contrast with *little* in line (4). There is no such person as *little Bob*, the origin of this phrase could be the child's wish to make *Bob little*, but he has now engaged in a practice session of adjectival substitution, using the antonyms *big* and *little*, as they appear in line (5) as the synthesis from the previous thesis *big* and antithesis *little*. In line (6) *little Bobby* could just be mention of the child's name, but line (7), *little Nancy*, when no such person exists, shows clearly that the substitution game continues, as line (8) also shows. Line (9) introduces a new pattern. While retaining the modifier in *big Bob*, it is not used with the other names, and the purpose of this line is primarily an enumeration and practice in the use of the conjunction *and*. A chain is formed, the climax of the preceding lines, where each line contains only a single name. *And* is used before every name except the first. This is corrected in line (10) where even the adjective *big* is dropped before *Bob*. *And* also appears in line (11), and now the enumeration has become refined to the point of actual counting, forming a new chain with ascending numerals. Even the plural morpheme is used with the noun to confirm this. Lines (12) and (13) go on counting, using only one numeral per noun, and echoing in line (12) the end of line (11). Counting has now become all-absorbing, and only the numeral remains, without the noun, ending the chain of grading. Since the concept of numbers was only in the early stages of acquisition by the child, *six* was probably the highest numeral he could think of at the moment. Hence, to terminate this particular activity, the child's version of "Say good night to Bobby" or "Say good night, Bobby", an imperative, appears in line (15), keeping the name *Bobby*, with which he has practised, still there. (It should be borne in mind that the initial consonant of "the" is /d/.) The two /b/'s in the last word of line (15), however, bring Anthony back again to his favorite *Big Bob* with three /b/'s, also typically returning to the beginning of the paragraph using a closed construction. In line (17) the /O/ phoneme is added two more times, also becoming the grand total of three. The /n/ in this line is probably a cue to the first word in line (18), *Nancy*, containing two /n/'s, followed by the echo of /En/ in *and* and *Wendy* which even alliterate further by the following /d/. The last word, *Wendy*, of line (18) is repeated as the first word of line (19) where the sequence /En/ reappears in *Anthony's*. The phoneme /g/ is also reintroduced and will again appear in line (22) and line (23) together with the sequence /En/ in *again* and *Nancy*. The possessive /s/ in *Anthony's* in line (19) can only be explained if we look at its consonant pattern /n-n-s/ which is identical with that of *Nancy*. Line (20) begins with [ɔn], contained in the last word of the previous line, and alliterating with the other word in the same line. *On Nancy* in turn is reminiscent of *only Nancy* because of its rhythm in line (21). *Only* plus a name plus *could* is a favorite saying of the child and it appears here. The /w/, which thus far has been confined to *Wendy*, now reappears in line (21) in *with* and in line (22) in *sweep*. *Kitty* is a repetition of the consonants /k-d/ of *could*.

An example of a combination of a grammatical exercise with sound play is the following paragraph occurring shortly after the child had been put to bed. We have indicated the first phonetic consonant of "throw" in brackets.

(E) (1) *Bobo's not throwing*   [t]
     (2) *Bobo can throw*   [θ]
     (3) *Bobo can throw it*   [θ]
     (4) *Bobo can throw*   [θ]
     (5) *Oh* (2×)
     (6) *Go* (3×)

Line (1) is a negative statement true to fact, a description of a state, with the phoneme /O/ occurring in four out of the five syllables. The first consonant of *throwing* is [t], a usual substitution for the standard English phoneme /θ/. Here perhaps [t] rather than [f], another substitute for /θ/, is chosen because of the final released [t] of *not*. In line (2) the first statement is amended to an imaginary statement of fact, the pronunciation of *throw* is corrected to conform to standard English with [θ], also avoiding the troublesome sequence *not throwing*. Here, as in line (1), a correct standard grammatical pattern is used, as they are also in the following two lines, line (4) being a complete echo of line (2). In line (3), however, the grammatical pattern has been expanded to include an additional slot in the pattern, making it more complex, but still grammatically correct. In terms of sound, this addition, *it*, ends in [tʳ], the same consonant as the original *not* which led the child astray in the first appearance of *throw*. Now the troublemaker is safely at the end of the sentence. The paradigmatic exercise of the first four lines is clear: *throwing, can throw, can throw it, can throw*. The significance of the repetition of /O/ in line (1) is borne out by line (5), phonetically [oʊ], showing the practice of a complex vowel nucleus, a feature imperfectly learned in the child's system. [oʊ] is repeated twice in line (5) and three times in line (6) where it is combined with /g/ making a pseudo-word of it. That the primary function of *go* is sound play rather than a referential or conative one is confirmed by the child's squealing pronunciation of this line, an indication of play, and not of intended denotative meaning. The selection of the velar /g/ is perhaps also not accidental in view of the previously repeated /k/ in *can*.

Following is a paragraph immediately preceding the child's dropping off to sleep, characterized also by his rocking back and forth in the crib, an activity often accompanying his speech, immediately preceding sleep:

(F)　(1) *Don't touch Mommy Daddy's desk*
　　　(2) *I should*
　　　(3) *He say so* (2×)
　　　(4) *Daddy's desk and Mommy's desk*
　　　(5) *Don't go on the desk*
　　　(6) *Don't take Daddy's glasses*
　　　(7) *Don't take it off*
　　　(8) *Don't take the glasses off*
　　　(9) *Daddy's wearing glasses*
　　(10) *Daddy always*
　　(11) *Dadada*
　　(12) *Leave it*
　　(13) *Daddy's glasses* (some whispering, banging, squealing)
　　(14) *Doggie, Mommy, cookie* (2×) (unintelligible low volume with much banging, hitting of microphone, squealing)
　　(15) *Mike* (15×) (Hitting of microphone, squealing)
　　　　　SLEEP

Interestingly enough, the things he is forbidden to do during the day preoccupy him at the moment of sleep. There are two very strict rules in the household: nothing on the parents' desks is to be touched, nor taken for play. No climbing on desks is permitted under any circumstances, although imitation of the cat who often walks on the desk is very tempting for the child. The other absolute, never to be tampered with, are eye-glasses which both parents wear, the father occasionally, the mother always. Line (1), then, is a repetition or reminder of a command the child has heard many times with great definiteness. The construction of the sentence is elliptic, the possessive does not appear with *Mommy*, and the conjunction *and* which we would expect between *Mommy* and *Daddy* is lacking too, probably in order to get more quickly to the alliterating *Daddy's desk*, the sound of which appeals to the child, and is also evocative of *don't*, the underlying idea of this paragraph. The indication of two possessors, *Mommy* and *Daddy*, is also typical of the child's thought pattern in pairs. Line (2) offers at first glance linguistically a contradiction to line (1) on the basis of standard English, but we believe this to be an erroneous interpretation. The rules for answers to negative statements or commands in English are rather complex, and the child has not yet learned them. *I should*, therefore, is to be interpreted as "I should not touch". The use of the pronoun *I* instead of the much more frequent "Anthony" when the child talks about himself and the occurrence of the modal *should*, which is rare in his speech, make this a very important sentence for Anthony in that he is trying to show that he is grown-up and understands what the adult has forbidden him, by using the adult's language which he understands very well, but usually does not use. In line (3) another infrequent personal pronoun appears, *he*, the distinction in substitutions of *he* or *she* not being well learned by the child, again an attempt at adult speech with pronouns. The attempt here, however, is not as successful as in line (2), the third person singular marker is missing, more consonant with the child's usual speech pattern. The selection of *say so*, both beginning with /s/ which is frequently confused with /š/ by the child, is probably also conditioned by the *should* of the previous line.

Line (4) completes the elliptic line (1), now expanding the paired idea, but the order of *Daddy's* and *Mommy's* is reversed for two reasons: the child prefers the alliterating *Daddy's desk* to *Mommy's desk* on the one hand, and the line conforms to the next seven lines by beginning with /d/. The following four lines (lines (5) through (8)), are not only tied by the initial /d/, but all have as their first word the negative command *don't*. In listing what he is not supposed to do, the child then continues with *don't go on* in line (5), a phonemically related sequence by repeating /O/ three times and the longer /On/ twice, continuing with *the desk* which again alliterates since the consonant of the definite article is /d/. The linguistic structure of negative imperatives has been learned quite well, since the child has no doubt heard them very frequently. The next negative command in line (6) substitutes a new verb, *take* replacing *touch* and *go* of the previous pattern sentences, repeating the alveolar /t/ of *touch* and echoing the velar of *go* by a voiceless /k/. The favorite *Daddy's* reappears, but *glasses* has been substituted for *desk* in the same slot in the pattern. The reason is twofold: the child has never been forbidden to *take* the *desk*, a physical impossibility for him; *glasses* repeats the vowel [æ] and consonant /s/ of *Daddy's* which ends in a voiceless sibilant. Lines (7) and (8) are a substitution pattern exercise, showing again weakness in the correct pronominal choice, and the adding of *off* to the pattern of line (6), that is echoing the phoneme /O/ played with previously, and also using *take off* in connection with *glasses*, a frequent activity which the child has observed and mentioned. Line (9) shows a change of the pattern, using the *-ing* verb construction correctly, the best-learned marked verb form. Since the mother, however, is the person who is the constant wearer of glasses, the following line (10) is not true to fact, and the occurrence of *Daddy* both in lines (9) and (10) is due to sound play as line (11) confirms. *Daddy always* of line (10) is a partial repetition of the consonants occurring in line (9), and since the child knows that Daddy does not always wear glasses, he drops the whole idea and goes on with just sound play in line (11). Line (12) now uses an affirmative command which parallels the meaning of the previous negative ones, and has as its object the pronoun *it*, the vowel phoneme of which is identical with that of *leave*, /I/. In line (13), *Daddy's glasses*, played with in line (6), is a substitution item for *it* of the previous line.

Following line (13), the recording becomes unintelligible. We can detect some whispering by the child which, however, is drowned out by his banging the side of the crib, and squeals follow. The next intelligible speech event is line (14), still having /d/ as its first consonant, but with a primarily phatic function. Three nouns are mentioned in sequence twice, all of which are of emotive content to the child, all also ending in /I/. In terms of sound pattern, the identical consonants /d/ of *Daddy* now have been dissimilated to /d-g/ of *doggie*, but identical consonants occur in the other two words, /m/ in *Mommy* and /k/ in *cookie*. Once again, some unintelligible speech follows, also accompanied by banging, squealing, and additional attention is focused on the microphone standing next to the crib, it being assaulted by various objects, judging by the recording. The last linguistic speech event, sounding like a phonograph record stuck in one place, is a repetition of the first syllable of the object which the child is hitting; the form *mike*, although frequent in standard English, is not a common expression in the household, and therefore not familiar to the child. Finally, after about fifteen repetitions of this syllable, Anthony has given up keeping the channel of communication open by linguistic means, he again resorts to throwing and squealing, and finally there is silence, sleep has overtaken him.

A type of paragraph which is infrequent, in that its primary function is narrative, is the following:
(G) (1) *See that*
     (2) *Walk with feet* (3×)
     (3) *Two feet*
     (4) *See*
     (5) *Twofeet and the horse*
     (6) *Like all other Indians*
     (7) *Twofeet had a horse* (2×)
     (8) *See cactus*
     (9) *And the grass*
    (10) *And flowers*
See that of line (1) could be interpreted as an imperative, or as an elliptic question which is more likely in view of the rising intonation contour which accompanies it and the context which follows it. Line (2) confirms that the child is pointing to or looking at something, namely his *feet*. Their observation evokes a statement of what they are used for, rather than a command which the form of line (2) would suggest.

Walk with feet is repeated three times, partially due to its alliteration, but primarily because of a statement of fact as line (3) also suggests. Observation of his *feet* has now made the child state that he has *two feet*, the numerical concept of *two* being already quite familiar to the child in distinction to higher numbers. Line (4) again has the rising intonation contour of line (1), suggesting a repetition of the question, omitting its second word. Sound association now takes over briefly to tie line (5) to line (3). *Twofeet* is a character in the child's favorite story at the time, an Indian boy who, after much hardship, acquired a horse *like all other Indians*, our line (6), a complete quotation from the story. Coming back to line (5), *Twofeet and the horse*, was the title of the book regularly read to the child before starting in on the story itself. We are also sure of our interpretation of line (3) as *two feet*, and of lines (5) and (7) as *Twofeet* because of the stress pattern. In line (3), both syllables carry phonemic stress, whereas in the two other instances, only the first syllable carries stress, the second being phonemically unstressed, a consistent pattern of the child's to distinguish between adjective plus noun phrases on the one hand, and compound nouns on the other.

Line (7), repeated twice, is the final line of the story, the happy ending, reiterated here, as this is more important to the child than the following three lines, also part of the story. The precedence of line (7) over lines (8)–(10) is determined emotively, but all these lines have as a common bond the child's recounting of the story. Needless to say, *see* in line (8) cannot be taken literally; the child does not have the book with the story in the crib with him, nor would the light level in the room permit the viewing of a drawing of a *cactus*, *grass*, or *flowers*; but *see* here repeats the pattern of lines (1) and (4), although the intonation contour is now a falling one. Lines (9) and (10) are quotations from the story, each appearing under the picture of the flora, and secondarily, they offer practice with the conjunction *and*.

Two other examples of interplay of sound and meaning follow. Here is one which also serves as a paradigmatic exercise for verbs, occurring half-way between the child's being put to bed and falling asleep:

(H) (1) *Anthony write*
     (2) *Pencil's always writing*
     (3) *And a*
     (4) *And a smiling*
     (5) *Anthony can smile*
     (6) *Can smile*
     (7) *Mrs. Kirs*
     (8) *Mrs. Kirsten*
     (9) *Kirsten* (2×)
   (10) *That's a good boy*
   (11) *Good boy*

Our assignment of the phonemic sequence /rAyt/ to "write" rather than "right" is based completely on line (2) where it reappears in the word *writing*, hence forming a paradigm, one of the functions of this paragraph. This line is a referential statement, evoked by the sound of *write* in line (1), stating a fact. The interpretation of the final sibilant /s/ in *pencil's* is of course open to question. It could be a plural marker, or the interpretation we have chosen, a form of "is". The whole line (3) is a reflection of the initial phonemes /ÉntE-/ of *Anthony* in line (1), here with the voiced alveolar stop, /ÉndE/, *and a*. The function of line (3) is phatic, analogous to a hesitation form in adult speech, like the proverbial "well". A new thread of thought is caught in line (4), although still non-sensical, but with a paradigmatic and a sound function. Its beginning is identical with that of line three, and *smiling* repeats the grammatical form of the previous *writing* with the vowel and glide phonemes being identical as well. Line (5) finally shows the accomplishment: we have a meaningful sentence, but by no means unrelated to what went on before. The pattern of the sentence is the same as in the first line of the paragraph, and the slot for the subject is even occupied by the same word, *Anthony*. The verb phrase, however, is expanded to a modal construction *can smile*, a fairly common pattern in the child's usage, and here a continuation of the paradigmatic exercise, and the verb is *smile*, introduced in line (4). Line (6) is an echo of the verb phrase of the immediately preceding line, a continuation of the paradigm, and perhaps also with some phatic function, judging by the following line (7) which again is devoid of referential meaning. *Kirsten*, as it appears in line (9), is the name of a friend of the Danish visitor who lives in the household, and the friend has perhaps made an impression on the child, although he has seen her infrequently. Line (7), however, is nonsense, since *Mrs.* has never been used with the name *Kirsten* which here also appears in a shorthand version. We can explain line (7) as sound play, repeating some of the consonants of line (6). Line (8) completes the name to *Kirsten*, and line (9) drops the *Mrs.* of lines (7) and (8), coming to the true name of the young girl, and the familiarity and reality is indicated by two repetitions. Line (10) refers back to lines (4) through (6), the *smiling*, for which the child commends himself, as adults often praise him for being friendly. Line (11) echoes the last two words of line (10), the important ones to the child before the volume of speech becomes too low to be intelligible.

Here is the other example which does not show the paradigmatic function, but is confined to the interplay of sound and meaning. It occurs shortly after the child has been put to bed.

(1)   (1) *Train*
     (2) *Anthony can see the plane*
     (3) *Plane* (2×)
     (4) *See bubble*
     (5) *Bubble's here*
     (6) *Bubbles*
     (7) *Flowers*
     (8) *Bed flowers*

Anthony has mixed feelings about a *train*. He is fascinated by its moving, but he intensely dislikes its noise which he has experienced at a railroad station. Line (2), then, changes to another moving object which he has seen only at a great distance, hence the element of noise is eliminated, and a *plane* is more pleasant than a *train*. Both move, however, and perhaps, even more important, they rhyme. The modal construction of line (2) is a usual one. The last word in the line, *plane*, is repeated in line (3) twice, which in turn leads to line (4) with *bubble*, repeating the sequence of bilabial stop plus /l/ together with an initial bilabial stop, but voiced this time. *See* which we encountered in line (2) reappears, but the pattern is highly elliptical. The last word of line (6) is repeated in line (5), a frequent practice within the paragraph, with the addition of the /z/ phoneme. Ambiguity results in whether this /z/ should be interpreted as the plural morpheme, or as the verb "is". We have chosen the latter interpretation in view of the following word *here*, thus resulting in a more meaningful sentence also as a follow-up of line (5). The interpretation of /z/ as a plural, however, seems preferable for line (6) in view of the following two lines. *Flowers* of line (7) resumes the play with the consonant plus /l/ cluster, this time a voiceless spirant is selected, as close as spirants come to the bilabial point of articulation, the labiodental. However, bilabiality and voicing are returned to in the first consonant of line (8), /b/ in *bed* which together with *flowers* of the previous line results in the elliptic phrase *bed flowers*, a familiar concept to the child.

Following is an example where Anthony's attempt at grammatical transformations and recombinations have non-grammatical results, also occurring shortly after the child has been put in his crib.

(J)   (1) *Step on the blanket*
        (2) *Where is Anthony's blanket* (2×) (falsetto)
        (3) *Where's hiding* (falsetto)
        (4) *Books*
        (5) *Down* (2×)
        (6) *Have the books today*
        (7) *I take the white blanket off*
        (8) *On the blanket*
        (9) *Under the blanket*
      (10) *Sleep go*
      (11) *What a blue blanket*
      (12) *What the take the blanket*

Blanket, which is a favorite object of his and is also with him in the crib, is the frame for lines (1) and (2). *Step* has overloud stress, showing the emotive rather than the conative function of the imperative to be primary. This is confirmed by the falsetto voice quality in the following two lines, so that these are certainly not questions for information, but play with language assuming here the roles of both participants of his imaginary dialogue. Anthony knows very well where the *blanket* is, but the pattern provides an opportunity to practise a question three times. The closer identification as *Anthony's blanket* rather than *the blanket* of the previous line is probably to show an even closer tie to the favorite object. However, the continuation of the question exercise in line (3) has led him astray grammatically which he probably knows, and he drops the pattern. *Books* in line (4) has a sustained intonation contour, suggesting some uncertainty. Possibly it was selected because of the labiality of /b/ due to lines (2) and (3) also starting with a labial, and, of course, it is also the initial consonant of *blanket*. After the hesitation of line (4), line (5) is definite, repeated twice. *Down* repeats the /d/ and the nasal of *hiding*, but primarily is associated with *books* which are often taken *down* from bookshelves. This in turn reminds him of line (6), formally an imperative, but we believe it is more correctly to be interpreted as part of a quotation form which he has heard frequently. The original sentence, as spoken by an adult, is more likely to have had a pronoun and modal precede *have the books today*. Since this is not a very fruitful pursuit, Anthony again turns to the favorite *blanket* as the object of line (7). This is a six-word grammatical sentence, a rather long one for him. The first person pronoun *I* appears, followed by context which is linguistically as well as referentially most familiar. The verb *take* in this construction does not require markers; except for the glide /y/, also contained in the preceding *I*, it is also the reverse of the second syllable of *blanket*, thus /tEyk/ and /-kEt/. Modification of nouns in this paragraph is quite consistent, and the definite article again appears, but modification becomes more elaborate, including the adjective *white*, one of the three colors assigned by Anthony to his blankets, partially based on reality, partially on imagination. He identifies them correctly, though, and if an adult makes a mistake in labelling, due to the blankets' non-descriptive colors, the adult is immediately corrected. The last word of the line, *off*, triggers the beginning of line (8), *on*, and since the use of the article thus far has been satisfactory, *the* follows, as does *blanket*. Line (9) contradicts line (8), and the antonym *under* replaces the preceding *on*, leaving the frame, *the blanket*, intact. The next line is produced by metonymy, *Sleep go*, albeit a fleeting one, as the rather imprecise construction shows. Anthony can do better on word order, his grammatical forte, and *go to sleep* or the elliptic *go sleep* are very frequent, all constructions, except for our example, in the correct order. Line (11) returns to the leitmotif *blanket*, always in final positions (except for line (7) because of the nature of the two-part verb), with *what* replacing the original *where* of lines (2) and (3). Grammaticality is still present, replacing the previous *the* by the indefinite *a*, and using now the alliterating modifier *blue*, another identifier of blankets. (Yellow, the third blanket, is missing in this paragraph.) The recombination of line (12), alas, is grammatically not successful and the combinatory rules have exceeded his linguistic capacity. Anthony tried to include too many things: the frame *what* of the preceding line, the thus far correct article *the*, the pleasing phonemic shape of *take* as well as the *blanket*, and grammatical failure results. However, not so in terms of sound play. Besides the glides and the vowel /O/ of *what*, only the vowel phoneme /E/ occurs, and all the consonants before *blanket* are alveolars and a velar, again repeated in the second syllable of his favorite object, *blanket*.

A number of functions appear in the following paragraph, which, although not the last, occurs only a few minutes before the onset of sleep.

(K) (1) *Like* (2×)
     (2) *One like*
     (3) *Two like*
     (4) *Three four like*
     (5) *One like*
     (6) *Monkey's like*
     (7) *Up* (2×)
     (8) *Light* (2×)
     (9) *Turn the light*
     (10) *Light*
     (11) *All gone* (2×)
     (12) *It's all gone* (2×)
     (13) *It's not all gone*
     (14) *It's not all*
     (15) *Stop it* (2×)
     (16) *There* (squealing, babbling [yayaya waʊ waʊ] [gigoʊboʊboʊ]) (2×)
     (17) *Now it's all gone*
     (18) *All gone* (falsetto)
     (19) *Go* (4×)
     (20) *All gone* (4×)
     (21) *Good luck*
     (22) *That's one*
     (23) *Two*
     (24) *Go* (4×) (falsetto)
     (25) *Close the door*
     (26) /gɪ/ (6×) (hitting, squealing)

The word *like* in the following lines is interpreted as indicating comparison, the child's most common usage for this phonemic sequence, although he also has it as a verb. The two repetitions in line (2) differ by their intonation contours: the first is rising, perhaps indicating hesitation or uncertainty, the second one is falling, more certain that this is the word he wants. The following four lines use *like* as the frame for numerals, in ascending order through line (4), coming back to *one* of line (2) in line (5). Both *three* and *four* precede the single *like* in line (4) where the gradation has reached its height. Line (6) shows a switch, counting is abandoned in favor of *monkey*, probably evoked by the phonemic sequence /ʌn/ of *one* contained in the first syllable of *monkey*. The interpretation of the /z/ morpheme must remain ambiguous as the plural or a form of "is", the possessive being unlikely since this is not a usually personified toy. Line (7) continues with the phoneme /ʌ/ and also shows the beginning of the play with voiceless stops, using this time a bilabial. Line (8) confirms the play with final stops, an alveolar is chosen (the velar occurred in *like*, thus using all three points of stop articulation), and the preceding phonemic sequence of *light* is identical to the one of *like*.

In considering *like* and *light*, we could speak of paranomasia as defined by Lausberg (1960): "...Spiel mit der Geringfügigkeit der lautlichen Änderung einerseits und der interessanten Bedeutungsspanne, die durch die lautliche Änderung hergestellt wird, andererseits." (p. 322) A minimum of sound substitution, /t/ for /k/, has occurred, pointing at the same time to an interesting relationship of meanings. *Light* is certainly a pleasant thought to the child since it means the opposite of sleep, social interaction with people important to him, daylight and what may be connected with it. The phonemic shape /lAyk/ represents two morphemes for the child: one, the verb "like" and the other the comparative "like". It could be argued that the latter has nothing in common with the notion of pleasantness, of loving. However, we do not believe this to be true. The child's *blanket like a lipstick* uses *like* formally as a word of comparison, but the emotional content of *blanket* is very high, and *like* is connected with it. We can also point to the German-American "ich gleiche" showing a clear connection between both morphemes "like". In our example, it is ambiguous which *like* is being used, although it seems that it is not the verb. Whichever it is, however, does not matter because both of them have a meaningful relationship to *light* far beyond sound.

Line (8) then serves as a build-up for line (9) which tells us what to do with a *light* in an elliptic way, using only the *turn* part of the verb. The article *the* is also added, thus showing an alveolar at the beginning of the first two words, and at the end of the last word. The line begins and ends in the voiceless /t/ with the voiced /d/ in the middle. Line (10) echoes the main phonemic sequence /lAy/ in *light*; however, there is no *light* for which the child uses the expression *all gone* in line (11), his usual way of indicating the absence of something. The two repetitions of the line are not identical, however, the /O/ in *all* in the first occurrence being overlong, one of the usual indications of a primarily emotive function. The completion of the originally elliptic sentence in line (11) to a complete one *It's all gone* in line (12) shows further concern over the absence of *light* by its two repetitions, and introduces a new pattern to play with. It is transformed into the negative in line (13), and the negative is repeated elliptically in line (14). Line (15) repeats the phonemes /Ap/ of line (7), and *it* again appears. Now the phatic function takes over in line (16); squealing accompanies the barely intelligible *there*, and the longest expansion of the pattern of lines (12) through (14) in line (17), *Now it's all gone*, with babbling interspersed as well. Falsetto is again the characteristic of line (18) which is also a reduction of the pattern to the semantic elements. The *go*, phonetically [gɔ], of line (19), together with line (20) is a paradigmatic exercise of the unmarked form and participle of the verb, a relationship just being learned. The repetitions of *all gone*, coming back to the part of the pattern important to the child in line (20), is first produced with longish vowels, very much exaggerated in the second repetition, and given with short vowels twice. *Good luck* of line (21) is a quotation form, coming in here because of its consonant phonemes: the order of /g/ and /l/ is now transposed, and the stops of the previous consonant play reappear. Moreover, *luck* is closely related to *like* of the original line (1), thus closing the construction and starting all over with *one* and *two* in the following two lines. The /d/ and /ts/ sequence also reappear again in *that's* of line (22), as does the numeral *one* from the original counting. *Two* in line (23) represents a new attempt at producing the ascending order, but the child is already too tired to continue, and line (24) returns to the four repetitions, falsetto, of [gɔ], just to keep on talking, but, interestingly, it is also a return to the former line (19). Play with [ɔ], the stops and /l/ are resumed once more in line (25), both *close* and *door* having a phonetic [ɔ]. The velar /g/ is still the consonant of the final line (26) where hitting accompanies the vocal means of trying to stay awake.

In the following paragraph, the child even uses the two English dialects which he imitates as an aid in sound play. As we have mentioned previously, both his /A/ and /O/ can appear in words like *what* due to the dialects he is exposed to.

(L) (1) *Wonderful*
(2) *What* (2×)
(3) *Ha what*
(4) *What*
(5) *He want to play*
(6) *Play*
(7) *Cobbers not night-night*
(8) *Yellow blanket please*

The paragraph starts with the pleasant word *wonderful* since pleasant things in particular seem to be on Anthony's mind at this very moment as the paragraph will show. However, an opportunity for sound play must not be missed, and line (2) are two repetitions of *what* beginning with the same two phonemes /wA/ as did the preceding word, also repeating its alveolar stop in the voiceless actualization, the most frequent one word-finally. The initial /h/ of line (3) is a recollection of a possible pronunciation of *what* with an initial cluster /hw/ which the child uses rarely, but his mother frequently, who also uses a low central vowel phoneme in this word. The epenthetic [a] between /h/ and /w/ is also repeated in a mora of length in the second syllable, and it conforms to *he* of line (5). In line (4) the child's other pronunciation of *what* appears, with /O/, and the intonation is rising suggesting uncertainty or a question. Line (5) returns in association to line (1), the pleasantness of *play*, in addition to the repetition of the phonemes of /w-nt/ in *want to* of the original *wonderful*, neutralizing the feature of voice in the stop. The third person singular marker does not appear since a sibilant would be an intruder in this play. The line also starts with *he*, a rare pronoun for the child, probably selected because of the initial /h/ of line (3). *Play*, the agreeable notion is echoed in line (6). The association is again continued in line (7), the dog, *Cobbers*, who is often the child's playmate, is *not night-night*, hence available for play. *Not* has overloud stress, emphasizing the nice idea, and the phonemes /n/ and /t/ of *not* are repeated as well in *night-night*. The vowel phoneme of *not* is /O/, staying within the dialect used at the moment to conform with *what*. The vowel plus /y/ repeats the phoneme sequence of *play*. But since Anthony really knows that this is not the time for *play* with *Cobbers*, he will be satisfied with something else that is pleasant, namely, the *blanket* which is the favorite of favorites, the *yellow*. He is not really asking for it since he has it in the crib, but *yellow blanket please* is a very common phrase for him, possibly due to its alliteration, except for the often irrelevant feature of voicing.

In one of the longest paragraphs in the monologue, which occurs at about the half-way point of an evening's repertoire, pronominal substitutions are the underlying theme for the major part.

(M)   (1) *Find it*
      (2) *With juice*
      (3) *Drink it* (2×)
      (4) *Juice*
      (5) *That's the right way*
      (6) *Right way*
      (7) *Where you going*
      (8) *I'm going*
      (9) *Shoe fixed*
   (10) *Talk to Mommy*
   (11) *Shoe fixed*
   (12) *See Antho*
   (13) *Anthony*
   (14) *Good night*
   (15) *See morrow morning*
   (16) *Shoe fixed* (4×)
   (17) *Fix it* (3×)
   (18) *Shoe fixed*
   (19) *It took it*
   (20) *Bring it back*
   (21) *Took them*
   (22) *Took it down* (4×)
   (23) *He took it* (2×)
   (24) *I'm going*
   (25) *Yellow one*
   (26) *Another one* (2×)
   (27) *Take a book*
   (28) *Another book*

(29) *A phone call*

(30) *Phone call book*

(31) *This phone call book* (3×)

(32) *This is the* (2×)

(33) *Book*

(34) *Another phone call book*

(35) *This is light*

(36) *One light*

(37) *This is light on it*

The paragraph starts out with an imperative, the syntactic pattern for the first four lines, keeping the pronominal frame *it* constant, and changing from *find* to *drink* in the verbs. After *find it* of line (1), line (2) *with juice* is a non-sequitur in regard to grammatical construction. *Juice*, here phonemically /yUs/, however, is used because the child is very fond of it, so he may as well *find juice*. The preceding *with* contains the phonemic shape /It/ of line (1), the /w/ reflecting the labiality of /f/ in line (1). Now *juice* evokes *drink* in line (3) which together with *it* repeat the pattern of line (1). The two repetitions of line (3) are not sufficient to convey the strength of the child's feelings, and another *juice* occurs in line (4), now without the preposition and clearly a substitution item for the imperative pattern used. Line (5) seems to refer to the drinking of juice from a glass rather than a bottle. Probably because of the new baby in the family, Anthony does not want to give up his bottle which is given to him upon "reasonable" request. However, he is also usually commended for drinking from a glass which he is capable of doing very well, of course, that this is *the right way* to go about it. Line (6) echoes the important part of line (5), *right way*, which in turn is the basis for the association in line (7) *where you going*. The intonation here is not rising which is some indication of the fact that a question for information is really not the primary function, but rather that *way* of the previous line has metonymic connection with *going*, and *where* starting with the same two phonemes /wE/ of *way*. But since a question pattern was formed, he answers himself in this dialogue with himself in line (8) *I'm going*, using this opportunity as a substitution exercise for *you* and *I*, something he knows about, but has not learned to use freely. In line (9) he completes in meaning line (8), namely, he is going to have the *shoe fixed*. Trips to the shoemaker with his mother were an enjoyable experience since it meant being with his mother and also going onto the university campus where the shoemaker was and where Mommy's office was as well. Also, he liked to watch the students milling around. Line (10) returns to the imperative pattern, *Mommy* is the person who goes to have *shoe fixed* and *talk to* was probably selected to echo the stops /k-t/ of *fixed* as /t-k-t/. *Shoe fixed* is again echoed in line (11), reinforcing the activity he is looking forward to or remembering fondly. The sibilants of this line are repeated in *see* of line (12), but the child is not quite sure what he wants to say and stops after having said the first two syllables of his name. He decides to complete it in line (13), and he is back to the idea of taking a walk with his mother to have the shoes fixed. However, he is in bed and he is supposed to sleep as the quotation form *good night* in line (14) as well as the more optimistic *see morrow morning* in line (15) indicate. The two expressions together were part of the ritual of putting the child to bed, the expressions being said in this order. Perhaps he had the second one in mind in line (12), but he was unable to produce it outside of the usual consecutive order, and hence the hesitant *Antho* after the word *see*. Line (16) returns to the task of having the *shoe fixed*, repeating it four times with almost cluster simplification, the /k/ being actualized weakly. This is once more a good occasion to return to the imperative and substitution exercise, with the resulting *fix it* repeated three times in line (17), also forming the usual paired association, and referring back to the frame *shoe fixed* in line (18). More substitution follows in line (19). *It* not only follows the verb but also precedes *it*, thus producing an indicative pattern, with the past verb form *took*, again using only the /t/ and /k/, limiting the vowels only to the high ones and a new pair is created with the previous line. Since the child does not want to have anything taken away, he commands *bring it back* in line (20), returning to the imperative pattern with the pronoun *it*, the pattern of line (1). *Bring back* also alliterates, and the final consonant is /k/, bringing him back to *took* in line (21), the order of words supporting the imperative structure, an impossibility because of the past from of the verb. The pronominal substitution continues with the unusual *them* of which he is not quite sure what it substitutes for. It is practised twice, but in line (22) he returns to the more comfortable *it*, echoing *them* in the alveolar and nasal of *down*. Since he probably realizes that he has not heard *took* in an imperative construction, he returns to the unambiguous indicative in line (23), practising the still hazy pronoun *he* twice. While he is at it, he may as well exercise with *I* again, but in the more familiar context of line (8), *I'm going* in line (24).

The pronominal substitution exercise is abandoned now for the remainder of the paragraph until we come to its last line, and a new topic comes up. It should perhaps be explained that *yellow* seems to be the child's favorite color, used more often than any other color adjectives. Also, when he is asked what kind of a balloon he would like, the answer most of the time is *yellow*. Line (25) then starts with the elliptic *yellow one*, followed by a substitution pattern with *another* as the modifier twice in line (26), with a falling intonation contour at first, a rising one with the repetition, perhaps suggesting the possibility of a question. In line (27) we are back to the /t/ and /k/ play in *take* and *book*, adding now the third point of stop articulation with /b/ in the latter. *Book* serves also as the substitution item with the frame *another* of line (26) in line (28). Line (29) is suggested by the initial vowel of the previous line, [ɛ] in *a*, the other vowels are now all the back rounded /O/, analogous to *book*; the labiality is also repeated in the /f/ of *phone*, and the final /k/ in the initial consonant of *call*. Combining now *phone call* with the model *book* in line (30) results in the new-formation of a compound. This is Anthony's usual word for "telephone book"; here it also ties in with *yellow* of line (25) since he knows the classified Yellow Pages quite well and because of its color, this telephone book appeals to him. A modification exercise is again undertaken in line (31) when, after these repetitions, he decides to try expanding the pattern to a sentence in line (32) but this would result in a six-word sentence, a length which he cannot handle readily. Therefore he stops with *this is the*, even though he tried it twice. Line (33) supplies the last word of the projected sentence which was never accomplished. He then decides to go to the exercise he is capable of handling, substitution of the modifier, with the resulting *another phone call book* in line (34). However, he still has not given up work with *this is*, and he uses it with the much simpler unmodified *light* in line (35). The need for modification, however, is satisfied in line (36) by *one*, and line (37) shows a last-ditch effort to produce a complete equational sentence but without grammatical success, although a meaningful, probably not intended sentence results. The modifier /wАn/ of the previous line has taken the shape /Оn/ following the noun, preserving rounding and nasality only, and *it* is the last word of the line, reflecting the last two phonemes of *light* as well as ending the paragraph with the original frame-word of line (1), thus coming back to the starting point, the frequent rondo construction of the paragraph. Within this large circle, however, smaller circles can be distinguished as well. For example, line (9) introduces *shoe fixed* which occurs for the last time in line (18), thus closing this circle. Or line (27) introduces *book*, the last word of the line, which is also the last word of line (34), bringing this round to a close.

It would be appropriate to show also a paragraph which is made up wholly of quotations, just a recital of sentences the child has heard, occurring at the beginning of one of the monologues:

(N) (1) *I hope so*
    (2) *Clean out the drawer*
    (3) *Excuse me*

The grammatical structures used in line (1) and (3) are not within the child's repertoire and we doubt that he knows their meaning. Line (2), although within the linguistic capacity of the child, contains the word *drawer*, an unlikely one in Anthony's active vocabulary, and the action referred to is hardly one that the child would be asked to do. Also, the occurrence of line (2) surrounded by two obvious quotation sentences points to its belonging in the same category.

The following paragraph, immediately preceding sleep, is interesting in that the child tells himself what an obedient child he is, as distinct from his playmate, the dog Cobbers. It is primarily based on association rather than linguistic play.

(O) (1) *Daddy*
    (2) *Cobbers crossed the street* (2×)
    (3) *Cobbers always cross the street* (2×)
    (4) *Look at Kitty*
    (5) *Come here Kitty*
    (6) *Make it all gone*
    (7) *That's the boy*

The person to whom Anthony is reporting all this is *Daddy*, the vocative in line (1). The fact he is reporting is contained in line (2), repeated twice, to make sure that he made his point. However, this still seems insufficient, and in line (3) he amplifies line (2), that is *Cobbers* not only *crossed* but he *always cross*, again repeated twice. The matter of crossing the street had been discussed with the child on several occasions, and he had been instructed very thoroughly that he was never to do it alone. Of course, the family dog engaged in this pursuit rather frequently, obviously to the child's displeasure. Now that he had taken care of *Cobbers*, the dog, in the first three lines, he turns to the other animal in the house, the cat, to report an activity of hers, probably preferably negative. In line (4) he calls attention to the cat, but apparently nothing to report on her occurs to him at the moment. Therefore line (5) is a pseudo-call for the cat, *come*, evoked by the initial /k/, the same consonant as *Kitty* on whom attention is focused, and *here* is the usual word to follow *come*. The child certainly has heard *come here* many times. In line (6) he turns to himself to report a positive action. He does it by using the sentence *Make it all gone* which he has heard frequently at mealtime, admonishing him to eat what is on his plate. The climax is reached in line (7), the assumption is that he had made it *all gone*, and he commends himself for the action. In lines (6) and (7) the child does not talk as Anthony, but as someone who talks to Anthony, thus assuming both the roles of dictum and dixit, making his dialogue pattern quite clear.

Negative parallelism, as described by Wallon, is typical of the following paragraph, occurring in about the middle of one of the soliloquies:
(P) (1) *Bobo has a hat*
(2) *Take off the hat*
(3) *Hat for Anthony and Bobo*
(4) *For Bobo, not for Anthony*
(5) *Hat for Anthony*
Line (1) is a statement of fact, phonemically interesting since it uses only two vowel phonemes: /O/ following /b/, and /E/ following /h/ and /z/. Both /b/ and /h/ are repeated twice. Line (2) asks for *the hat* to be removed so that the statement in line (1) would no longer be true, and a negatively paired association is produced. Line (3), however, again reassigns the hat to *Bobo*, but also includes *Anthony* this time, thus combining two concepts. That is contradicted in line (4) by a division where *Bobo* is to be the sole possessor of the hat, and not *Anthony*. Line (5) in turn contradicts the previous line, the *hat* is after all *for Anthony*, probably stating the child's wish all along.

The following paragraph is one of the longest for various substitution exercises, occurring very close to the end of a monologue.
(Q) (1) *Alice* (calling)
(2) *Mommy* (4× – calling)
(3) *Mommy's too weak*

(4) *Alice strong*

(5) *Alice too weak* (2×)

(6) *Daddy's too weak*

(7) *Mommy's too weak*

(8) *Too weak with Barbara*

(9) *Be careful Barbara*

(10) *Barbara can broke*

(11) *Careful broke the* [rámì]

(12) *Careful broke Anthony*

(13) *Careful broke it* (2×)

(14) *Careful broke the*

(15) *Broke the finger*

(16) *Broke the Bobo*

(17) *Broke the vacuum clean*

(18) *The broke*

(19) [bégì phú]

(20) *Get some broke*

(21) *Broke the*

(22) *Alice broke the baby fruit*

(23) *Alice almost dropped*

(24) *It's David fruit*

(25) *Look* (2×)

(26) *All right*

(27) *Lady*

(28) *Mama*

Line (1) is identified as a call by an overlong vowel in the second syllable of *Alice*;
the same is true of line (2) with *Mommy*. Alice is a girl who helps in the household,
and after first calling for her, the child decides that he would prefer *Mommy* and
indicates this by four repetitions. Since he knows that nobody will respond to his
call, he decides that the reason for it is that *Mommy's too weak* in line (3). This was
often given as an excuse to the child when he asked to be carried or lifted by his
mother. *Alice* did not use this excuse; therefore, she was *strong* in line (4). But *Alice*
is not coming either, and perhaps negative parallelism is also instrumental in producing line (5), repeated twice. Phonetically, an additional vowel is added to *weak*
[ı], repeated in lines (6) and (7) as well, reduplicating the word and repeating the vowel
of the second syllable of the names once more. In lines (6) and (7) the substitution
exercise is continued, now in a clearly unambiguous construction. Both *Mommy* and
Daddy are used as substitution items ascribing the quality of weakness to all the adults
in the household. The phrase *too weak* with the added [ı] is now moved to the
beginning of line (8) and *with*, or the phonemes /wɪt/ are added as well, in order to
continue the sound play. *Barbara* is one of the few three-syllable names which the
child knows, and he needs three syllables to balance the first part of the line. Moreover,

just as the vowel phonemes in the first three syllables are characterized by the highness of /I/ and /U/, so are the vowel phonemes in the last three syllables even identical, the low /A/. Primarily a sound association is assigned to *Barbara* because there is nothing to our knowledge which would otherwise have brought this particular name or person to the child's mind. Line (9) continues with the sound play in terms of number of syllables as well as consonants: /b/ is the initial consonant of the first and fourth syllable, another labial is added, /f/, and a liquid. Line (10) tells us why *Barbara* was to be *careful*, namely because she *can broke*, a continuation of the sound play with /b, r, k/. It should be noted that the form *broke* in the child's language was the unmarked form of the verb. In line (11) the frame for substitution becomes *careful broke*, no doubt an important thought to the child. Since [rámi] follows the definite article, we assume it belongs to the form class of nouns, but we do not know its meaning. The substitution item of line (12), *Anthony*, is open to good psychological interpretation in this particular context. Line (13), by using the pronoun *it* which is never used as the pronominal substitute for *Anthony*, he is apparently trying to get away from the thought of the preceding line; line (13) is also repeated twice, as reinforcement. Line (14) is elliptic, the noun substitution item is missing, but the pattern still remains clear by the line's ending in *the*. The next three lines provide the substitution items, but the pattern has been shortened, omitting *careful*, probably because its original length taxes the child's linguistic capacity too much as shown also by the preceding ellipsis. The substitution items in line (15) *finger*, in line (16) *Bobo*, and in line (17) *vacuum clean* (one of the child's names for the microphone) all begin with a labial, repeating this feature of *broke*, the first word in the line. The elliptic *clean* occurs in line (17), probably again because of the length of the line, since the child usually produces this compound noun form non-elliptically. The attempted transformation of line (18) is unsuccessful grammatically, but is indicative of the child's awareness of the possibility of English verb and noun transformations. We again do not understand the meaning of line (19). In any event, the voiced and voiceless bilabial stops are again there. Line (21) returns to the grammatical *broke the*, using *broke* correctly as a verb, transforming line (18) back again to the productive pattern, and line (22) gives a non-elliptic statement with the pattern *broke the* contained in it. *Alice* would be the most likely person to drop a jar of *baby fruit*, food not intended for Anthony, but for his younger brother, so that the idea of the food not reaching the latter would not be averse to the former. In *baby fruit*, again both words begin in labials. The thought of losing the fruit is modified in line (23) by *Alice almost dropped*, changing the linguistic pattern. So that there is no misunderstanding whose food is being discussed, line (24) offers an explicit statement that *David fruit* is at issue, the possessive omitted in *David* which would put it into the class of non-personalized nouns. *Look* in line (25) is repeated twice, once with rising, once with falling intonation. *All right* in the next line confirms the previous thoughts, and also reuses the /l/ which had been introduced in *Alice* in lines (22) and (23), repeated in *almost* and *look*, and occurring again in *lady* of line (27) which also uses the same syllable nucleus as *David*, /Ey/, and the alveolar /d/. But since it is really not a *lady* who deals with *David*, but his mother, *Mama* is the last line of the paragraph, with the first /m/ overlong, stressing again the labiality of the consonant.

The following paragraph is one of the longest in the corpus; it occurred shortly after the child had been put to bed and after his father had visited him, hence the underlying theme of *Daddy*.

(R) (1) *That's for he*
      (2) *Mamamama with Daddy*
      (3) *Milk for Daddy*
      (4) *OK*
      (5) *Daddy dance* (2×)
      (6) *Hi Daddy*
      (7) *Only Anthony*
      (8) *Daddy dance* (2×)
      (9) *Daddy give it*
    (10) *Daddy not for Anthony*
    (11) *No*
    (12) *Daddy*
    (13) *Daddy got*
    (14) *Look at Daddy* (falsetto)
    (15) *Look at Daddy here*
    (16) *Look at Daddy*
    (17) *Milk in the bottle*
    (18) *I spilled it*
    (19) *Only for Daddy*
    (20) *Up*
    (21) *That's for Daddy*
    (22) *Let Daddy have it*
    (23) *Take off* (2×)
    (24) *The*
    (25) *Turn around* (2×)
    (26) *Look at donkey*
    (27) *That's the boy*
    (28) *That's the donkey*
    (29) [dæn] *Daddy* [dæn]
    (30) *Pick up the* [dən]
    (31) *I can pick up*
    (32) *I can*
    (33) *How about*
    (34) *How about the Daddy*
    (35) *OK*

(36) *Daddy's two foot*

(37) *Daddy had some feet*

(38) [bí:bə̀]

(39) *Put on a record for you*

(40) *What Daddy got*

(41) *Daddy got*

(42) *On the plane*

(43) *Look at pillow*

(44) *What color pillow*

(45) *What color*

(46) *Is not black*

(47) *It's yellow*

(48) *Daddy dance*

(49) *Ah, Daddy*

(50) *Take it to Daddy*

(51) *Daddy put on a hat*

(52) *Daddy put on a coat*

(53) *Only Daddy can*

(54) *I put this in here*

(55) *See the doggie here*

(56) *See the doggie*

(57) *I see the doggie* (2×) (falsetto)

(58) *Kitty likes doggie*

(59) *Lights up here*

(60) *Daddy dance* (3×)

(61) *With Bobo*

(62) *What color's Bobo* (2×)

Line (1) probably refers to the father who has just left, asserting the child's desire as to whom *Daddy* belongs. This is somewhat modified in accordance with reality in line (2), with two repetitions of *Mama* showing the certainty with whom *Daddy* really is and pointing to the struggle within the nuclear family as was so well described by Parsons (1955). The prepositional construction of line (1) is repeated with the substitution item *Daddy*, the most important word here, in line (3), assigning *milk* to *Daddy*, a very precious item to the child. Line (4) confirms the previous line, namely it is *OK* for *Daddy* to have the *milk*. Sound play produces line (5), repeated twice, with the alliteration obviously pleasing the child. Line (6) *Hi Daddy* is another attempt to establish contact for *Only Anthony* of line (7), coming back to the idea of possession. Line (8) repeats line (5), and in line (9) the syntactic pattern is changed in requesting *Daddy* to *give it*. The theme of possession appears again in line (10), *Daddy not for Anthony*, confirmed in line (11) by *No*. But the child still wants to play with the word *Daddy* even if he cannot have *Daddy*, hence the build-up sequence of lines (12) and (13), and the longer chain of lines (14), (15), and (16). The falsetto used in line (14) is a further indication of the intent of play. Since it is clear to Anthony that he cannot have Daddy at the moment, he is willing to take a pleasant substitute, *Milk in the bottle*, that is to say not only *milk* which he had assigned to *Daddy* in line (3), but *in the bottle* which is additionally gratifying. But the child is afraid that the fate of the milk will be the same as that of *Daddy*, and he projects that he *spilled it* in line (18). It is interesting that *I* occurs here rather than the more babyish construction with the child's name, perhaps an attempt to approximate the adult *Daddy* to whom he returns in line (19). It is still *for Daddy*, but now to the exclusion of everyone else, *only*. Line (20), with rising intonation, perhaps is not the word *up* but rather an elliptic form of something for Daddy, the *that* of line (21). Line (22) says the same thing as line (21), in a syntactic construction which appears to be a quotation from adult speech. The theme of *Daddy* is temporarily abandoned in line (23), *Take off* which with line (24) *the* forms a still elliptic completion sequence; apparently no noun occurs to the child at the moment to follow *the*. He therefore returns to another imperative with a verb beginning again in /t/ in line (25), repeated twice. The imperative pattern continues in line (26), the two-part verb now ends in /t/ and the noun begins in the voiced counterpart, the consonant of *Daddy*. The same consonant begins the frame for substitutions in lines (27) and (28); *that's the boy* is a sentence heard frequently as praise by the child, but he is able to decompose it and substitute *donkey* to return to the preferred consonant phoneme /d/. That sound is of utmost importance as shown in line (29) which is similar to the previous *Daddy dance* in terms of sound. In line (30) *donkey* appears abbreviated to conform to the previous line, but the phonemes /k/ and /I/ are included in *pick* with the following *up* repeating the initial /p/ of *pick* finally. Line (31) again reiterates a grown-up's ability in *I can* followed by *pick up*, and only *I can* in line (32). Adults in the house also frequently ask Anthony to do something by a pseudo-question introduced by *how about* which appears in line (33). But for the child the active use of this linguistic pattern exceeds his language capacity, resulting in the non-grammatical sentence of line (34) with *Daddy* reappearing in an unusual position, after the definite article *the*. The importance of *Daddy* is reaffirmed by *OK* in line (35) and a description of *Daddy* results in line (36): that he has *two foot*, the non-grammatical selection of *foot* partially based on the preceding vowel /U/ in *two*, but perhaps more importantly it is due to the child's frequent reduction of number redundancies, that is, the omission of the plural morpheme when the noun is modified by a numeral. The child's plural of *foot*, however, has been well-enough learned so that he does not feel comfortable with line (36), and the result is the grammatical, but non-sensical line (37), with no definite numerical modifier, using *some* instead. Line (38) could be a recollection of what he thought he had heard on one of his records which he is fond of playing, and the imperative of line (39) is an indication of the desire of putting on a *record*. The preposition *for* also reappears, and *you* is misused due to the child's inability to handle pronominal substitutions adequately. In line (40) we are back to *Daddy* in a clumsy construction which refers to the record which *Daddy got*. The importance of the giver is reiterated in the repetition of *Daddy got* in line (41), and *On the plane* of line (42) refers to the gift of a record which his father brought him after returning from a trip by plane. Since *plane*, however, is a less familiar and further removed object than a *pillow*, this is the next association, repeating the /p/ and /l/ of *plane* in *pillow*, and the /l/ also in *look*. The *what* of line (40) reminds him of the favorite question pattern which appears in lines (44) and (45). He provides the answer to his question by negative parallelism, first stating in line (40) that the color of the pillow is not *black*, thus repeating the initial sequence of the phonemes of *plane* with the neutralization of the feature of voicing, and stating in line (47) the correct color of his pillow, *yellow*. Back to the play *Daddy dance* in line (48), a somewhat different play in line (49), and *Daddy* is now the object of line (50) in an imperative construction with the voiceless alveolar /t/ in *take*, *it*, and *to*, so that except for the /k/ of *take*, all the consonants in the line are alveolar stops. The substitution exercise of lines (51) and (52) also serves to indicate what the child is to take to *Daddy*, *hat* and *coat*, some usual items of clothing requested, both again ending in /t/. Line (53) returns to the exclusiveness of *Daddy* with *only*, emphasizing his ability, *can*, to perform the activities described in the previous two lines. Line (54) is again a partial quotation form, serving the child's adult imitating desire. His own more typical pattern is culled from it in the break-down sequence of lines (55) and (56), the noun still beginning in /d/. That Anthony is conscious of the adult style of *I* and that he plays with it, is apparent from its use in line (57) where at first it is practised seriously, taking the other person's role in the imaginary dialogue by answering line (56), but in the second repetition falsetto is used, an unmistakable sign of play. Since belonging and hence love are one of the underlying themes of the paragraph, line (58) makes a statement *Kitty likes doggie* which is more of a wish than a fact in regard to reality. The cat and dog in the household do get along fairly well, but to say that they like each other would be charitable. *Likes* of line (58) produces *lights* of line (59), with a substitution of the more favored alveolar for the velar stop, and showing once again the child's play with these two words. The previous frame word *here* also reappears. In line (60) it is back again to the sound play *Daddy dance*, repeated three times, the dancing partner being suggested in line (61), *with Bobo*. The glide /w/ and the final /t/ of *with* suggest the favorite question word *what* to the child in line (62) which again refers to *Bobo* of the previous line, and it is repeated twice. The paragraph is inter-tupted here by the child's hurting himself somehow, and the consequent reappearance of his father to look in on him.

The rondo-like construction of the paragraph is clear. Here are more examples: The important *for me* of the first line reappears as *for Anthony* in line (10); in lines (16) and (21) it is *for Daddy*, and the *for you* in line (39), which brings this circle back to its starting point, is only linguistically different from *for me* in line (1) due to the imperfect learning of pronouns. *Only* in line (7) finds its counterpart in lines (19) and (53), but first it is *Anthony*, then twice *Daddy*; *What color pillow* of line (46) reappears as *What color's Bobo* in the last line of the paragraph.

CONCLUSIONS

In summarizing the findings, we will divide our conclusions into two parts: first, the features of the phonology, morphology, and syntax which have not been learned well as yet by the child will be pointed out, without dwelling on what has been learned. Our conclusions in this respect will be negative, based on the linguistic demands within the corpus in regard to the combinations of articulatory features and of morphemes into words and sentences, but not in regard to the selection of structural entities into higher units. Second, we will summarize what we have found as characteristic of the paragraph and hence of the monologues in general, this being an over-all resumé.

PHONOLOGY

The prosodic features of intonation are still unstable, although pauses are quite consistent, but contours are only occasionally and not reliably contrastive. The distinction is made between stress and no stress, without using various levels distinctively. In regard to vowels, the feature of tenseness *versus* laxness has not been learned in its contrastive function. The absence of the /ə/ as a phoneme can perhaps be attributed to the lack of vowel reduction in syntactic patterns, also reflected in the stress pattern. Active linguistic practice by the child on the establishment of new phonemic contrasts in order to conform to standard English usage was noticed in an attempt to learn the phoneme /æ/ and /θ/. As for the non-vowels, the use of glides is still very unstable; they fluctuate freely with length and/or zero, hence the distinction between simple and complex syllabic nuclei has not been well learned. In regard to consonants, the over-all characteristic is the non-use of the feature of voice, particularly word-finally. The contrastive use of the interdental place of articulation has not yet been mastered, although here also a conscious attempt by the child to learn to produce this feature consistently can be observed. Except for /č/, none of the palatals are stable phonemes. Medially and finally, the voiced labiodental spirant /v/ is frequently replaced by the voiced bilabial stop /b/. Of the consonant clusters called for by the vocabulary of the corpus, /l/ in a word-final cluster does not occur, and the combination of the velar nasal /ŋ/ with the voiced velar stop /g/ is very rare. Most other cluster simplifications occur side by side with standard clusters, thus perhaps representing an earlier stage in the child's linguistic development.

For the purpose of comparing proportions of phoneme events with those of standard English, because of differing analyses, only consonants are truly comparable. The proportion of alveolars in our corpus is almost double that for standard English. A similar discrepancy is found in terms of manner of articulation where stops in our data account for almost 50% of events, compared to slightly less than 30% for the standard language. Due to the child's neutralization of the feature of voicing, our proportion of voiceless consonants is about 20% higher than that of standard English studies. The proportions of various phonemic shapes of words are comparable to standard English, with the predominance of shorter designs.

Except for the learning of /æ/ and /θ/, the combination of features into phonemes was not practised by the child in an attempt to approximate the phonemic system of standard English. However, as is evident from the statistical comparison with standard English, certain phonemes were selected as a means of play, and their combinations into higher units, morphemes and words was a purposeful activity in many instances.

GRAMMAR

Morphology

In the morphology of the noun, the possessive case is restricted to "personalized" nouns. The use of the plural morpheme at times follows the child's own rules of usage, e.g., it may not appear if a numeral precedes the noun, or it may be used only with the last item in an enumeration. The adjectives are not inflected, that is to say, no gradation appears. In regard to verbs, the *-ing* form has been mastered grammatically but not phonetically, and it is a true paradigmatic form. The past, however, shows a paradigmatic awareness within the marked and unmarked form of a particular verb only, and the past paradigm as a whole has not yet been generalized in the child's linguistic system. On the level of derivation, new-formations with bound morphemes are practically non-existent, but compounding of words has been learned fairly well.

In comparing word events with word designs, the proportion of events of nouns and verbs are about the same. However, in terms of designs, nouns outnumber verbs considerably. This is consistent with the usually greater paradigmatic association of nouns which are also the most frequent substitution items in the structured patterns of the soliloquies.

Syntax

The imperative sentence is the most frequent type, followed by declaratives and interrogatives, with a great number of structurally ambiguous sentences which, due to their elliptic constructions, cannot be readily classified. In addition, occurrences of non-grammatical utterances are frequent. Mistakes in modifiers of a noun phrase are infrequent. Several modal constructions are used consistently in verb phrases, but some modals and other "small" words are often omitted. Although the *do* constructions have been well learned for the negative imperative, they are very unstable in negative declarative sentences and questions. Interrogative pronouns are the most reliable indication of a question construction, all other signals being still unstable in the system. The production of a sentence at first try often overtaxes the child's linguistic capacity, and speech measures from the intended sentence may appear, preceding or following it; unauthorized pauses sometimes also intrude and separate phrases intended to be a single sentence resulting in build-up, break-down, and completion sequences respectively.

As to sentence length, two- and three-word sentences are the most frequent; four- and five-word sentences show a considerable drop-off, six-word sentences are rare, and there are no true sentences beyond the seven-word length.

Vocabulary

The choice of vocabulary in the monologues is very limited, as compared to the child's lexical capacity during the day. Within this restricted vocabulary, the toy-interlocutor *Bobo* has the greatest number of noun occurrences, followed by *blanket*, the child's most favored object. Color epithets outnumber by far any other descriptive adjectives. In regard to verbs, *go* and its marked forms have been selected more often than any other verb by a considerable margin.

THE PARAGRAPH

The best summary to characterize the nature of the paragraph or for that matter of all the material is Freud's description of the joke technique "sense in nonsense" (1960). Just as the enjoyment of a joke can be derived from play with words, so does the child enjoy play with words, by repetitions of similar sounds, by his rediscovery of what is familiar to him. But analogous to the joke, where there is sense in nonsense in the deliberate use of word play, the child's play also has sense: the pleasure of play is structured so that it serves as a linguistic exercise. The role of content in most cases is subordinated to linguistic form, or the content serves the form, as Vinogradov (1930) pointed out. That there is linguistic structure in Nonsense has been demonstrated by Sewell's (1952) excellent analysis of the works of E. Lear and L. Carrol, and of nursery rhymes. Her definition of Nonsense as "a collection of words which in their internal composition of letters and syllables or in their selection and sequence do not conform to the conventional patterns of language to which the particular mind is accustomed" (p. 2) fits exactly our set of data. Sound is what is played with, and it is done within the framework of paradigmatic and syntagmatic exercises. It is a world out of language, similar to the one described by Kaper (1959) for older children. That is not to say that secondary ludic symbolism as discussed by Piaget (1951) is not present, but our concern is primarily the overt linguistic structure of the paragraph. It is not within our province to decide whether the non-occurrence of certain past forms of the verb, for example, are due to the child's suppression of certain past events, but what we can determine is the role of the past paradigm of the verb in the structure of the monologues. It is being consciously practised, just as are other grammatical combinations and selections, so that at times we have the feeling of listening in on a foreign language lesson with extensive pattern practice. The substitution lists used by the child are very limited; the vocabulary of nouns is primarily made up of names of objects within his immediate surroundings, the crib and room, except for some "personalized" nouns. Play with epithets, frequent in nursery rhymes, is mainly confined to colors used in substitution patterns in the monologues. Another common usage of adjectives is that of negative parallelism, but that too fits into a paradigmatic set. Paradigmatic relationships are transposed into sequences, a characteristic only of the poetic function of language with adults, but not so with the child. Paradigms, however, are not the only linguistic exercise, the exploration of combinatory possibilities and the resulting syntagmatic exercises shed still more light on the sense in nonsense. At times the combinations do lead to grammatical nonsense as well, but these are the hazards of exploration.

The selection of substitution items is not based on semantic synonymity, but on grammatical parallelism. The items either belong to the same form class, and then sound play is the basis of selection within the form class, or they are pronominal substitutes. The use of the semantically precisely defined numerals used imprecisely serves as an excellent framework for substitution in the monologues, also part of the structure of Nonsense in Sewell's analysis. The paradigmatic use of nouns as substitution items is more pronounced than that of any other form class. With verbs, grammatical markers are more frequently selected as the items to be changed in a pattern, be it the *-ing* form or the past alternating with the unmarked form.

But the selection in the paradigm and the building of longer grammatical combinations are not the only typical aspects of the paragraph construction. Paired association as described by Wallon (1945) is characteristic in either negative parallelism as already mentioned, or in associations, or in linguistic parallelism. A sentence with a noun object followed by a sentence with a pronoun object is a paired association, so typical of the thought process of the young child. Following Steinitz' classification of paired constructions in folkloric poetry, we can also distinguish several pairs analogous to his: the contrastive pair which consists either of two antonyms, or of a statement and its contradiction; the varying pair which goes from the simple to the complex, or vice versa; and the enumerative pair which results in a chain. The chain complex, as a matter of fact, is most descriptive of our data. As characterized by Vygotsky, it is "a dynamic, consecutive joining of individual links into a single chain... The decisive attribute keeps changing during the entire process. There is no consistency in the type of the bonds or in the manner in which a link of the chain is joined with the one that precedes and the one that follows it. The original sample has no central significance. Each link, once included in a chain complex, is as important as the first and may become the magnet for a series of other objects." (p. 64) Anthony's paragraphs are just such a chain, and a number of functional criteria have to be applied in order to understand the structure of this unit.

In these linguistic sessions the child does not assume only the role of the student, however, for he is the other participant in the language learning situation, the model, as well. It is really inaccurate to call these soliloquies monologues, because outside of the fact that they are produced while the child is physically isolated, he becomes his own interlocutor and produces the equivalent of a dialogue spoken by a single person. He can switch roles in this interchange readily – he asks a question and provides the answer, he performs a linguistic task and commends himself on the accomplishment, he produces a linguistic event and explicitly corrects himself. The importance of the conative function as shown by the great number of imperatives, supports clearly the premise of a social aspect of this vocalized inner speech as Vygotsky (1962) has suggested it, or as Peirce (1933) has characterized thought.

Besides the conative, two other functions of language as outlined by Jakobson (1960) are particularly characteristic of our data. One, the metalingual as shown by the child's preoccupation to practise the language he is learning, and the other, the poetic, which the play with words and sounds illustrates. But there is even more of the latter structured in our nonsense than just play. Alliterations are frequent and paronomastic images emerge, often connecting the individual lines of the paragraph. That both these functions are predominant in the monologues is consistent with the nature of the language of a young child where these two functions often merge, contrary to adult speech.

However, the paragraph at times is not only delimited by a change of topic or by a change of linguistic exercise, but by a larger circular, rondo-like construction. Frequently, it ends just as it began. Moreover, smaller closed constructions occur, as part of the larger circle, and, after we have been led back to the beginning, a new round just like the completed one may be started, a structure parallel to rounds in songs. There is linguistic sense in the child's nonsense, that is our conclusion.

APPENDIX

Following is the complete corpus in rough phonetics as transcribed from the tape recordings. Included are also comments as to the intelligibility of the signal made at the time of transcription, and the number of echo repetitions occurring.

Each sentence or non-grammatical utterance is on a separate line. A question mark is used to indicate an unintelligible portion of a sentence. The abbreviations FC, RC, SC stand for falling, rising, and sustained contours respectively. Only the latter two will be indicated regularly; all utterances without contour markings are falling contours. However, FC will be used in instances where it occurs together with one of the other two contours.

The phonetic symbols for vowels and non-vowels are those used commonly in American linguistic works. The symbols for stress are [á â à], in descending order, the weakest stress being unmarked. Overloud stress is marked [ắ]; length, depending on its duration, has the symbols [· : :: :::], from slightly long to very long. A short pause within a sentence is represented by a single slanted line. Aspiration and release of stops are indicated by [ʰ] and [ʳ] respectively, following the consonant.

ǽntənɪ gètʰə́pʳ

gò làį dáųn

lâį dáųn

làį dáųn | bóųbò

làį dáų:n

áplsôs

ắplsôs

gôų tʰʊ̀ nʊ̀yɔ́kʳ

yélòų

yɛ́lòų

nô blú:

nô: blú:

óųkʰɛ́·į

yǽŋkʳ (SC)

yaŋkʳ (SC)

ya:ŋkʳ (SC)

yæ:ŋkʳ (SC)

yaŋkʳ (SC)

ya:ŋkʳ (SC)

yæ:ŋkʳ (6×) (SC)

yaæŋkʳ (SC)

yæ:ŋkʳ (2×) (SC)

yaæŋkʳ (SC)

yæ:ŋkʳ (SC)

yæŋkʳ

klɔ́kʳ ɔ́·f

kləkʳ

ɔf (decrease in loudness)

àpdé:r (2×)

? àpdé:r

òvə héər

heᵊr (2×)

bóu̯bò dêr

gô· àpdé:r

heər (great definiteness)

bóu̯bò | kʰàmɔ́f

mɔ́r mɪlkʳ (RC) (ten times, with increasing urgency, until he is given milk; silence
   follows)

mámì·

mámì gǽv sə̀m mílkʳ

mámì (more urgent) (SC)

lʊ́kʳ θrû: ðə wínòu̯ (2×)

lʊ́kʳ θrû: ɔ̀ldə wínᵈou̯ (3×)

álìs

ã́lìs

yêlòu̯ bláŋkʰɛ̀tʳ (RC)

bóu̯bò (RC)

ǽntənɪ putʰɔ̀n də blǽŋkʰɛ̀tʳ (RC)

pʰʊ́l də stɔ́mɛ̀kʳ | ín: (3×)

ɔ́:l də fíŋɛ̀rs

ɔ́:l də fíŋɛrs | ín·

tam

dɛ̀ts ə tám:

dɛ̀ts ə θám:

ə fíŋə̀r

ðé:r ìz də tàm

nɔ́t hér

ðê:r ìz də θám:

ðé:r ìz ðə àdə θám

ðə fíŋèr

pʰʊ́tʳ də fîŋèr àpdé:r bàị̆ dɛ láịtʳ (RC)

dé:rz dɛ làịtʳ

hwé:r ìz dè làịtʳ (SC)

wèrz dɛ láịt (RC)

hí:rəz dè làịtʳ

hí:rz láịtʳ

wán pʰɛ́ɪpər

tʰʊ́ʊ̯ pʰɛ́ɪpɛrs (SC)

ɔ́:l dè pʰɛ̀ịpərs

ɛ̀ mǽ:n

mǽ:n gìvìtʳ tʰʊ̀ mámì

mǽn dú: détʳ

mámì gìv dè mǽ·n

mámì

fər mámì

ìn stɔ́:r

dét bèkəs mámì

bétsìs mámìs nɔ́t hóʊ̯m

ǽn fríkəs mámís nɔ́tʳ hoʊ̯m

bétsìs mámì s nɔ́tʳ hóʊ̯m

mámì

tʰêịkʳ mámì

báịbàị̆ wìtʳ mámì

bétsìs kʰáə̯r

čəŋkʳ (RC)

ɔ̀čɔ́kʳ (RC)

čəŋkʳ (RC)

tʰakʳ (2×)

kʰịûmàkétʳ (2×) (RC)

ǽntənìs rí:dən

béịkìn ə kʰɛ́ịkʳ (RC)

tʰə̂rnèráʊ̯nd (RC)

yú tʰə̀rnèráʊ̯nd (2×)

gétʰèwéị (RC)

gètʰèwéị (2×)

lʊ́kʰèt dòʊ̯z pʰáịnépl (2×) (RC)

ìn ɛ̀ prîtʰ̀ì bɔ́ks

ǽnt kʰéịks (RC)

wɔ̀tʰɛ̀ stíks fər kʰéịks (RC)

fə̀r dè klík^r

frí̧ bótəl

fó:r bótəls

ǽnt tʰù: lítəl (SC)

místɛ́ stóy̧

ǽnt tʰú: spórtkʰə̀r

θrí: wán tʰú: fə̀rtkʰá:r (RC)

wán tʰù kʰá:rs

mámì prítɟ pʰílòy̧s

wót^r ə̀r yý tʰɔ́kìn èbáy̧t^r (RC)

rí:dìn ə bǔk^r

bí kʰèrfəl

kʰáps ɔ̀l gɔ́:n

wót^r kʰálə̀^r (SC)

wót^r kʰálə̀^r blǽŋkʰèt^r (RC)

wɔ̀t^r kʰâlɛ́^r móp^r (RC)

wót^r kʰálə̀ glǽ:s (RC)

mámí: (2×)

mámìs rí:də̀n dè pʰéi̧pʰɛ́ (RC)

ènádə̀ bíg bótəl (RC)

bí:g bótəl (SC)

wɔ̀t^r kʰálèr tʰí:ví: (RC)

rɛ́t ǽnt (SC)

fáyè^r

lái̧kʰè lípstík^r (SC)

bəlǽŋkèt

lái̧kʰè lípstìk^r

bík^r tʰú: tráks

θri: tráks (2×)

ènádè^r bí·g trák

kʰɔ́bə̀s (SC)

gárbìčmǽn (2×) (SC)

lái̧k dè gá:rbìčmǽn

ə bí:k^r trák^r

wɔ̀t^r hèpèn tʰʊ mǽn (RC)

wɔ̀t^r hépèn tʰʊ léi̧dì (RC)

álí:s (2×)

óy̧ | bók^r tʰə́^rnáy̧t^r

kʰəlóp^r

šə́tʰə̀p^r

blèŋkét^r

náy̧ dè blú blǽŋkèt^r

pʰìlə̀kʰéi̯s (RC)

pʰísìs pʰìlə̀kʰéi̯s

wàn nέkʳ (RC)

θrí: nέkʳ (RC)

fɔ́:r nέkʳ (RC)

gétʳ fánìs

fánì bói̯

wótʳ kʰálə̀ tʰí:bí: (RC)

wôtʳ kʰálə̀ hɔ́:rsì (RC)

dέn | wôtʳ kʰálə̀ tʰéi̯bə̀l (RC)

dèn wə̀t kʰâlə̀ʳ fáyέr (RC)

wít ə̀l dè wú:dz

hí:r yélə̀ṳ spú:n (RC)

èntʰə̀nɪ tʰéi̯kʳ dè (SC)

téi̯kʳ dè bʊ́kʳ

wótè bʊ́kʳ (RC)

wótè bʊ́kʳ

tʰéi̯kʳ dè bʊ́kʳ

wə̀tʳ kʰálə bʊ̆k (RC)

dè bɔ́:i̯ (RC)

ǽntə̀nɪ tʰéi̯kʳ dè bʊkʳ

tʰéi̯kʳ dè bʊ́kʳ ɔ́f

pʰéi̯pə̀ ɔ́:n

ái̯ hèf tʰṳ rí:d (RC)

nótʳ pʰéi̯pə̀ ɔ́·f

dís wàn

(unintelligible whisper)

ma (4×)

ə̀l dè čérs

wì hǽ·vìtʳ | álìs

nóṳ sîɡə̀réts (2×) (RC)

nóṳ sîɡə̀réts (2×)

âi̯m lṳ̀kʰìn frə̀m dénìs

mámí::

mámì

fei̯s (3×)

mámí::

mámà

kʰàm wìt má·mì (2×) (RC)

kʰɔ́·làp mámì (RC)

kʰɔ́làp mámì sɔ́l ɡɔ́:n (2×) (RC)

ɔ́:l ɡɔ́:n (2×) (SC)

kʰɔ́làp mámì (3×) (RC)

ápʳ (3×) (RC)

ǽntənɪ gò ápʳ (RC)

tʰə̀déi̧

tʰə̀dés mándèi̧

gɔ́ tʰʊ̀ sǽtʰə̀rdéi̧

sǽtʰə̀rdéi̧ (RC)

mándéi̧ (2×) (RC)

mámì (RC)

mámì wέnt bái̧bái̧ (RC)

mámì (RC)

mámì wέntʳ

nílə̀

nílá (8×) (RC)

mámìs gɔ́yìn bâi̧bái̧ (RC)

mámìs gɔ́yìn tʰʊ̀ ɔ́fí·s (RC)

sátʰə̀rdéi̧

frái̧déi̧ (3×) (RC)

tʰʊ̀déi̧s frái̧déi̧

sátʰə̀rdéi̧ (3×) (RC)

wái̧tʳ blǽŋkʰétʳ (staccato)

màmí (2×) (RC)

gó bái̧bái̧ (RC)

gó bái̧bái̧ sántònì (RC)

góu̧ bài̧bái̧ wìt mámí ǽn dɔ́gí:

pʰéní:

dèt pʰéní: (2×) (RC)

pʰéní (4×) (RC)

dèt dɔ́gí: pʰéní

pʰéní: (2×) (indication of surprise)

dìd pʰéní· wɔ́nts wɔ́:tər (RC)

kʰábə̀s àu̧tsái̧d

dèt pʰènì: (RC)

pʰéní (2×)

hʊkʳ (6×) (RC)

tʰéi̧kʰìn ɔ́:l dè pʰéi̧pʰés

lái̧kʳ ɛ̀ hóu̧l (2×) (RC)

tʰʊ̀mɔ́rò sátʰə̀rdéi̧

kʰálə̀r (2×)

ɔ́l dè blǽŋkʰètʳ

blû blǽŋkìtʳ

pʰú̧tʳ dè blù blǽŋkʰétʳ ɔ́n

pʰʊ̀tʳ àpʳ dὲ wâi̯t blǽŋkìtʳ

blǽŋkìtʳ

líf bóu̯bò

dɛ́ts bóu̯bòs tʰói̯

yus (2×) (RC)

yú slípʳ æn ræ̣̀stʳ (2×)

dὲ hǽtʳ

wáns bóbò (RC)

dǽts dὲ bói̯

bóbò | gôu̯ tʰèi̯kʳ ə̀f dὲ hǽtʳ

bóu̯bò tʰʊ́k ə̀f dὲ hǽtʳ

ɔ́·l dὲ dɔ́·gz

tʰɔ́rnɔ́n dὲ blǽŋkʰètʳ (RC)

bóu̯bòs réstʳ

ɔ́ bóu̯bò

lái̯ dáu̯n ə̀n dὲ pʰílə̀ (2×)

bóu̯bòs lái̯n dáu̯n

ǽntəni gɔ́tʰə̀n bóu̯bóu̯ (RC)

lí:píŋkʳ bóu̯bóu̯

éts ὲ bói̯

ìz dὲt bóu̯bóu̯ (RC)

bóu̯bòstɔ́mákʳ

hái̯ bóu̯bò (RC)

bóu̯bò tʰéi̯kʳ ə̀f dὲ blǽŋkʰètʳ

tʰéi̯kʰìn bóu̯bóu̯ (SC)

bóu̯bò dú: dɛ́·tʳ (RC)

nú: réd réč

pʰʊ́tʳ ə̀nὲ blǽŋkʰétʳ (RC)

wái̯t blǽŋkʰítʳ (RC)

ênd yélòu̯ blǽŋkʰɪtʳ (RC)

wèrs yélòu̯ blǽŋkʰìtʳ (RC)

ǽntəni gètʳ (SC)

gʊ́dái̯diə̀

dɛ́ts dὲ tʰái̯gə̀r

háyù | tʰái̯gə̀r (2×)

wèrs dὲ blù blǽŋkʰètʳ

wái̯tʳ

nɔ́t dὲ blù wàn

híərs dὲ blú:

pʊ̀tʳ ɔ́n dὲ blǽŋkʰètʳ

blǽŋkʰètʳ

ɔ́l dὲ blǽŋkʰètʳ

bóbòs m: (SC)

áṳ (RC)

frís ǽntɔ̀nì yámp (2×)

há:ị̀ (RC)

kʰídì

blǽ·ŋkʰèt˞ | bóṳbò tʰʊ́k˞ ɔ́f hɚr blǽŋkʰèt˞ (RC)

bóṳbòṳs ìn ǽntɔ̀nì pʰílòṳ

ap˞ (2×) (RC)

bóṳbòs stǽndìŋ ɔ́n hís íəs (RC)

mámì | bóbòs nɔ̀t gèt˞ʰɔ́f

láị̀ dáṳn ég̣éị̀n (2×)

óṳ | bóṳbóṳ (2×) (1RC, 1FC)

bóṳbóṳ (SC)

tʰóị̀lèt˞

ǽntəni kʰɛ́n rí:ts kʰɛ́n rí:ts dè tʰɔ́p˞

rí:č dè tʰɔ́p˞

kʰɛ̀n yú: rí:č dè tʰɔ́p˞ (RC)

ǽnd bóṳbóṳ (RC)

hìmsélf (RC)

léts wéị̀k˞ wéị̀t˞

yélòṳ blǽŋkʰèt˞

dìs wèị̀ wít˞ (RC)

wit˞

wérs dì yélòṳ blǽŋkʰèt˞ (RC)

wíl klóṳzìt˞

náṳ wì pʰʊ̂t˞ dè tʰɔ́p

fít

sét˞ʰìt

ǽnt˞ pʰʊ́t˞ʰìt (RC)

áp˞ déər (RC)

léft˞ʰɔ́n

dǽts dè bóị̀

náṳ dè blǽŋkʰèt˞

óṳ | ɛ̀ntənɪ kʰɛ́n rí:č dɛ tʰɔ́p

nóu yʊ́ (signal unintelligible) bʊ́·k (RC)

ɛ̀ntənɪ dzámp

fá:ị̀n

ǽntəni dᶻámp (2×)

dá:ṳn

ɛ̀ntənɪ dᶻámp˞

džǎ:mp˞ (SC)

dᶻámp˞

áʊtʳ
êntəni dᶻámpʳ áʊtʳ
áʊtʳ ɛgéịn (RC)
áʊtʳ ɛgéịn
dᶻámpʳ áʊtʳ ɛgéịn (3×)
láị dáʊn ɛn slíəpʳ
ǽntɔ̀nì žámpʳ áʊtʳ ɛgéịn
ɔ̀ntɔ̀ní yampʳ
ǽntɔ̀nì áʊtʳ ǽn bóʊbɔ̀
bóʊbɔ̀ dzámp (RC)
áʊtʳ | áʊtʳ | bóʊbɔ̀ | ɛ̀ntəni yámp aʊtʳ
bóʊbɔ̀s gɔ̀ìn tə slípʳ | ɪŋk
áʊ (RC) (5×)
fɔ̀ní | tʰʊ̀déị | áʊtʳ ɛn yámpʳ
náʊ yámpʳ áʊtʳ ɛgéịn (RC)
ɔ̀ʊsgɛ̀dáʊn bóʊbɔ̀
dì ádɔ̀r wèị
džámpʳ áʊtʳ
ǽʊ:tʳ
gètʳ ɔ̀n ɛgéịn (RC)
dᶻámpʳ (RC)
a::: (very long| RC and FC| 2×)
dɔ́ntʳ dᶻámpɔ̀ (2×)
bóʊbɔ̀ (RC)
dɛ̀ métˢ (SC)
bléŋkʰètʳ (SC)
métˢ (SC)
a:: (RC)
dídìtʳ
náʊ (RC)
ǽntʰɔ̀nì dú: détʳ (RC)
ɔ̀ pʰílɔ̀ déʳ
tʰéịkʳ ɔ́f dɛ̀ blǽŋkʰèt
góʊ tʰʊ̀slípʳ
tʰéịkʳ bóʊbɔ̀ ɛ̀n stɛ́n ɔ́n ítʳ (RC)
góʊ tʰʊ̀slípʳ ìndì (SC)
ìndì (SC)
bóʊbɔ̀s yélòʊ nɛ́tʳ
bóʊbɔ̀
góʊ ɔ́ndɛ̀ blǽŋkʰètʳ
ha:: (RC) (2×)
pʰʊ́tʳ ìtʳ déʳ (RC)

lúkìn bóʊ̥bò

wán | tʰú:: | θrí | fɔ́:r (RCs)

wán | tʰú: (RCs)

wán | tʰú: | θrí | fɔ́·r (2 RCs| 2 FCs)

wán | tʰú· | θəri· (2 RCs| 1 FC)

æntʰɔ̀nì kʰaʊ́ntʰɛ̀n

gʊ́d bóɪ̥ yú

wán | tʰú: | θrí:

gɛ́t dɛ̀ pʰílòʊ̥

aʊ̥ (RC) (3×)

æntʰɔ̀nìs bíg šì:tʳ (RC)

lɛ́tʳ bóʊ̥bò stɛ́ɪ̥ ɔ́n dɛ̀ blǽŋkʰɛ̀tʳ

a | láɪ̥ dáʊ̥n

bóʊ̥bəs ɔ́ndɛ̀ flɔ́·r

bóʊ̥bòs nɔ́tʳ stɛ́ɪ̥n

bóʊ̥bòs gɔ́s | tʰʊ́dɛ̀ bɛ́θrʊ́m

klí:nɔ́f

nɔ́ goʊ̥

go go gogo go goʊ̥ (RCs)

dɛ́t láɪ̥t

nɔ́s vǽkyum | klí:nɛ̀r

láɪ̥kʳ ɛ̀ vǽkiúm | klí:nɛ̀r hí:r

mámì tʰʊ́kʳ dɛ̀ myúsìk ɔ́·l fíkstʳ

ǽnt rɛ́kɔ̀t plɛ́ɪ̥s nɔ́t fíkstʳ

náʊ̥ ìts fíkstʳ

myú:zìks nɔ́tʳ fíkstʳ

myúzìk stɔ́pʳ

fíksít

stɔ́·pʳ

dɔ́ŋkì

lív dɛ̀ dó·r óʊ̥pə́n wìt dɛ̀ stíkʳ

dríŋkʳ

wɔ̀tʳ kʰálər

wɔ̀tʳ kʰálər (RC)

bráʊ̥n

íz dísə pʰílóʊ̥ ìn dɛ̀ bɛ́kʳ

ɔ́hə́m (2×)

bóʊ̥bòs nɔ́tʳ tróʊ̥ə̀ŋ

bóʊ̥bò kʰɛ̀n θróʊ̥

bóʊ̥bò kʰɛ̀n θróʊ̥ítʳ

bóʊ̥bə kʰɛ̀n θróʊ̥ (RC)

óʊ̥ (2×)

góṳ (3×)

kʰábès èn kʰídì (laughter)

yampʳ (2×)

blǽŋkʰèt láịkʰè lípstìkʳ

óṳː (4×)

fə́nì

blǽŋkʰètʳ láịkʰè lípstík

sít dáṳn (2×)

ìn dè blǽŋkɛt

áṳtʳ

apʳ (RC)

ǽntənɪ gétʰápʳ

hə́rì ápʳ

hápls hǽf tʰṳgóṳ

wə́rkʳ (RC)

góṳ tṳ̀ wə́rkʳ

twáịs

ìs yέlə̀ pʰéịpə̀ (2×)

íz ənádə́

nóṳgṳ́·d

náŋgṳ́·d

náŋgə́s (2×)

sítʰápʳ

ápʳ

ápʳ bóṳbə̀

gétʰàpʳ

ɔ́l frú | ɔ́l dán

wɔ́ts détʳ (RC)

wɔ́tʳ kʰálə̀r (RC) (2×)

nóṳétʳ (RC)

wɔ́ts àpʳ dé·r (RC)

bóṳbə̀ wéịtə́ŋ

mámì | stópʰítʳ

stópʳ dét čéŋk

náṳ ə̀l frù

či

tʰɪ

tráị

tráyə̀ŋk (2×)

ɔ́l dè έpls

wìtʳ pʰéịpə̀ ɔ́n

wítʳ pʰéịpə̀s

námθíŋ
nóʊ nóʊ pʰéɪ̯pə̀ (3 FC)
nóʊ pʰéɪ̯pə̀s
pʰéɪ̯pə̀s ɔ̀n dɛ̀ blǽŋkʰɛ̀tʳ
wáɪ̯tʳ
goʊ (RC)
wérs dɛ̀ láɪ̯tʳ (2×)
góʊ (RC)
éɪ̯tʳ
wérs dɛ̀ láɪ̯tʳ góʊ
vékʰúm klínə̀r
tʰʊ (SC) (5×)
mámìs róʊ̯pʳ
nə:
nɔ́tʳ mámì
álìs
dʸámpʳ
tʰʊ̀déɪ̯
dánséŋk
nɔ̀t dʸámpʳ
ápʳ (2×)
dʸámpìn ɔ̀n dɛ́ yélò blǽŋkʰɛtʳ
áʊ̯tʳ
dʸámpʳ ɔ̀n yélòʊ blǽŋkʰɛ̀tʳ
ɛ̀géɪ̯n
daʊ (5×, 4 RCs, 1 FC) (squealing)
fání (RC)
ɛ̀ntənɪ kʰɛn lʊ́kʳ (2×)
sí (RC)
ǽntənɪ dʸámps wɔ́čìn dɛ̀ rɛ́kʰɔ̀tʳ
a::: (RC)
yélə̀
hàníkʳ (2×) (RC)
hàníkʳ
háɪ̯nàkʳ
bégə̀v háɪ̯nàk
hàɪ̯níkʳ
hàɪ̯nákʳ
wéɪ̯
nɔ́tʰɛ̀wéɪ̯ (2×) (squealing)
dáʊn
sít dáʊn

SLEEP

áʊ·

nɔ̀t dè yέlòʊ blǽŋkʰèt^r

dè wáịt^r

wáịt^r

háị bóʊbò

dέ::ts è̀ gʊ́d bɔ́·ị

áp^r

áp^r dér ɔ̀ndɛ blǽŋkèt^r

tʰéịk^r ɔ̀f dè ɛ̀ blέk^r blǽŋkèt^r

tʰéịk^r ɔ́f dè blǽŋkèt^r (RC)

nɔ́ | tʰéịk^r ɔ́f dè blǽŋkèt^r (2 FC)

tʰéịk^r ɔ́f dè blǽŋkèt áp^r (RC)

aʊ: (RC)

ὲnáp^r déᵊr (RC)

sídέ (SC)

sídè bíg háʊs (RC)

dǽdí: (RC)

màị néịl pʰɔ́liš (4×)

déts rɔ́ŋ néịl pʰɔ́líš

tʰʊ̀ néịl máị néịl pʰɔ́lìš

néịl pʰɔ́lìš

gét^r sám:ɔ́r mɪlk^r (RC)

áʊ::

blǽŋkèt^r

u::: (RC)

áị fàgɔ́t^r (3×)

plap^r (2×)

nóʊ (RC)

mịúzìk^r (RC)

blǽŋkʰèts háịdèŋ

kʰɔ́fì

gét sàm kʰɔ́fì (2×)

nɔ́ mílk^r

gét sàm kʰɔ́fì fɔr ὲntəni

gét sóʊp^r

soʊp^r (4×)

góʊ gèt^r kʰɔ́fì

góʊ bàị sám kʰɔ́fì

stǽp^r ɔ́ndè blǽŋkèt^r

wér ìs ǽntɔ̀nìs blǽŋkʰɛt^r (2×) (falsetto)

wérs háịdɪŋk (falsetto)

bʊ́ks (SC)

dáʊn (2×)

hév dè bʊ̀ks tʰʊ̀déi̯

ài̯ tʰéi̯kʳ dè wái̯tʳ blǽŋkʰɛtʳ ɔ́f

ɔ̀n dè blǽŋkʰɛtʳ

ándər dè blǽŋkʰɛ̀tʳ

slìpʳ gòʊ (SC)

wɔ́tè blú blǽŋkʰɛ̀tʳ

wɔ́t dè tʰéi̯kʳ dè blǽŋkʰɛ̀tʳ

kʊíkʳ

gɔ́ kʊíkʳ

hái̯ bìg bɔ́b

dèts bɔ́·b (2×)

bìg bɔ́b (2×)

bìg bɔ́·b (RC)

líʔəl bɔ́·b

bíg ɛ̀n líʔəl

líʔəl bɔ́·bì

líʔəl nénsì (SC)

bíg nénsì

bíg bɔ́·b ɛ̀nd nénsì ɛ̀nd bɔ́·bì

ǽnd bə·bʳ

ɛ̀n tʰú: θrí: bɔ́·bìs

θrí: bɔ́·bis

fóʊr bɔ́bìs

síks

tʰél dè nai̯tʳ | bɔ́·bì

bíg bɔ́·b (SC)

bíg bɔ́·b nə̀tʳ hóʊm

né·nsì ɛ̀nd wèndì

wéndì géi̯v ǽntənìs

ɔ́n né·nsì

óʊnlì né·nsì kʰʊdʳ wídè kʰídì

mámì góʊ sʊí·p

áʊ nénsì gén

gètʰɔ́n

ɔ́·l dè yámpʳ

yélòʊ blǽŋkɛ̀tʳ (SC)

stéi̯ déər

stéi̯ déər blǽŋkɛ̀tʳ

lài̯kʰè lípstìkʳ

ái̯ tʰoʊld mí: (2×)

hái̯dɪn déər

góṵìn háịdìn déᵊr
dóṵntʳ gèthɔ́f ɛ̀n háịdìn déᵊr
dóṵntʳ (2×)
mámì
góṵ tʰṵ́ ʔi·tʳ ɛ̀ndɛ́n tʰṵ́ béd
fɔ́ʳstʳ tʰṵ́ ʔɔ́fìs
dɛ̀n fɔ́ʳstʳ lá·nč | dɛ́n ɔ́·fis
dóṵntʳ dɛ̀ ʔɔ́·fìs
fɔ́ʳstʳ lánč
ə̀ntnɪ kʰóṵm tʰṵ̀máč
tʰṵ̀ máč héᵊr
bḭ́:g héᵊr
bḭ́·g
lḭ́ʔəl héᵊr
déts kʰéni
ɛ̀ntənɪ tʰéịkʰɔ̀l dɛ̀ kʰénìs
ɔ̀l dɛ̀ kʰénis
ìndɛ̀ bɔ́·ks
dóṵntʰéịkʰénis ɔ́l bə·ks
tʰṵ̀ hóṵlz
dís wéị (RC)
óṵ
dù détʳ láịkʰɛ̀ líps
lṵ̀kʰín fɔ́r dɛ̀ blǽŋkʰɛ̀tʳ
nòṵ tʰṵ́kʰìtʰɔ́f
ɛ̀ntəni tʰéịkʰìtʰɔ́f
ɛ̀n bóṵbòṵ (RC)
ɛ̀ntə̀nì dṵ̀ dét
ɛ̀nɪ yámpʳ
ɛ̀nənɪ wɔ́kʳ dʸámpʳ
ɛ̂ntəni tráị kəlábʳ ápʳ (SC)
nóṵ dáṵn
ándər dɛ̀ blú· blǽŋkɛt
wə·ntʳ
dᶻámpʳ (4×)
wɔ́tʳ kʰálər (3×) (RC)
yélóṵ
kʰálər
wɔ́tʳ kʰálər dí:yèn (2×) (RC)
mèịkʳ tʰú: máč nóịs
æntʳ (RC)
nóṵtìs čáịnə blákʳ (falsetto)

kʰídì

frɔ́m dè (signal unintelligible)

nóʊ̯

síː dè háʊ̯s

áɪ̯ wɔ́ntə góʊ̯ tʰʊ mámìs háʊ̯s

nɔ́t yélòʊ̯ | rétʳ

góʊ̯ tʰʊ̀ tʰɔ́ɪ̯lɛt

góʊ̯ láɪ̯k

ìz détʳ ráɪ̯tʳ

bɔ́ːtʰɪt

ʔɔ́ːː

ʔáhá

mámì (2×)

náʊ̯ dís

nóʊ̯ dís

déts ìnáf (3×)

ǽndè bíg réd (2×)

tʰú bìg rèd wàns

wɔ́ts dè métər

tʰú bíg líəl

híꞏrɪt (RC)

dérs sám

wèrs léɪ̯dì léɪ̯dì

wèrz láɪ̯tʳ

háɪ̯ (3×) (some unintelligible whisper)

ɔ́pənítʳ

bʊ́kʳ

SLEEP

tʰíkl (3×)

ǽntənì tʰíkl tʰíkl (RC)

déts dè bɔ́ɪ̯

dèts ɛ̀ gʊ́d bɔ́ɪ̯

tʰéɪ̯kʳ békʳ dè vékʰúm | kliːnər

kʰɔ́bès nɔ́tʳ ɔ́n

mámì hébìtʳ ɔ́n (2×)

vékʰùm kíːnər (2×)

vékʰʊ̀m klíꞏnər ɔ́ꞏn

SLEEP

hántʰì dántʰì

áɪ̯ gɔ́tʰɛ̀ blɛŋkʰɛtʳ láɪ̯kʰɛ̀ lípstìkʳ (2×)

ɛ̀ntənɪ (signal unintelligible)

dɔ́gìs méɪ̯kʰən ɔ́l dèt nɔ́ɪ̯s

háɪ̯ dóɡì

wêr yù góʊ̯ə̀n

vékʰʊ̀m vékʰʊ̀m klí·nə̀r (3×)

tʰú: máč

tʰɔ̀·kʳ tʰú: máč

tʰú: máč

lɔ́kʳ dè dóʊ̯r

mèɪ̯l ɔ́·l dè læ·də̀r

méɪ̯lmǽn

dóɡì kʰɛ̀n báɪ̯tʳ dè méɪ̯lmǽn

baɪ̯tʳ ɔ́·l dè lǽ·də̀rs

méɪ̯lmə̀n hévè báɪ̯tʳ

báɪ̯tʳ dè lǽ·də̀rs

m:: nú: bʊ́kʳ

nú: bʊ́:kʳ (2×)

wán dètʳ sǽlì mèɪ̯dʳ

sí· bánì lípstɪkʳ èndè léɪ̯dì èndɔ́ɡì

kʰàms póʊ̯nì·

dèr kʰáms (SC)

mámìs kʰámìn (2×)

(unintelligible signal) bóʊ̯bò (RC)

bóʊ̯bə̀ làɪ̯ dàʊ̯n

dérs dè wàɪ̯tʳ blæŋkʰɛtʳ bóʊ̯bə

yélòʊ̯ blǽŋkʰɛ̀tʳ

dè flávə̀r

ènd náʊ̯ (RC)

si: (RC)

òʊ̯ yá (4×) (3 FCs, 1 RC)

óʊ̯ (RC)

nòʊ̯ blǽŋkèt

dì yélòʊ̯

yélòʊ̯

èndì yélòʊ̯ yélòʊ̯

èndís wàn

ɔ́ní ɔ́ní dís wéɪ̯

àns wɔ́čìn léɪ̯dìs èn mǽn

mǽn tʰʊ̀kʰɛ́tʳ

sètə̀rbéɪ̯

èndè gréɪ̯ kʰápʳ

háɪ̯ bóʊ̯bò

wìt bóʊ̯bə̀ slí·pèŋ

bóʊ̯bə̀ stàrtìd slí·pèn

slípìn (2×)

slí·pìŋ (2×)

ìz hì· slí·pə̀ŋ

tʰéi̯kʳ dɛ̀ blǽŋ dóg

dɛ́ts dɛ̀ bò̤i̯ (whisper)

m: (RC)

bóṳbə̀

tʰə̀rnìtʰɔ́f

tʰéi̯kʳ ìtʰɔ́f

bóṳbə

sɛ́tʳ bóṳbə̀

bóṳbə̀

gò̀tʰáyə̀

ɛ̀ntənìs šṳɛ́tər

bóṳbə kʰɛ́ntʳ

bóṳbə̀ hɛ́tṳ̀ kʰí·pʳ

fái̯nìt

wìt yṳ́·s

dríŋkʰìtʳ (2×)

yṳ́·s

dɛ̀ts dɛ̀ rái̯tʳ wɛ́i̯

rài̯t wɛ́i̯

wèr yṳ̀ góṳìn

ái̯m góṳìn

šu· fíkstʳ

tʰɔ̀kʳ tʰṳ̀ mámì

šṳ́ fíkstʳ

sí· ǽntɔ̀ni

ǽntɔ̀ní

gṳ̀nái̯tʳ

sí· mə̀ròṳ mɔ́·rnìn

šṳ́ fíᵏstʳ (4×)

fíksìt (3×)

šṳ́· fíkstʳ

ìtʰṳ́kʰìtʳ

bríŋìtʳ bǽkʳ

tʰṳ́k dɛ́m (2×) (RC)

tʰṳ́kʰìtʳ dáṳn (4×) (RC)

hìtʰṳ́kʰìtʳ (2×) (1 RC, 1 FC)

ái̯m góṳìn

yɛ́lòṳ wàn

ɛ̀nádə̀r wàn (2×) (1 FC, 1 RC)

tʰéi̯kʰɛ̀ bʊ́kʳ

ɛ̀nádər bʊ́kʳ

ɛ̀ fɔ̀n kʰɔ́·l (RC)

fóʊ̯n kʰɔ́·l bʊ́k

dís fóʊ̯n kʰɔ́·l bʊ́kʳ (3×)

dísìsdɛ̀ (2×)

bʊ́kʳ (RC)

ɛ̀nádər fóʊ̯n kʰɔ́·l bʊ́kʳ

dìsìz lái̯tʳ (RC)

wán lái̯tʳ

dìsìz lái̯tʳ ɔ́nìtʳ

déts ɔ́fìs (2×)

lʊ́kʳ sɔ́fì

dɛ̀tsɔ́fì

kʰám lâstʳ nái̯tʳ

gʊ̀d bɔ́i̯

gɔ̀ fɔ̀r glǽsìs

gɔ́ fɔ́rɛ̀m

góʊ̯ tʰʊ̀dɛ̀ tʰɔ́pʳ

gɔ̀ θróʊ̯

gòʊ̯ fɔ̀r bláʊ̯s

pʰǽ:nts (RC)

gòʊ̯ fɔ̀r šú:s (RC)

pʰáʊ̯dər (RC)

snɔ́tʳ drái̯

gétʳ pʰáʊ̯dər ɔ̀n

šú· fíkstʳ (2×)

ɛ̀ndɛ̀ šú: (RC)

sám pʰáʊ̯dər

ɔ̀ndɛ̀ lé·g (RC)

ǽntɔ̀nìs lé·g

pʰʊ́tʰìn dǽdìs légz

pʰʊ́tʳ sɔ̀m mámìs légz

mámìs légz (2×) (1 RC, 1 FC)

mámì gétsám (2×) (SC)

sóʊ̯pʳ

mámì tʰʊ́kʰɛ̀ šáʊ̯ér

tʰèi̯kʳ sɔ̀m sóʊ̯pʳ

dáʊ̯n

ɛ̀n pʰíkʳ dɛ̀m ɛ̀ báč

snɔ́tʳ fɔ̀r ɛ̀ntɔnɪ

sfɔ̀r nílà

lúkʰètʳ dét (2×)

éntònì tʰèįkʰín

wòzdétʳ

wòzdétʳ fròm détʳ (3×)

wòzdétʳ (RC)

détʳ fròm détʳ

fláy̯ərs à:r bróy̯kʰə́n

gètʳ dè (SC)

lítʰəl šávəl

gètʳ dèm fí·kst

stéį (SC)

áįm fíksən dè dóy̯r

dó·rsòpòn

áįm lókʰən bóy̯bò

dís wèį

dís wèį déər

bóy̯bòslí·pèŋ

béįŋgè béįŋgè bíkʰì

béįŋgè béįŋgè

wán pʰílòy̯ àpdéər

wòt wìl hǽpòn

dóy̯ntʳ gètʰóf

ìnè pʰílòy̯

góy̯òn tʰỳ blǽŋkʰètʳ (2×)

tʰéįkʰín dè wáįtʳ blǽŋkʰétʳ

bóy̯bòstéįkìn hǽtʳ

tʰéįkʳ dè rékʰètʳ

hí·rzèhǽtʳ

hí·rzènádòr

bá:į (RC)

èn bóy̯bò (RC)

hí·rz hǽtʳ

hí·rzènádòr hǽtʳ

dètsè hǽtʳ

ráįtʳ

lèts tʰéįkʰòf dè hǽtʳ

wèrs dè blǽŋkètʳ

bóy̯bò hèzèhǽtʳ

tʰéįkʰóf dè hǽtʳ

hǽtʳ fòr ǽntònì èn bóy̯bò

fòr bóy̯bò | nótʳ fòr ǽntònì

hǽtʳ fòr èntənɪ

óʊ· (RC)

láįkʰè šábl

bóʊbə̀ stén

pʰʊ́tʰə̀n dè blǽŋkʰèt‸

bóʊbə̀ stábʊ̀ìk (2×)

wèrz hámptì

blú: (2×)

nɔ́ (2×)

nɔ́t‸ dè blǽŋkʰèt‸ láįkʰè lípstìk‸

dì àdə̀r

yú

yú tʰèįkʰɔ́f ɔ̀ldè máŋkìs

èn kʰídìs

èn fílìs èn hámptì dámptì

ɛ́nd máŋkì ɛ̀nd hɔ́rsì

ɛ́nd vǽkįùm klí·nə̀r

ɛ̀nd fífì

ɛ̀nd hɔ́rsì

nòʊ háʊs (RC)

ɛ̀nd háʊs (2×) (1 FC, 1 RC)

nòʊ rékʰə̀ts

ɛ̀ndè blú· blǽŋkèt

dìs dè blú· blǽŋkèt

pʰə̀ndí pʰə̀ndí pʰɔ́dí

ǽntə̀nì gét‸ bóʊbóʊ

ǽntə̀nì kʰɪk‸ (RC)

ɛ̀ntənɪ gètʰáp

àbéįméįn (3×)

bíŋk‸ (2×)

lèt‸ bóubə̀ bíŋk‸

bíŋk‸ bɛ́n bíŋk

blú·kìŋ

bóʊbə̀

sténdɔ́n dè blǽŋkʰèt‸

háįdə́ŋ

wáįpíŋk‸ ɔ́ldè blɛ́k‸

dèn tʰéįkʰíŋk‸ tʰéįkìn dáʊn blǽŋkèt

á::

hí·rzè lídə̀l

àį gɔ́dèm

tʰéįk‸ dèmɔ́f

wɔ́dz dè mǽdə̀r

ɔ·l ìs fíkstʳ

óʊkʰéịʳ

nú: (RC)

bàị dè héd

détsítʳ

wí: pʰùtʰí (falsetto)

wér yù pʰʊ̀tʰìn bɔ́ị

kʰɛ́č

láịkʰɛ̀ pʰígìbǽŋk (2×)

hédɛ̀ píŋkʳ ši·tʳ ɔ́·n

dɛ̀ gréị pígʳ áʊtʳ

lǽdɚz

háị dɔ́gì

àị góʊ àpʳ déɚr (2×)

áị góʊ (SC)

šì góʊ àpʳ déɚr

SLEEP

pʰɪgʳ ìndɛ̀ | dìs kʰɔ́rnɚr

dè mǽtʰɚr pʰígì

pʰígì hɛ̀dʳ tʰʊ́

lʊ̀kʰétʳ dè wɔ́lɐ

ɔ̀l frì· pʰígì nóʊ čéịnčìn

nóʊ čéịn

čéịnč ɛ̀ntɐnɪs dáịpʰɚr

fɚstʳ gɛ̀tʳ sɐm pʰáʊdɐ

u::: (SC)

a:: (SC)

ə:: (SC)

nɔ̀nɔ̀mú: (SC)

gɔ (4×) (SC)

m:: (4×) (SC)

ə: (SC)

u: (SC)

yómín yómín yógí (SC)

udi

uzi

wɔ (2×)

ma (3×)

tʰa (4×)

i:tʳ (2×)

i: (2×)

tʰí

tʰísədž

bìbín gétʰìn ápʳ

áʋm

ai̯ gótʰɛ̀ (signal unintelligible)

lái̯kʰɛ̀ tʰá:š

kʰá·š

flò·r sʋíč

góʋ bái̯

hɛ̀v tʰʋ̀ gòʋ bái̯

hɛ̀v tʰʋ̀ bái̯ létʰɛ̀rz

hǽtʳ fɔ̀r ǽntɔ̀nì

pi̯áʋ (2×)

a: (SC)

bábí (2×)

wɔ̀tʳ kʰálə́r

ìndɛ̀ tʰói̯lɛ̀tʳ (2×)

déts tʰói̯lɛtʳ

nə̀ pɔ̀síbl gɛ̀tʳ sàm·ɔ́r

nɔ́tʳ mɔ́·r

nɔ́tʳ pɔ́sìbl

márkʰɛ̀tʳ

gɔ́ slí·pʳ

bóʋbɔ̀ (2×)

SLEEP

kʰɛ́·č dɛ̀tʳ (2×)

bóʋbɔ̀

ɛ̀n kʰídì

dɔ́gì

dí̯ərz dɛ̀ dɔ́gì

dɔ́gì

dérz dɛ̀ dɔ́gì nɔ̀tʳ yɛ̀tʳ dérz dɛ̀ dɔ́gì

dérz dérz dɔ́gì

dɔ́ktʰər fi̯úks (3×)

ìz dəktʰər fi̯úkʳ

ə̀ndɛ̀ mǽtʳ (2×)

déts dɔ́ktʰər déi̯vìs

álɨs

ái̯ gétʰìtʳ

dínər wìtʰálɨs

dáŋkʰì lì·v dò·r óʋpʰə̀n

hǽtʰʋ̀ klóʋz dì dó·r

klóʋzítʳ

klóʊ̯z dè dó·r
lók^r dè skrìn dó·r
skrí::n (3×)
skrí:n pʰʊ̯tʰón
tʰéi̯k^r sə̀m rélìbéròʊ̯ (2×)
hóʊ̯mák^r (2×)
ʔu (5×)
gèt^r šàmpʰú: (2×)
tréi̯n (RC)
šǽmpʰú· (10×)
šʊ̯ìmìŋ pʰú:l (3×)
wònt^r sə̀m wó·tʰə̀r dédì
dédì
sái̯s hæt^r
ə̀ntə̀nì wóntʰéi̯kʰìt^r
tʰéi̯kʰìt^r
nóʊ̯ dèts dædìs mámìs
tʰéi̯kʰìt^r mámìs
mámì pʰʊ̯tʰón hə́r (RC)
hái̯ (RC)
ámámá
mámá
pʰʊ̯tʰón dè hæt^r
góʊ̯ tʰʊ̀ rài̯t^r sái̯d^r góʊ̯
wíč sài̯d^r góʊ̯
rái̯t^r sài̯d^r góʊ̯
sái̯d^r góʊ̯ góʊ̯ (2×)
rái̯t^r sái̯d góʊ̯
ìndè mái̯ə̀r èdz (2×)
mámìz góʊ̯ìn tʰə kʰʊ̯́k^r

SLEEP

bóʊ̯bə̀sítʰìn ə̀n pʰílóʊ̯
dètsè bíg bʊ́k^r
nòʊ̯ dèts lídə̀l bʊk^r
yèlò
léi̯dì
dèn dè léi̯dì pʰíŋk^r
lʊ̀kʰèt^r dè léi̯dì stèndìn órìnč
ènádə̀r léi̯dì (SC)
wóts krái̯éŋ
ènádə̀r léi̯dì
dèts mámì

nóʊ̯ | nɔ́tʳ mámà (2 FCs)

dèts bábə̀

dèts mámà

ə::: (3×) (SC)

gétʰən bóʊ̯bə̀ (2×)

nái̯sèn wɔ́·rm

véki̯ʊ̀m klí:nər

mə·r mɪ́lkʳ (2×)

ǽi̯·s (4×)

ʔɔ́líb

dɔ́ŋkì hɔ̀ldèdó·r óʊ̯pʰə́n

dè vǽki̯ʊ̀m klínər

áʊ̯ʔ

lʊ́kʳ

ǽlí·s

mǽmí̃ (4×)

mámìstʊ́ wìkʳ

álìstrɔ́·ŋg

álìs tʰú· wí·kʰì (2×)

dǽdìs tʰú: wí·kʰì

mámìs tʰú· wí·kʰì

tʰú: wí·kʰì wítʳ bá·rbə̀rà

bì· kʰɛ́rfʊ̀l bárbə̀rà

bárbə̀rà kʰɛ̀n bróʊ̯kʳ

kʰɛ́rfʊ̀l bròʊ̯kʳ dè rámì

kʰɛ́rfʊ̀l bróʊ̯kʳ ʔǽntə̀nî

kʰɛ́rfʊ̀l bróʊ̯kʰìtʳ (2×)

kʰɛ́rfʊ̀l bróʊ̯kʳ dè

bróʊ̯k dè fíŋə

bróʊ̯kʳ dè bóʊ̯bə̀

bróʊ̯kʳ dè vǽki̯ʊ̀m klí·n

dè bróʊ̯kʳ

bégì pʰʊ́

gétʳ sə̀m bróʊ̯kʳ

bróʊ̯kʳ dè (SC)

ǽlìs bróʊ̯kʳ dè béi̯bì frú·tʳ

ǽlìs ə·lmóʊ̯stʳ drɔ́ptʳ

ìts déi̯vìd frú·tʳ

lʊ́kʳ (2×) (1 RC, 1 FC)

ɔ̀lrái̯tʳ

léi̯dí·

m::ámà

bí:::

ìzmέ::

blálà

pʰæ::

nóʊ̯ lài̯tʳ hǽtʳ (2×)

nù lái̯tʳ

lʊ́kʳ

dὲtsὲ nʊ̀ bʊ́kʳ

léi̯dì léi̯dì (signal unintelligible)

kʰátən wɔ́·rm

kʰátʰɔ̀ló·n

kʰátʰὲló·n

wìdǽdì mámìnǽlìs

déts fər dǽ·dí

lʊ́kʰɔ̀l dὲtʳ pʰílòʊ̯z (2×)

nài̯tʰí·bí·

tʰái̯pər

έbən tʰái̯pə́r

lʊ́kʰὲtʳ dὲtʳ klɔ́kʳ

nóʊ̯ mílkʳ (RC)

óʊ̯vər dérz ɔ̀ldὲ klɔ́kʳ

wɔ̀tʳ klɔ́ks dét

góʊ̯ sóʊ̯ dárkʳ

ìtˢ ʔóʊ̯kʰéi̯

ɔ̀ldὲ gɔ̀rlz óʊ̯kʰéi̯

έ·g yɔ́·bi̯á·m (SC)

yém yá::m

lám::

li:

blὲm yí::: (2×)

yám

yi::: (SC)

díní::: (SC)

mὲmὲm::: (SC)

mám:ám:::

bim

m::: (SC)

ʔəʔəʔə (SC)

i::: (SC)

a::: (SC)

dὲts rái̯tʳ hí:r

ə::: (SC)

a::: (SC)

ə::: (SC)

a::: (SC)

i::: (SC)

fífì

héví:: (2×)

ɛ::: (SC)

dè léi̯dìsə̀·l klí·n

ə̀nlì ɔ́m:éi̯n

mámámá::: (RC)

m:::

ə:::

ʔau̯ʔ

gòu̯ tʰu̯bèd náu̯

mɔ́r mílkʳ

dɔ́ktʰər déi̯vís

m::: (SC)

hírz dè blǽŋkʰètʳ

mámá álámámá lá (SC)

ál mámá (2×)

lálámámá (SC)

ál mámá (3×) (SC)

ə̀ldè héts góu̯ìn dáu̯n

fə̀r léi̯dí

fə̀r léi̯dì kʰèi̯m fə̀r pou̯stmèn

wə̀tʳ kʰài̯nd léi̯dì

wə̀tʳ kʰái̯nd (SC)

wə̀tʳ kʰálər

sám tʰú: hǽts

óu̯nlì hǽtʳ

sám ɔ́ldè hǽts

plis

mə̀r mɨlkʳ

èndè méi̯lmən

dèts ǽnádər hɛtʳ (2×)

SLEEP
FATHER PRESENT

ou̯nlí lísén

lísén

lísən ìndì mi̯ú:zìkʳ   To what, the records?

ìndì mi̯ú:zìkʳ

pléi̯ dè blǽkʳ mi̯ú:zɪkʳ (2×)

lísən tʰùmórôʊ

sǽtʰùrdéi̯
                               That is right, tomorrow is Saturday.
                               That is absolutely right, Anthony.

 èntənɪ méi̯kʰâpʳ è ši:tʳ
                               You took off the sheet? What for?

vǽki̯ùm klí:nər
                               You want to put it back in Daddy's
                               pocket?

kʰátʰìtʳ (2×)
                               No, you don't cut it. You want to put it
                               back in Daddy's pocket?

pʰṵ̀š

mámì tʰùdéi̯
                               Hm?

wénzdéi̯

pʰṵ́tʰìtʳ

pʰṵ́šìtʳ
                               Push it in. Did you go out with Mommy
                               today?

ǽntənɪ sɔ́: dè tréi̯n
                               That's right.

ǽnd (2×) (RC)

lísən rékʰəts (2×)
                               Tomorrow morning. The records went
                               night-night.

lísén (2×)
                               No, they went night-night.

pʰṵ́tʰìtʳ békʳ
                               Daddy is going to have his dinner.

pʰṵ́tʰìtʳ ìn dǽdìs pʰɔ́kʰétʳ
                               Go ahead.

dì ádər wéi̯
                               No, you had it right the first time. The
                               other way. That's right.

dì ádər wéi̯ (2×)

gètʰɔ́f
                               Shouldn't you wear your pajamas?

pìyámàs

pìdᶻáməs (2×)
                               Put′on the pajamas.

pʰṵ́tʰɔ́n dè pìdᶻáməs

mɔ́·r mílkʳ (5×) (SC)   (crying a little)

yéló̯ʊ blǽŋkʰètʳ (2×)

dè blǽŋkʰètʳ (2×)

pʰṵ́tʰɔ́n dè šú·s

pʰṵ́tʰɔ́n dè pìyámás

dì grí:n

grí:n

réd
                               Now Anthony's right arm. The right one.

rái̯tʳ (2×)
                               That's left.

rái̯tʳ

léftʳ

rái̯tʳ (3×) (RC)

léft (3×) (RC)

dís wéi̯

dǽ:ts dè bɔ́i̥

wèrz dè bátʰən (RC)

dɛ́rz dè bátʰən

ɔ́u̥pʰən dè bátʰən   Now your left foot.

rái̥tʳ (2×) (RC)

rái̥tʳ (RC)

lɛftʳ (RC)

rái̥tʳ (RC)

rái̥ts ɔ́lrədì ín

gètʰɔ́f (2×)

tʰɔ́rn dè róu̥b (2×)

gètʰɔ́f

góu̥ sí: dǽ:dì

góu̥ sí: àlí·s   Alice went to a dance.

dǽns (2×)   Alice will be back tomorrow morning.

dínər mái̥ər   No, she's not having dinner there.

álìs wìt mái̥ər

góu̥ sí: ái̥dì

gètʰɔ́f

pʰu̥tʰɔ́n dè ší:tʳ (2×)   First the pajamas.

tʰɔ́rnèráu̥nd   Stand up.

dèn pʰu̥tʰɔ́n dè róu̥bʳ (2×)   No, no.

pʰu̥tʰɔ́n dè róu̥bʳ (2×)

pʰu̥tʰɔ́n réd róu̥bʳ (4×)

réd róu̥b (3×)

èntəni mú·vìndè kʰɔ́rnər (3×)

góu̥ ìndè kʰɔ́rnɔ́r (2×)   It's all done

mɔ́·r mílkʳ (4×)   O.K.
                                        FATHER LEAVES

ya̕ (SC)

mámà

mámì drɔ́pʳ ít (2×)

mɔ́·r dzú·s (SC)

álí:s (SC)

kírstɛ́n (4×) (SC)

álɪ:s (SC)

dárkʳ gréi̥ (2×)

mɔ́·r yús

álís (2×) (SC)

ìndè bɔ́i̥frɛ́nd (2×)

álìs ìndè dǽns (2×)

lái̥dàu̥n bóu̥bə

náʊ̯ yú lʊ́kʳ
tʰʊ́· máč
è̯ lídəl
nɔ̀tʳ dís | nɔ̀t détʳ

óʊ̯pʰə̀n
wɔ̀ntʰʊ̀ lísə́:n (2×) (RC)
dǽdì | wɔ́ntʰʊ̀ lísə́:n
dáŋkìs klòʊ̯zìn dè̯ də·r
lísə̀n tʰʊ̀ wán

lísə̀n tʰʊ̀ blú·wàn (2×)

màị̯ dínə̀r
klóʊ̯zd
lí·vɪtʳ óʊ̯pʰə̀n
klóʊ̯zd
dáŋkì kə́rtʰɛ́n
m::: (SC)
nimananaňana (SC)
ňəm ňəm (7×)
m:::
m::: (SC)
ňaňaňa (SC)
atʰaňaňa
ča
tʰéịkʳ bóʊ̯bə̀
tʰéịkʳ èwéị̯
æ:::
lʊ́kʳ
lʊ́kʳ bóʊ̯bɔ́
dè̯ bɔ́tl
bóʊ̯bə̀
lʊ́kʳ
bóʊ̯bə̀ slí·pʰìn
bóʊ̯bə̀ gètʰápʳ
hí·r wìgóʊ̯

MOTHER PRESENT
Do you want me to close this one for
you or leave it open?

To what?
To what?

Tomorrow we'll listen to records. Daddy
will have his dinner now.
MOTHER LEAVES
FATHER COMES
I'm going to have my dinner now,
Anthony.
FATHER LEAVES

mámìskʰámìn

mámí

dér kʰámz jŏní·

wŏtʳ

á·tʰápʳ

m::: (SC)

u::: (SC) (2×)

(Tape dead for about five minutes)

ìts léi̯tʳ (2×)

kʰǽtʳ bróy̯ks (2×)

á·pʳ

kʰǽtʳ broy̯kʳ

kʰǽt bʉ̀ks

tʰɔ́rnərȧy̯nd (4×)

ǽntənìs tʰɔ́rndərȧy̯nd (2×)

ǽntənì tʰɔ́rnərȧy̯nd

dì ébèlòy̯pʳ

méi̯l lǽdər

lái̯tʳ

sí yélòy̯ blǽŋkʰètʳ

àpdér sí yélòy̯ lái̯tʳ

òy̯vèr détʳ

sí· bʉ́kʳ (SC)

óy̯pʰénìtʳ

lʉ́kʰètʳ dè hɔ́rs (2×)

kʰǽtʳ mílkʳ (3×)

glàs mílkʳ

di (4×)

goy̯ (8×)

nɔ̀tʳ dètʳ wéi̯

dì ádər wèi̯

détʳ wèi̯

gètʰápʳ (7×)

SLEEP

mái̯krəfóy̯n (2×)

kʰàmìn (2×)

véki̯ʉ̀m klí·nər

mái̯krəfóy̯n (2×)

o· oy̯· u· (3×)

lái̯kʳ mámà

mámà

sóy̯ìŋ məšĭ·n

məší·n

síŋ

náʊ̯ síŋ

rɔ́kʳ kʰǽndì máʊ̯ntʰə̀r

áwʊ́pʳ

wʊ́pʳ

nɔ́tʳ bóʊ̯bə̀

dáʊ̯n bóʊ̯bə̀

ǽntə̀nì pʰʊ́ts hìs fíːtʳ ɔ́n bóʊ̯bə̀

sífíːtʳ (signal unintelligible) (RC)

á· vérì gʊ́dʳ (3×)

hæː

hiː

bóʊ̯bóʊ̯ (5×) (RC)

lʊ́kʳ lʊ́kʳ

wán tʰú θri (3 FCs)

vé·rì gʊ́d

òʊ̯kʰé (2×)

wáf (2×)

ìtʳ kʰǽn gòʊ̯ ɔ́f

gòʊ̯ àpʳ dé·r

détsètréi̯n

gòʊ̯ ɔ́f tʰʊ̀ sku·l

ɔ́fìs

dǽdìzìnɔ́fìs

fáyə̀

dǽdì (4×)

hái̯ (2×)

wéi̯tʳ

nó·ʊ̯

náʊ̯ òʊ̯pʰə̀n dìs

ápʳ (3×)

góʊ̯z yèlòʊ̯ blǽŋkʰètʳ

nái̯s

pʰʊ̀tʰɔ́n dè rékʰə̀tʳ (3×)

pʰʊ̀tʰɔ́n dè rékʰə̀tʳ | dǽdì

pʰʊ̀tʰɔ́n rékʰə̀tʳ

   (Child drops his bottle)

bɔ́tl (6×)

pìkʰáp dè bɔ́tə̀l dǽdì

dérz nɔ́ sígə̀réts

sígə̀ré·ts (SC)

pʰʊ́tʰɪ̀tʳ ɔ́n dǽdì

pʰʊ̀tʰɔ́n dɛ̀ bɛ́s

pʰóʊ̯n

ɛ̀n kʰídì bɛ́d

kʰídì ìn bɛ́d

ɛ̀ndɛ̀ tʰɔ́i̯ ɛ̀ndɛ̀ bánì

bánì plí·z

ɛ̀ndɛ̀ bɛ́lɛ̀tʰʊ́· (2×)

náʊ̯ pʰʊ̀tʰɔ́n dì bɛ́lɛ̀tʳ

pʰʊ̀tʰɔ́n

ɛ̀ndɛ̀ rɔ́kʰìŋ čɛ́r ɔ̀ndɛ̀ bɛ́dʳ

tʰʊ̀ hɛ́ví·

tʰɛ́i̯k dɛ̀ bɔ́·tl dɛ̀n tʰʊ́·

wɔ̀tʳ kʰɔ́lɔ́·r

dɔ́tʳ (RC)

wɔ̀tʳ kʰálɔ́·r dɔ́·ts

blú

rɛ́dən yɛ́lò

wɔ̀tʳ kʰálɔ́·r dɔ́·ts

blú·

ɛ̀n blú·

grí:n (SC)

rɛ́d (SC)

dɛ́ər

ɛ̀n lʊ̀kʳ (RC)

bʊ́kʰìs bróʊ̯kʰən

wɔ̀tʳ kʰálɔr čɛ́·r fɔ̀r dɛ̀ éi̯g

lʊ́kʰɛ̀tʳ dì ɛ́·g tʰʊ́·

ɛ̀n číkʰən

lʊ́kʰɛ̀tʳ dɛ̀ bákʰɛ́tʳ

kʰábɔ̀s kʰámín (3×)

lʊ́kʳ

dɛ̀ts ǽntɔ̀nì

lʊ́kʰɛ̀tʳ ǽntɔ̀nì

wɛ́i̯tíŋ (4×)

wɛ́i̯tín fɔ̀r bɔ́b

blɔ́kʳ

yɛ́lòʊ̯ blɔ́kʳ

lʊ́kʰɛ̀tʳ ɔ́ldì yɛ́lòʊ̯ blɔ́kʳ

dìsìzèdɔ́tʳ

wɔ̀tʳ kʰàlɔr dɔ́tʳ

dɛ̀ lɛ́ftʳ wán

léftʳ dɔ́tʳ

dèts dè léftʳ wán

dè nékstʳ wán

twáįs blɔ́kʳ (2×)

sí· dè blɔ́ks

ìndè bɔ́·ks (RC)

èndèn pʰʊ́tʳ dís wàn ràįtʳ dé·r

a:: (SC)

ǽntònìs ádèr blɔ́kʳ (SC)

wĭč wán

tʰú·

wán

ráįtʳ wán

nóʊ̯ | lèft wán

si:: (RC)

dìs wán (RC)

fóʊ̯r (RC)

ya· (RC)

  (Dog's barking drowns out speech)

kʰábès

ǽ·nd dĭš wán

dìs blɔ́kʳ góʊz dís wàn

òʊ̯kʰé (RC)

déts ítʳ

wàn óʊ̯vèr déᵊr (RC)

èndʳ ápʳ (RC)

àpʳ déᵊr

ìndə éč (2×)

nòʊ̯ déᵊr (RC)

wèr gòʊ̯ ìn dér

tʰɔ́į gòʊ̯ dèr

ðndè sáįdʳ wìtʰɔ́į

lʊ́kʰètʳ dè kʰídì ìndè dáįč

dóʊ̯ntʳ méįkʰè prézəntʳ ìndè fí·tʳ (2×)

lʊ́kʰètʳ kʰídì

tʰéįkʳ dè kʰídì kʰídì kʰídì (RC) (falsetto)

híᵊr

àyá kʰídì

lʊ́kʰètʳ déᵊr

láįtʳ hès kʰàmɔ́n

grì·n láįtʳ

lʊ́kʰètʳ láįtʳ

áɪ̯m tʰéɪ̯kʰən dì yélòυ̯ blǽŋkʰèt˞

tʰù·má·č

áɪ̯yèv dì yélòυ̯ blǽŋkʰèt˞

dáυ̯n

doυ̯nt˞ stópʰìndè blǽŋkʰèt˞

yú stéɪ̯

sté::ɪ̯

kʰídí (RC)

stéɪ̯ (2×) (RC)

tʰéɪ̯kʰè sáɪ̯d˞ (RC)

méɪ̯bì láɪ̯t˞ (2×)

kʰídì (2×) (1 FC, 1 RC)

sí· láɪ̯t˞ (RC)

sì dè kʰídì (3×)

sí kʰídì (RC)

kʰídì (SC)

k̟ʰídì èn kʰábə̀s

dádà (5×)

kʰídì ǰamp˞

ǰamp˞ áp˞

dáυ̯n

lύ̯kʰáυ̯t˞

tʰú:

déts dè bóɪ̯

lύ̯kʰáυ̯t˞

si: (3×) (RC)

dáυ̯n

ǽntònìz góυ̯ìn ófɪs

àɪ̯kʰèn gètʰáp˞

háυ̯s

détsè háυ̯s

tʰúbǽd

nò̀t˞ fífì

ná·ɪ̯s fífì

fífì (SC) (signal unintelligible, long silence)

bóbí· (2×) (SC)

bób (SC)

pʰὺtʰón dè rékʰə̀t˞

ǽntònì kʰɛn plèɪ̯ dè rékʰə̀t˞

wóts dís (2×)

dǽdì (6×)

dǽdì | pʰὺtʰón dè rékʰə̀t˞ (2 FCs)

rὲkʰə́tʳ (RC)

lísə̀n tʰʊ̀ rέkʰə́tʳ

dǽdì lìsə̀n rέkʰə́tʳ

háį dǽdì

góʊ̀ìn tʰʊ̀ (SC)

góʊ̀ìn tʰʊ̀ gárdə̀n wìdǽdì tʰə̀mɔ́róʊ̯ (2×) (RC)

pʰʊ̀tʰɔ́n rέkʰə̀tʳ

pʰʊ́tʰìtʳ ɔ́n

mámìz góʊ̀ìn tʰʊ̀ ɔ́fìs   No, we're going to a party.

ὲ pʰártʰì (SC)

góʊ̀ìn (2×)

mámì mùv dὲ bέg (4×)

    (unintelligible whisper)

dǽdì (RC)

dǽdìz góʊ̀ìn tʰʊ̀ pʰártʰì

    (unintelligible whisper)

dὲts í:

í:

dàbl yú

í:

áį

tʰʊ̀mɔ́róʊ̯ àį gòʊ̯ tʰʊ̀ bǽθ

tʰə́rnìtʳ ɔ́f

a: (2×)

mámí (17×) (SC)

bɔ́tʰə́l (2×)

kʰréį (5×)

tʰréį (9×)

àpʰréį

áp

ápʰí

wὲrz də̀ bɔ́tl

dὲ bɔ́tʰə̀l (SC)

mámì brɔ́·tʰítʳ

yílòʊ̯

yέlòʊ̯

álís (SC)

mámí (SC)

                                              SLEEP

gòʊ̯ áʊ̯tʰʊ̀ də̀ gárdə̀n

gárdə̀n

ìndὲgárdə̀n

gò̞ʊtʰʊ̀gárdən

tʰéi̞kʰìtʳ áʊ̞tʳ (4×)

æ̀ntənɪ wɔ̀nts tʰʊ̀tʰɔ́·kʳ tʰʊ̀ dǽdɪ

gò̞ʊ tʰʊ̀ gárdən wìdǽdɪ

èndáŋkʰì èn fífì

èntʰái̞gər

èndɔ́·gì

dɔ́·gì èndè tʰái̞gər

èŋkʰídì

dázntʳ mǽtʰə̀r

fífì

èndè dɔ́ŋkʰì dèr

dǽdì (3×)

bɔ́ks ìndèr tʰú·

èndè bɔ́ks ìndéˀr

grí·n bɔ́ks

è blɔ́kʳ

dérzè blɔ́kʳ

wán tʰú θrí (3 RCs)

tʰú· (RC)

wán

θrí (2×) (RC)

fóʊ̞r (RC)

wán

náʊ̞ kʰáʊ̞ntʳ dís wàn

wán tʰú θrí· fóʊ̞r fái̞v (5 FCs)

tʰéi̞kʰɔ́f dè blɔ́kʳ náʊ̞

náʊ̞ kʰámz dèréd

wán tʰú θrí fóʊ̞r fái̞v síks sévén (7 RCs)

éi̞tʳ ná·i̞n (2 RCs)

náʊ̞ dǽdì kʰáʊ̞ntʳ dèm

æ̀ntònì wɔ̀ndè blú wàn

wán tʰú· (2 RCs)

náʊ̞ dǽdì kʰáʊ̞ntʳ dèm

dǽdì kʰàʊ̞ntʳ dè blú wàn

náʊ̞ kʰáʊ̞ntʳ dè dɔ́ts

wán tʰú· (2 RCs)

nóʊ̞ | dǽdì kʰáʊ̞ntʰìtʳ (2 FCs)

dǽdì kʰàʊ̞ntʳ dèm (RC)

wán tʰú· θrí (3 FCs)

kʰábə̀s bárkʰín

bárkʳ (SC)

bárkʰìn ɔ̀ndè móʊtʰɔ̀sáɪ̯kl

móʊtʰɔ̀sáɪ̯kl

ǽntənɪ wɔ̀nts ɛ̀nádɚ bɔ́ks tʰúˑ

ɛ̀nádɚ bɔ́ks (SC)

tʰúˑ blɔ́ks ìn bɔ́ks

bɔ́ks plíˑz (2×)

ɔ́ldè bɔ́ks

blɔ́kʳ plíˑz tʰúˑ

lʊ́kʰètʳ dè bɔ́tʰɘlz

dìs gòʊz ìndè ráɪ̯tʳ wán

wáɪ̯ (4×) (RC)

klòʊz dɪbɔ́ks (3×)

àɪ̯ kʰǽn klɔ́ʊz dè bɔ́ks

pʰʊ́tʰìtʳ ráɪ̯tʳ déˑr (SC)

nóʊ

àɪ̯ sɔ́ˑ dè bɔ́ks

ǽntɔ̀nì (SC)

ɔ́ʊkʰé

wán tʰúˑ θrí fóʊr fáɪ̯v (3 RCs, 2 FCs)
  (signal unintelligible)

nóʊ blɔ́kʳ

wán tʰúˑ (2 FCs)

góʊ náɪ̯tʳ náɪ̯tʳ bótl

góʊ náɪ̯tʳ náɪ̯tʳ hǽtʳ

blúˑ blǽŋkʰètʳ

dèn lɔ́kʰétʳ (2×)

máɪ̯ (2×)

ǽntɔ̀nì kʰám

láɪ̯tʳ (RC)

síˑdèláɪ̯tʳ (RC)

blúˑ

wáɪ̯tʳ

ǽntɔ̀nìz núˑ slípʰɚs

tʰéɪ̯kʰɔ́f slípʰɘs

pʰʊ́tʳ dèm ɔ́n

ràɪ̯tʳ bǽkʳ

síˑ (RC)

dǽdí (SC)

kʰábɘs kʰrɔ́stʳ dè stríˑtʳ (2×)

kʰábɘs ɔ́ˑlwéɪ̯s kʰrɔ̀s dè stríˑtʳ (2×)

lʊ́kʰètʳ kʰídì

kʰàm híˑr kʰídì

méɪkʰìtʳ ɔ́·l gɔ́·n

déts dè bɔ́ɪ̰

SLEEP

klóʊ̰z dè bʊ́kʳ (2×) (SC)

bʊ́kʳ (RC)

klóʊ̰z dè bʊ́kʳ (2×) (SC)

dáʊ̰n (squealing)

háɪ̰ kʰídì

bʊ́kʳ

ɔ́·l gɔ́n

múvàʊ̰tʳ dè láɪ̰tʳ híᵊr

bóʊ̰bə gòʊ̰ʔɔ̀n pʰígì

pʰígì (squealing)

wáɪ̰tʳ ší·tʳ

á:: gʊ̀déɪ̰

réɪ̰

ʔám·áʔ (2×)

(signal unintelligible) nàɪ̰tʳ náɪ̰tʳ

láɪ̰dàʊ̰n

èndèbóks

gìv dè tʰɔ́pʳ

blǽŋkʰétʳ plí·z (3×) (SC)

nóʊ̰ (RC) (squealing)

ápʳ (RC)

blá:::

ǽntənɪ gɔ̀tʳ sám slípʳ híᵊr

ǽntənɪ gɔ̀tʳ

máɪ̰krəfòʊ̰n gòʊ̰ náɪ̰tʳ náɪ̰tʳ

pʰʊ̀tʰɔ́n dè rékʰə̀tʳ

óʊ̰nlì wàɪ̰ər pʰʊ̀tʰɔ̀n rékʰétʳ

dǽdí (2×) (SC)

mɔ́r mílkʳ (SC)

plí·z (SC)

mɔ̀r mílkʳ (RC) (signal unintelligible)

ɔ̀·ldè gɔ́rlz (2×)

ar (RC)

rékʰə̀tʳ

rékʰə̀tʳ pléɪ̰ər

   (signal unintelligible)

gòʊ̰ áʊ̰tʳ (2×)

ɔ̀·ldè bə̀rdz (1 FC, 1 RC) (2×)

ɔ̀·ldè bə́rdz àr

détʳ ə·ldè bɔ́rdz (2×)
lʊ́kʰètʳ ɔ̀ldè bɔ́rdz
álìs
ɔ̀ldè bɔ́rdz (2×)
slí·pə̀ŋ
tʰéi̯kʰìtʳ áu̯tsái̯dʳ (2×)
dèts lài̯kʳ márgə̀rètʳ
álìs
bá
dɔ́ŋkì
kʰrápʰètʳ
m:: (RC)
nə̀gɔ́tʳ
rái̯tʳ dɛ́·r
gèthápʳ (4×)
    (signal unintelligible)
dèts dè gréi̯ tʰápʳ
hái̯fífì
stǽndápʳ
fífì stǽndʳ ápʳ
stǽndàpʳ (3×)
dáu̯n (4×)
lʊ̀kʰáu̯tʳ (RC)
hì·r kʰáms fífì (RC)
mámì
lʊ̀kʰáu̯tʳ lài̯kʳ fífì
lʊ́kʳ áu̯tʳ
lʊ̀kʰáu̯tʳ
fífì stǽndə̀ŋ
fífì lʊ́kʰáu̯tʳ
tʰɔ́pʳ
ɔ́ldè bɔ́rdz
tʰɔ́pʳ
dáu̯n
dâu̯ndâu̯ndáu̯n
dètsè gûdʳ bói̯
ʔá:ʔ (3×)
fífì
lʊ́kʰètʳ ɔ̀ldè bɔ́rd
déts ɔ̀ldè bɔ́rd
óu̯ nóu̯
óu̯pʰə̀n dè (SC)

kʰábə̀s

dè lájtʰìzò̀n

májkrə̀fòʊ̯n

yélòʊ̯ blǽŋkʰèt‍ʳ (2×)

yélòʊ̯ blǽŋkʰèt‍ʳ plí·z (2×)

blǽŋkʰèt‍ʳ plí·z (2×)

hájfífì

hájbóʊ̯bə̀

wándə̀rfə̀l

wát‍ʳ (2×)

hàwá:t‍ʳ

wɔ́t‍ʳ (RC)

hì wò̀ntʰʊ̯́ pléị̀

pléị̀

kʰábə̀s nɔ̃́t‍ʳ nájt‍ʳ nájt‍ʳ

yélò blǽŋkʰèt‍ʳ plí·z

gívìt‍ʳ

mílèt‍ʳ

rát‍ʳ

hí·rz lájt‍ʳ (SC)

   (whisper, signal unintelligible)

tʰàkʰàblá

m::blá

m::

bíbè

góʊ̯

hǽnd (RC)

kʰábə̀s bárkʰìn

wɔ́wɔ́ (4×)

wáf

wáwá

wɔ́

wɔ́wɔ́wɔ́

wáf (3×)

yélòʊ̯ blǽŋkʰèt‍ʳ plí·z (2×)

bóʊ̯bə̀ nájt‍ʳ nájt‍ʳ

o:: (RC)

dè bárdz ò̀n (2×)

sì·dè bɔ́·rdz

ə̀ldè bárdz ìz ò̀n

ə̀ldè pʰúr bárdz (SC)

pʰúr bárdz (RC)

pʰúˑr (RC)

a:: (3×) (2 FCs, 1 RC)

ápʰán (2×)

óʊ̯ mámì

ìndè máị̀ (SC)

máị̀ (SC)

máị̀krɔ̀fóʊ̯n

yélòʊ̯ blǽŋkèt plíˑz (RC)

yélòʊ̯ blǽŋkèt (RC)

mɔ́r ᵈyùs plíˑz

mɔ́r mìlkʳ pliˑz (3×)

bóʊ̯bɔ̀ (2×)

mílkʳ

bóʊ̯bɔ̀

ráị̀tʳ

déts dè ráị̀tʳ

síˑdèfíˑtʳ

hiᵊr

gètʰìmɔ́f

bíˑ (4×)

bá

dèrz yápʳ (3×)

yápʳ

déᵊr góʊ̯ (2×)

déᵊr kʰám

   (signal unintelligible)

màị̀nèná

kʰídì

àị̀ dòʊ̯ntʳ síˑ dè kʰídì

kʰídìz áʊ̯tʳsáị̀dʳ

θrú dì ádᵊr doᵊr

góʊ̯ìn tʰʊ̀gètʳ mámìskɔ́rtʳ (2×)

wìt mị̀úzìkʳ

dǽdí

dǽdì | bákʰètʳ plíˑz

ɛ̀nàdᵊr àdᵊr búkʳ plíˑz

dáŋkì

fìks dè dáŋkì

ɛ̀ndè blú bɔ́ks ɛ̀ndè bíg bɔ́ks

déts dárkʳ

dárkʳ (2×)

pʰʊ̀tʰɔ́n dè láị̀tʳ

ɔ̀ldɛ̀ dárkʳ dárkʳ

nóʊ̯ (5×)

dǽdí

dǽdì

lɔ́kʳ dɛ̀ dóᵊr

dǽdì (3×) (RC)

nádᵊr bɔ́ks plí·z

nádᵊr plí·z

wái̯tʳ bɔ́ks plí·z (2×)

déts dǽdì

wán

ɛ̀ndís wán

ǽntənì mèi̯dɛ̀ més

ɛ̀ndɛ̀ bɔ́ks plí·z (2×)

tʰú·

dɛ̀ bɔ́ks plí·z tʰú·

dǽtsítʳ

dís wàn (2×) (RC)

dǽdí

ɔ̀ldɛ̀ blǽŋkʰɛ̀tʳ

ɔ̀ldɛ̀ blǽŋkʰɛ̀tʳ ɔ́lsòʊ̯

ɔ́lsòʊ̯

   (throwing, squealing)

blǽŋkɛ̀t (RC)

lʊ́kʰɛ̀tʳ kʰídìs fí·tʳ

kʰídìs θrí·fí·tʳ

dǽdìs (4×)

dǽdí (3×)

dǽdì (4×)

àyáyáyá

fɜ̀rstʳ góʊ̯

méi̯kʰɛ̀ prézɜ̀ntʳ dǽdì

góʊ̯ (RC)

θǽŋk yú (5×)

θǽŋk yú fɜ̀r dɛ̀bérí

góʊ̯bæ̀kʳ mámì

bék ʳ fɔ́r dɛ̀béríz

ɔ́lgɔ́n (2×)

fɜ̀rdɛ̀ bérì·z

a: (SC)

wìkʰʊ́d álìs

gʊ́d (RC)

dèts gúd

bérìz

lúkʰìn bérìz

bǽkʳ plí·z

bérìz

nɔ́tʳ bǽrìz

bǽrìz (2×)

nɔ́tʳ bǽrìz

bɛ́·rí·z

bǽ (2×)

yélòꭒ blǽŋkʰètʳ plí·z (8×)

bɔ́·l

sí dè bɔ́·l

yélòꭒ blǽŋkʰètʳ plí·z (2×)

bámbám

kʰídìkʰídìkʰídì

bámbám

kʰídìkʰídìkʰídì (3×)

yélò blǽŋkʰètʳ plí·z

SLEEP

nóꭒ· (RC)

lísàn | kʰídì

dè jǽkʰètʳ

ápʳ góꭒz dè wíl (3×)

θrí píŋkʳ dɔ́ts

mǽč

θrí píŋkʳ

mǽč

hír kʰám tʰúmájs (2×)

θrí blájn májs (2×) (3 FCs)

θrí wán májs (3 FCs)

frí θrí kʰájnd májs (4 FCs)

wèrz dè stíkʳ

wàrkʰɔ́nítʳ

òꭒnòꭒnòꭒnóꭒ

dérz dè féjs

dóꭒntʳ góꭒ ìndè rájtʳ wán

gòꭒ ìndís wán

wátʳ wɔ́z gúd

wátʳ wɔ́z stártʳ (2×)

slí·pʳ (2×) (RC)

   (unintelligible whisper)

góʊ tʰʊ̀ slí·pʳ

nɔ́tʳ góʊ tʰʊ́slípʳ

gètʰáʊtʳ

mámì (RC)

blǽŋkʰètʳ

ɔ́ldè θìŋks áʊtʳ

  (signal unintelligible)

blǽŋkʰèts nái̯tʳ (2×)

hɛ́lòʊ (2×)

  (squealing)

álɔ́s

álɪ́s

bábí (2×)

hái̯ déi̯vìdʳ (2×)

gəgəgə

gigigigigi

gə́gə̀gə̀

gʊgʊgʊgi (RC)

gadigadi (SC) (falsetto)

kaklikaklɔku

bəbəbəbə

lalalalali (RC)

gagaga

mamamama

gigigi

lʊ́kʰètʳ dè bɔ́tl

góʊìn tʰʊ̀dè mái̯krɔ̀fòʊn

déts dè mái̯krɔ̀fòʊn áʊtʰɔ̀v dɛ́·r

pʰʊ̀tʰìtʳ ɔ́·n (2×)

plágìtʳ áʊtʳ (2×)

  (signal unintelligible)

lʊ̀kʰètʳ bóʊbə̀ dè̀ᵊr

lʊ́kʰètʳ ìtʳ

bú::: (SC)

lʊ́kʰètʳ bóʊbə̀ dɛ́·r

bóʊbə̀ dɛ́ᵊr

lʊ́kʳ wə̀tʳ bóʊbə̀ díd

  (squealing)

á·búts bóʊbə̀

méi̯dìtʳ

lʊ̀kʳ wə̀tʳ bôʊbə̀ díd (2×)

sí· wə̀tʳ bóʊbə díd

(squealing)

lûkʳ wàtʳ bóу̥bə̀ díd

bóу̥bə̀zə̀ndὲ

(signal unintelligible)

bóу̥bə̀zɔ́·n

bóу̥bə̀zìn bêθrùm

wìtʳ dὲ tʰɔ́i̯z

sí· bóу̥bə̀ (RC)

bóу̥bə̀

(squealing, unintelligible signal)

gétʰə̀f dὲ tʰɔ́pʳ

sí· smóу̥kʰì (RC)

dὲts dὲ béi̯tʳ

détsὲ mí·rə̀

lûkʰὲt dὲ

lú·kʳ

lʊ́kʳ hírz dὲ yélòу̥ ὲndὲ wái̯tʳ

wôtʳ kʰálə̀r

smóу̥kʰìs fí·tʳ

smóу̥kʰì kʰὲn kʰɛ́č

kʰὲn kʰɛ̂č (2×) (RC)

gὲtʰáp

i̯ə̀st wàn kʰís ɔ́nlì

áу̥tʳ tʰʊ̀dé·r

góу̥ gêtʳ smóу̥kʰì (2×)

gétʳ

klí·nə̀pʳ

tʰéi̯kʳ dὲ fóу̥n ên gὲtʳ smóу̥kʰì déə̯r

lûkʳ wàtʳ smóу̥kʰì díd

ə̀n kʰábə̀s

mámí

dǽdí (3×)

mámì

mámí (5×) (RC)

dǽdí (2×)

mámì (2×)

dǽdì (4×)

pʰʊ́tʰɔ́n dὲ béi̯ðìŋ

béi̯ðìŋ rʊ̀m

nóу̥ | lèts gòу̥ bɛ́kʳ

dэ́tsítʳ

(signal unintelligible)

ápˢ gòʊ̯z dè (SC)

sí: dè máŋkʰì apdé·r

ɛn wìtˢ dè smôʊ̯kʰì ápˢ

nɔ́tˢ gòʊ̯ìn tʰʊ̯béd

tʰéi̯kˢ dè máŋkʰì

tʰéi̯kʰìtˢ

stɔ́pʰìtˢ

  (squealing, unintelligible signal)

kʰírstən

nóʊ̯ dédì | nɔ́tˢ kʰírstèn

ãĺís (2×)

kʰám (RC)

kʰám hí·r

bi:::didi

ãĺís

wə́wə́wə́

wəgigigigi (RC) (falsetto)

ǰəmpˢ mái̯krəfòʊ̯n

tʰʊ̯ (4×)

  (falsetto)

sálì dóʊ̯ntˢ

àntənɪ wònts tʰəsèi̯ hɛ́lòʊ̯ tʰʊ̯ sálì

gu (4×)

bəbəbəba

gòʊ̯ ǰámpˢ

  (squealing)

kʰàmɔ́n

stɔ́pˢ

hɛ́ftʰʊ̯ stɔ́pˢ

stɔ́pˢ

stɔ́pʰìtˢ

stɔ́pˢ dè bɔ́·l

stɔ́pʰìtˢ

stɔ́pˢ dɛ́ bɔ́·l plí·z

tʰéi̯kʰìtˢ

stɔ́pʰìtˢ

yú tʰéi̯kʰìtˢ

plí·s tʰéi̯kʰìtˢ

gògògó

nòʊ̯nòʊ̯nóʊ̯

nóʊ̯ (13×)

dɛ́ts ǰə́mpˢ

óʊ̀vèr

óʊ̀vèr ǰə́mpᵣ

SLEEP

sí: dè blǽŋkʰètᵣ dètᵣ áị fáʊ̀nd

détsèbóị

mámí (RC)

blókᵣ

máŋkʰì

nótᵣ dɛ́:r

á:::wə̀

wə́

ìts dá·kᵣ

dá·kᵣ

dákᵣ

kʰí

hítᵣ də̀ máịkrə́fóʊ̀n (2×)

ə máịkrə̀fóʊ̀n (2×)

máịkrə̀ʔə̀ʔə̀ʔə̀ʔ

máịkrə̀

  (squealing)

kʰábə̀s hèzítᵣ

nóʊ̀ | kʰábə̀s hèzìtᵣ

hí héz

hórs

ándịén

bə̀t tʰʊ́fì·tᵣ hèd nóʊ̀ hórsì

wíš (SC)

wíš hǽdè hórsì

bót hǽdè hórsì

wíš hǽdè hórsì (2×)

wìní·d stró·bə̀rìs

kʰə̀món béịbì (2×) (1 RC, 1 FC)

pʰʊ́tʰìtᵣ ɔ́·n

ʔa

ʔa:

ʔə

ʔa:kᵣ

ʔá:kʰéị

ák

kʰàmɔ́·n béịbì

a::

  (squealing)

lúks láɪkʰɛ̀
gigigigigi (3×)
  (falsetto)
gə (4×)
gaga
ráɪtʳ
déts skrǽčtʳ
ràɪtʳ híə̯r
ré:i̯d
ɔ̀l ní·d
ɔ̀lgɔ́tʳ
ɔ̀l ní·d
  (signal unintelligible)
áʊtsàɪdʳ déə̯r
àpsáɪd
áʊtsàɪdé·r
blákʳ (4×)
nó·ʊ̯
ɔ́·l frù
ɔ́·l màɪ̯ bláks
óʊ̯ (RC)
a
o·ʊ̯ (RC)
šúə̯r (3×)
àɪ̯ gɔ́tʰìtʳ (2×)
nóʊ̯
méɪkʰə̀
yɔ́
  (squealing)
óʊ̯ (4×)
ɔ́ (4×)
bɔ́ (4×)
  (falsetto)
áɪ̯m hfə̯r (2×)
láɪkʳ (2×) (1 RC, 1 FC)
wán láɪkʳ
tʰú: láɪkʳ
θrí fóʊ̯r láɪkʳ
wán láɪkʳ
máŋkɪ̀z láɪkʳ
ə́pʳ (2×)
láɪ̯tʳ (2×)

tʰə̀rn dè láḭtʳ

láḭtʳ

ɔ́::l gɔ́·n

ɔ́l gɔ̂n

ìts ɔ́:l gɔ́·n (2×)

ìts nɔ́tʳ ɔ́:l gɔ̀:n

ìts nɔ́tʳ ə·l

stápʰìtʳ (2×)

déᵊr

yayayawa̤ṵwa̤ṵ
   (squealing)

gígòṵbóṵbòṵ (2×)

náṵ ìts ɔ́:l gɔ́·n

ɔ́:l gɔ́:n (falsetto)

gɔ (4×) (SC)

ɔ́:l gɔ́:n

ɔ́::l gɔ́::n

ɔ́lgɔ́n (2×)

gʊ́d lákʳ

dèts wán

tʰú·

gɔ (4×)
   (falsetto)

klɔ́z dè dɔ́ᵊr

gígîgí (2×)
   (hitting, squealing)

hèḭhé·ḭ

áḭ dû: ìtʳ

héḭhéḭ
   (squealing)

áḭ láḭk tʰṵ̀ (2×)

gɔ́ŋ gɔ́ŋ blǽn

blǽŋkʰètʳ láḭkʰè lípstìkʳ

blǽŋkʰìtʳ

óṵ (2×)

a:

fáḭər sàḭn

ìz nɔ́tʳ (2×)

ìz nɔ́tʳ sámtèn

góṵ tʰṵ̀s (SC)

slí·pʳ

stíkʳ

ráʊnd gòʊ dè stík˥ (SC)

ɔ́n kʰár

si: (RC)

góʊ dè stík˥

lídəl

stík˥

gòʊ gêt˥ də yêlòʊ stík˥

híᵊrìz yélòʊ

góʊ blǽk˥

yi:::

  (squealing)

ái̧ (3×)

díd

gi (4×)

də béi̧bì (3×)

  (Baby is crying in adjoining room)

béi̧bì də béi̧bì béi̧bì (6×)

ɪ:::

béi̧bì (3×)

bɛ́·i̧

béi̧bì

béi̧·

hǽpì béi̧bì

dèts dè béi̧bì

bɛ́:i̧ (SC)

béi̧bì

déts dè béi̧bì

béi̧ bí· (SC)

ya:: (SC)

a:: (SC)

  (squealing)

SLEEP

blǽk˥

mái̧krə̀

ɔ́ŋkì pʰɔ́·l pléi̧ dè mái̧krə̀fòʊn

mái̧krə̀fòʊn

ǽntə̀nìz dʊ́ìŋ

FATHER PRESENT IN THE ROOM

dǽdìz góʊìn ə̀ndè tréi̧n

dǽdì góʊzòndə̀ tréi̧n

ɛ̀ndéi̧vìd

kʰɔ́bə̀rs

ìnsájd
óʊnlì dɔ́gì
èn bóʊbɔ̀ góʊzɔ̀ndè tréịn
èn dǽdì góʊzɔ̀ndè tréịn
ènɛ́ktʰáị góʊzɔ̀ndè tréịn
wáịtʳ
blǽkʳ dɔ́ts
láịtʳ gréị dɔ́ts
làịtʳ gréị
wɔ̀tʳ kʰálɚz bóʊbɔ̀ (2×)
wɔ̀t kʰálɚr
mílkʰìn dè bɔ́tʰəl
áịm dríŋkìn dǽdìs
tʰápʳ fɔ́r dè bóʊbɔ̀

FATHER LEAVES

dɛ́ts fɔ́r mí:
màmàmàmá wìtʳ dǽdì
mílkʳ fɔ̀r dǽdì
óʊkʰéị (RC)
dǽdì dǽns (2×)
háị dǽdì
óʊnlì ǽntənì
dǽdì dǽns (2×)
dǽdì gívìtʳ
dǽdì nɔ̂tʳ fɔ̀r ǽntənì
nóʊ
dǽdì
dǽdì gɔ́tʳ
lʊ́kʰèt ʳ dǽdì
   (falsetto)
lʊ́kʰèt dǽdì híᵊr
lʊ́kʰèt dǽdì
mílkʰìndɔ̀ bɔ́tl
áị spíldìtʳ
óʊnlì fɔ̀r dǽdì
ápʳ (RC)
dɛ́ts fɔ̀r dǽdì
lɛ́tʳ dǽdì hévìtʳ
tʰéịkʰɔ́f (2×)
dɛ́·
tʰɔ́rnèráʊnd (2×)
lʊ́kʰètʳ dɔ́ŋkì

déts də bóɪ̯

dêts də dóŋkì

dǽn dǽdì dǽn

pʰíkʰə̀pʳ dè dón

áɪ̯kʰén pʰìkʰə̀pʳ

áɪ̯kʰèn

háʊ̯bàʊ̯tʳ

háʊ̯bàʊ̯tʳ də dǽdì

óʊ̯kʰéɪ̯ (RC)

dǽdìs tʰú: fʊ́tʳ

dédì hèd sə̀m fí:tʳ

bí:bə

pʰʊ̀tʰɔ́nèrékʰə̀tʳ fə̀r yú

wɔ́tʳ dǽdì gɔ́tʳ

dǽdì gɔ́tʳ

ɔ̀ndə pléɪ̯n

lʊ́kʰètʳ pʰílòʊ̯

wɔ́tʳ kʰálə̀r pʰílòʊ̯ (RC)

wɔ́tʳ kʰálə̀r (RC)

ìznɔ̂tʳ blǽkʳ

íts yélòʊ̯

dǽdì dǽns

á dǽdì

tʰéɪ̯kʰìtʊ̀ dǽdì

dǽdì pʰʊ̀tʰɔ́n ə̀ hǽtʳ

dǽdì pʰʊ̀tʰɔ́nə̀kʰóʊ̯tʳ

óʊ̯nlì dǽdì kʰên

áɪ̯ pʰʊ̀tʳ dìsìn hìəʳ

sí: də dɔ́:gì hí·r (RC)

sí:də̀dɔ́:gì (RC)

áɪ̯ sí: də dɔ́:gì (2×, 1 falsetto)

kʰídì láɪ̯ks dɔ́:gì

láɪ̯ts ə̀pʳ hí:r

dǽdì dǽns (3×) (SC)

wítʳ bóʊ̯bo (SC)

wɔ́tʳ kʰálə̀rz bóʊ̯bò (2×) (SC)

dǽdì blóʊ̯ (SC)

FATHER COMES

dǽdì pʰʊ̀tʰɔ́n dè hǽtʳ

óʊ̯nlì dǽdìs kʰʊ́dʳ

nóʊ̯ dǽdì

FATHER LEAVES

lúkʰètʳ dǽdì (2×) (falsetto)
wótʳ kʰálə̀r (RC)
wótʳ kʰálə̀rə̀r díś rúm (RC)
wótʳ kʰálə̀r tʰáʋ̩ə̀lz

SLEEP

aị (2×) (squealing)
klóʋ̩z ín dɛ́ bó·tʰə̀l (2×)
klóʋ̩z dɛ́ bó·tʰə̀l plí:z
háʋ̩ bàʋ̩tʳ gɛ̀tʳ də̀ bó·tl | álìs (2 FCs)
kʰɪ (4×)
wi::
kʰʋ̩í (4×)
yélòʋ̩ blǽ:ŋkʰètʳ
háịdə̀s ìndè wó·tʰə̀r
yélò blǽŋkʰètʳ (2×) (SC)
blǽŋkʰètʳ (SC)
wéə̀r tʰʋ̩pʰútʳ də̀ blǽŋkʰètʳ (SC)
wéə̀r tʰʋ̩pʰútʳ ìtʳ (3×)
wéə̀r tʰʋ̩ pʰû̩t də̀ blǽŋkʰètʳ (2×)
blǽŋkʰètʳ (6×)
mámì
blǽŋkʰètʳ (3×)
gôʋ̩ tʰʋ̩ skú:l
m (4×)
m::
mór mílkʳ plí:z (8×)
híə̀rz dè bótl
mór mílkʳ plí:z
mámì tʰéịkʳ dè bótʰə̀l (squealing)
mámì
hátʳ (3×)
pʰɔ́pʳ (3×)
pʰɔ̀pʰɔ̀pʰí:
go (9×)
pʰʋ̩tʰɔ́nə̀ blǽkʳ róʋ̩bʳ (3×)
óʋ̩pʰə̀n də̀ wín ᵈòʋ̩
pʰútʰɔ́nə̀
pʰútʰɔ́n də̀máịkrə̀fóʋ̩n (4×) (SC)
m::: (SC)
pʰa (4×) (SC)
pʰa::
kʰɪ (4×) (SC)

mámì (RC)

dǽdì (7×) (RC)

sí: də̀ fíŋ góʊ̯ (RC)

yá

sí: də̀ fíŋ góʊ̯ (RC)

wɔ́ts dís (RC)

wɔ́tʰə̀ (2×)

ántə̀nì (SC)

dís

tʰɔ́i̯ (3×)

sái̯

sái̯də̀r

ápʰə̀l sái̯də̀r

sái̯dὲr

dís íz

dɛ́ts yú°r

ántə̀nì

mái̯ stɔ́mὲkꝛ

hɔ́rtꝛ (2×) (RC)

mái̯ hɔ́rt stɔ́mὲkꝛ

ápʰə̀l

hɔ́rtꝛ

lʊ́kꝛ wɔ́tꝛ bóʊ̯bə̀ dídꝛ

wé°rs bóʊ̯bə̀

bóʊ̯bə̀ (RC)

bábà (2×)

góʊ̯ gétꝛ bóʊ̯bə̀

tʰʊ̀ márkʰὲtꝛ

wítꝛ bóʊ̯bə̀

góʊ̯ bái̯bài̯ (squealing)

nái̯tꝛ (4×)

dóʊ̯ntꝛ tʰə́č mámì dǽdìs déskꝛ

ái̯ šú:d (RC)

hì: séi̯ sòʊ̯ (2×)

dǽdìs déskꝛ ὲn mámìs déskꝛ

dóʊ̯ntꝛ góʊ̯ ə̀ndə̀ déskꝛ

dóʊ̯ntꝛ tʰéi̯kꝛ dǽdìs glǽsə̀z

dóʊ̯ntꝛ tʰéi̯kʰìtꝛ ɔ́f

dóʊ̯ntꝛ tʰéi̯kꝛ də̀ glǽsə̀z ə̀f

dǽdìs wérìn glǽsə̀z

dǽdì ɔ́lwèi̯s

dàdádà

líːbìtʳ

dǽdìs glǽsə̀z (some whispering, banging, squealing)

dɔ́ˑgɪ mámì kʰʊ́kì: (2×) (unintelligible low volume with much banging, hitting of microphone, squealing)

mái̯kʳ (15×) (hitting of microphone, squealing)

SLEEP

pʰʊ̀tʰìtʰɔ́n èndʳ pʰʊ̀tʰɔ́n rékʰə̀tʳ

nái̯sǽnd kʰúːl

mi̯úˑzìkʳ

ǽntə̀nìs mi̯úˑzìkʳ

ǽntə̀nìz bráʊ̯n mi̯úzìkʳ (2×)

ǽntə̀nì rái̯tʳ

pʰénsə̀lzɔ́lwèi̯z rái̯tʰì̯ŋ

éndè

éndè smái̯lìn

ǽntə̀nì kʰèn smái̯l

kʰén smái̯ˑl

mísìz kʰírs

mísìz kʰírstén

kʰíˑrstén (2×)

détsè gʊ̀dʳ bɔ́i̯

gʊ̀dʳ bɔ́i̯ (signal unintelligible, volume too low)

tréi̯n

ǽntə̀nì kʰǽn síˑ dè pléi̯n

pléi̯n (2×)

síˑ báːbl

báːblz híˑr

báːblz

fláʊ̯ə̀rz

bèd fláʊ̯ə̀rz

hɔ́tʳ dɔ́g

góʊ̯tʰʊ̀ wínòʊ̯z nái̯tʳ nái̯tʳ

góʊ̯ nái̯tʳ nái̯tʳ wìθ léi̯dì (signal unintelligible)

wér dè wái̯tʳ wàn gó

híˑrz dè wái̯tʳ wán

blǽŋkʰètʳ

ɔ́ˑldè blǽŋkʰètʳ àpʳ déᵊr

wèr ári̯ù blǽŋkʰètʳ

lái̯kʰè̀ lípstìkʳ

híᵊr

híˑr yʊ̀ àr

híᵊr

góṳ síˑ máị blǽŋkʰèt^r

múv dè yèlòṳ blǽŋkèt (SC)

blú wàn

yélòṳ blǽŋkʰèt^r láịkʰè lípstìk^r

tʰṳ̀ˑ hàt^r (RC)

nòt^r tʰú hót^r

nòt^r tʰù gúd^r

dís wàn (RC)

gòṳtʰṳ́ márkʰèt^r wìt^r mámì

wóts dǽt^r (RC)

ǽntənì fáṳndìt^r

dáŋkʰì kʰíkt^r ít^r

kʰám bóṳbə̀

kʰídìkʰídìkʰíd^r

SLEEP

tʰə́rnìt^r óf

bə̀ˑrn (RC)

wówó (2×) (a dog is barking outside)

dǽdì (2×)

dǽdì mòṳ sə̀m fláṳə̀rz

détsè bróṳkʰèn kʰárt^r

dǽˑdíˑ (4×) (RC)

dǽdìdǽdì (3×)

dís èndét^r (unintelligible whisper)

dè bóịz (RC)

wán (RC)

sébən

núgí (2×)

déts míˑ (RC)

nóṳ

ə̀lóṳnìˑ

gét^r

kʰólóp^r (RC)

lìp^r

lǽp^r

ámíˑ

hǽnə̀r (3×)

yá wóf (a dog is barking outside)

SLEEP

bátʰə̀n brúk^r

láṳtsə̀n brúk^r

ófìs (2×)

nɔ́dá

ó:::

máč tʰéi̯kʰə̀n

díšíš

gív ǽntə̀nì bátʰə̀l

mámìs tráŋkʳ

lìftʰápʳ (RC)

tʰéi̯kʳ bóy̱bɔ̀

bóy̱bɔ̀ bétʰèr gróy̱ ítʳ

àbí::

bí·š

ní·š

bíš (2×)

tʰú: wái̯tʳ ètʳ dè bí·š

bábétʳ

békʳ híə̯r

wétʳ

àbíkʰí

klóy̱zìtʳ

ɔ́·l (SC)

híə̯r

ɔ́·l hí:r (2×)

àkʰídí

híə̯rz wán

bɔ́bí

bɔ́bábábá

rɔ̀kʰái̯n

bí:::

wédì

lʊ̀kʰètʳ dè dɔ́·g: ègén

ə̀š kʰábə̀s

ə̀š

yélòy̱ blǽŋkʰètʳ plí·z (2×) (RC)

blǽŋkʰètʳ plí·z

dapʳ

dáptʰì

dápʳ

yélòy̱ blǽŋkʰètʳ plí·z

dáptʰì (2×)

dápʳ

lʊ́kʳ wòtʳ bòy̱bɔ̀ dídʳ (2×)

dáptʰì (4×)

dápʳ (2×)

yúr ɔ́·l wétʳ (RC)

čéịnǰ dè pʰǽnts (4×) (SC)

mámà | čéịnǰ dè pʰǽnts (1 FC, 1 SC)

ǽntɔ́ní (2×)

blǽŋkʰètʳ plí:z (4×) (SC)

déts lɔ́lìpʰɔ́pʳ (3×)

sí· détʳ (RC)

wɔ́·kʳ wìθ fí·tʳ (3×)

tʰú fí·tʳ

sí· (RC)

tʰúfìtʳ ɛ̀ndè hɔ́·rs

láịkʳ ɔ́l ádə̀r ìndyènz

tʰúfìtʳ hédè hɔ́rs (2×)

sí· kʰɛ́ktʰə̀s

ɛ̀ndè grá·s

ɛ̀n fláᶹə̀rz

nǽnsì (RC)

lúkʰètʳ dì ɛ́s

m::: (3×) (SC)

wáʔ

m::: (2×) (SC)

dɔ́gì báịtʳ

tʰákʳ tʰàkʳ tʰíkʳ

ə̀š::

kʰábə̀s kʰɛ́rì dè hóᶹl

bɔ́tʰə̀l àpʳ déə̀r

àị pʰùtʳ dè bɔ́ks ápʳ

wáf wá (5×)

dàwá (4×) (RC)

čéịnǰ dè pʰǽnts (RC)

máị (RC)

pʰùtʰɔ́n dè fə́rstʳ wɔ́tʰə̀r

dǽị (3×)

dǽdì (RC)

wɔ́tʳ kʰálə̀r vékịᶷm klí·nə̀r

wɔ́tʳ kʰálə̀r máịkrə̀fóᶷn

nóᶷ gréị

á:::r

ɔ́:: (3×)

lúkʰètʳ fífì ɛ̀n bóᶷbə̀

fífì ɛ̀n bóᶷbə̀

ɛ̀n tʰái̯gə̀r

ɛ̀n bélèt^r

ɛ̀ndɛ̀ bélèt^r (3×) (2 FCs, 1 RC)

náy̯dɛ̀ (SC)

náy̯dɛ̀ kʰídì tʰú

ɛ̀ndɛ̀ kʰídì

náy̯dɛ̀ kʰídì

bə̀lóy̯nì

blóy̯ní·

ɛ̀n hái̯ dɛ̀ búks

ǽntənɪ wònts dɛ̀ bélèt^r plí·z

bélèt^r plí·z

hái̯ bóy̯bə̀

mái̯krə̀fóy̯n

kʰə́dí

mís kʰə́dì

gét^hàp^r

héndz

gét^r á::p^r

gét^r (2×) (falsetto)

gét^hàp^r (falsetto)

gét^háp^r (5×)

gét^hìm á·p^r | kʰídí (2 FCs)

gét^hìm áp^r ɛ̀t nái̯nɔ́klɔ́k^r | fífì (2 FCs)

héyù

pʰə̀tʰétə̀

gív dɛ̀t^r hí·r

híᵊr

nǽ:n

ná^ʔ

nǽ:n

ǽntənì wónt^hɛ̀ búk^r plí·z

ɔ́y̯nlì (SC)

ɔ́y̯nlì dǽdì tʰéi̯k^r dɛ̀ búk^r

óy̯nlì tʰɔ́mì (2×)

óy̯nlì dǽdì

kʰâmón

wéi̯t^r (2×)

fífì

nà̯y̯fífì

náy̯ dɛ̀ bɔ́tl

wé·i̯ (3×) (RC) (falsetto)

mέlὲ mí:

ǽntənì wɔ́nts dὲ bɔ́tʰəl plí·z

wɔ̀ts dὲ mǽtʰə̀r wídìt ʳ

áp ʳ déi̯ déi̯ (SC)

tʰɔ́rέ

tʰɔ́rέi̯

  (whisper, signal unintelligible)

nà̯u̯dὲ blǽŋkὲts ɔ́lgɔ́n

dὲ blǽŋkʰὲts ɔ́·l gɔ́n

yέlò̯u̯ blǽŋkʰὲts ɔ́l gɔ́n

dᶻámp ʳ

blǽŋkʰὲts ǰàmp ʳ

bɔ́u̯bɔ̀

há̯u̯bá̯u̯t ʳ bɔ́u̯bɔ̀ ǰámp ʳ

ɔ́ldὲ krái̯

hέv dὲ bɔ́tʰəl

ná̯u̯ bɔ́u̯bɔ̀ gɔ́tʰìt ʳ

bɔ́u̯bɔ̀ šɪt ʳ dá̯u̯nègéi̯n

sít ʳ dà̯u̯n ègéi̯n

blǽŋkʰὲt ʳ plí·z (2×)

yέlò̯u̯ blǽŋkʰὲt ʳ plí·z (3×)

máŋkʰì (3×)

détsὲ (2×) (SC)

détsὲ kʰídì

déts fífì hí·r

déts tʰédìbéə r

έn béi̯bì

dǽdì | yέlò̯u̯ blǽŋkʰὲt ʳ fɔ̀r ǽntənì

blǽŋkʰὲt ʳ fɔ̀r ǽntənì

blǽŋkʰὲt ʳ plí·z (2×)

mɔ̀r mílk ʳ (3×)

sánìz šánìŋ

nɔ́t ʳ dὲ grǽ·s

déts dὲ bɔ́i̯

blǽŋkʰὲt ʳ plí·z (3×) (squealing)

bέlὲt ʳ plí·z (3×)

ǽntənì wɔ̀nts dὲ bέlὲt ʳ

bέlὲt ʳ plí·z (2×)

ǽntənì wɔ́nts dὲ bέlὲt ʳ plí·z

bέlὲt ʳ plí·z (2×)

  (signal unintelligible)

tʰám (3×)

bám tʰám tʰám

bám (6×)

bélèt^r plí·z (4×) (1 SC, 3 FCs)

dǽdəm (3×)

yέy (RC)

rέdì (9×)

rέd (2×)

rέ:d

rέdì (2×)

rέd (2×)

æ:: (3×)

háʔ (4×)

blǽŋkʰèt^r plí·z (2×)

blǽŋkʰèt^r ὲndὲ bélèt^r (2×)

blǽŋkʰèt^s wái̯nìŋ

gwái̯n

stópʰít^r (2×)

stέpʰít^r

stέpʰìt^r déᵊr

m::: (RC)

blǽŋkʰèt^r plí·z (2×)

bótʰəl ìndὲkʰá·r (signal partially unintelligible)

góу̯ bài̯bài̯

ìn trák^r

óу̯pʰὲn dὲ wínóу̯

góу̯ drái̯v

méi̯kʰὲn dὲ ší·t^r (squealing)

blǽŋkʰèt^r plí·z (3×)

lái̯k^r mi̯úzìk^r

   (music is playing)

blǽŋkʰèt^r plí·z (5×)

ʔaʔ

hí·r mi̯úzìk^r

lái̯kʰìt^r

dóу̯nt^r lái̯kʰìt^r

lái̯kʰìt^r dǽdì

dǽdí

ǽlís

dǽᴅí̃

                                         SLEEP

mái̯krəfóу̯n (3×)

dὲts fɔ̀r dὲ mái̯krɔ̀fòу̯n

mámì blóʊ̯ (3×) (SC)

mòr jûs ìndè bóthə̀l (3×)

mòr mîlkʳ ìndè bóthə́l (2×)

m::: (RC)

mísɨs fíšə̀r (2×)

nɔ́tʳ dɔ̀kthə̀r déi̯vìs

mísìs fíš

mísɨs fíšə̀r

séi̯ hélóʊ̯ thʊ̀ mìsɨs fíš

sèi̯ hélòʊ̯ thʊ̀ mísɨs fíšə̀r (2×)

hélóʊ̯ thʊ̀ mísɪs fɪšə̀r (4×)

ɛ̀nts khíkhìn

sí: dè mìlk (2×) (RC)

mɔ́·r mílkʳ (signal unintelligible)

khʊ̀ (4×)

l::: (RC)

wʊ́f (2×) (a dog is barking outside)

rúrúrúrú:θ

héi̯ rúθ (4×)

m:::

ɛ̀ntì khám

wèrzæ̀n | mámì

khámín (10×) (6 FCs, 4 RCs)

gòʊ̯s èwéi̯ dè bánì

mɛ́kʳ

mɔ́s

hú ìz khámìŋ

wér ìz dètʳ

mésìn

mámìs khámìŋ wáns

lái̯khɛ̀ lípstìkʳ

nóʊ̯ blæ̀ŋkhètʳ lái̯khɛ̀ lípstìkʳ

khábə̀s mú·vèn

krɔ́s strí:tʳ

khábə̀s krɔ́sìn strí:tʳ

dóʊ̯ntʳ krɔ́s

dè strí:kʳ

   (signal unintelligible)

dóʊ̯ntʳ ǰámpʳ (RC)

ǰámpʳ

ə̀kláklá (3×)

pháphə̀

fífì

ɔ̀ldè tʰɔ́i̯s

mái̯kʰɔ̀fóy̯n (4×)

ǰámpʳ

tʰy̯dè mái̯krɔ̀fòy̯n (2×)

nɔ̀nɔ̀ blǽŋkʰèt̚ʳ

ápʳ

pʰám (3×)

lìsɔ̀n tʰy̯mái̯krɔ̀fòy̯n

góy̯ tʰy̯ mái̯krɔ̀fòy̯n

á: | kʰídì kʰídì

ɛ̂ntɔnì ǰámpʳ

ǰámpʳ (2×)

óy̯vé tʰy̯ mái̯krɔ̀fòy̯n

bíg ǰámpʳ stérz

lìsén máŋkì

gɔ̀n wìt̚ʳ fífì

a:: (RC)

góy̯ fífì

a:: (RC)

bu (RC)

fífì | blǽŋkʰèt̚ʳ ápʳ

gòy̯ tʰy̯sí:

ápʳ gòy̯z blǽŋkʰèt̚ʳ

gù: ná·i̯t̚ʳ

ápʳ gòy̯z dè (RC)

ái̯ hóy̯pʳ sóy̯

klí:náy̯t̚ʳ ɔ̀ldè drɔ́·ɔr

ɔ̀kski̯úz mì

bóy̯bɔ̀

dòy̯nt̚ʳ tʰíklìš

gi

gɔ̀ndúdèt̚ʳ

wɔ̀tʰái̯m

bám bóy̯bɔ̀ (2×)

bóy̯bɔ̀ àndɔr dè blǽŋkʰèt̚ʳ (2×)

bóy̯bɔ̀

ápʳ bóy̯bɔ̀

bóy̯bɔ̀ kʰámén

nɔ́t̚ʳ bóy̯bɔ̀ (2×)

lúkʰèt̚ʳ ǽntʰɔnì

bɔ́tʰɔl spúf

bɔ́tʰəl jǎmpˊ

ápˊ dɛ̀ bɔ́tʰəl

pʰʊ́tʰɔ́n dɛ̀ šíːtˊ (8×) (crying)

ápˊ wìt bóʊbə̀ dɛ̀ šíːtˊ

jǎmpˊ bóʊbə̀

dɛ̀ts mǎikrə̀fòʊn híːr

dɛ̀ts mámì

dɛ̀ts mámì pʰʊ́tʰɔ́n hə̀r šúːz

dɛ̀ts mámì pʰʊ́tʰɔ́n ǽntə̀nìs slípʰə̀rs

dís kʰɔ́rnə̀r | ǽntə̀nì rɔ́kʰìn

dɛ́tˊ kʰɔ́rnə̀r

pʰʊ́tʰɔ́n dì šíːtˊ (6×) (crying)

blǽːnkʰɛ́tˊ plíːz (8×) (SC)

ǽntə̀nì wɔ̀ndɛ̀ bɔ́ːl plíːz (SC)

bɔ́ːl zìndɛ̀ bǽ·θrʊ́·m

ìndɛ̀ bǽ·θrʊ́·m

bìg rɛ̀dˊ bɔ́·l (RC)

lídə̀l rɛ̀dˊ bɔ́·l

mámì blóʊ (5×) (crying)

yʊ̀r wɛ́lkʰàm

òʊvə̀r dɛ́ híl flǎi

gòʊ bóʊbə̀ òʊvə̀r dɛ̀ hìl flǎi (2×)

sí krǽkʰə̀r

ái dòʊntˊ híˑr yʊ̀

rɔ́kʰǽndì máʊntʰə̀r

aːːː (singing)

rɔ́kˊ

rɔ́kʰǽndì

bóʊbə̀ ɔ́ndì wáit blǽŋkʰìtˊ

blǽŋkʰɛ̀tˊ díˑr

wɛ̀r dìd ǽntə̀nɪ góʊ

tʰʊ̀ slíːːpˊ

ìz slí·pìŋ

bóʊbə̀ slí·pˊ

ɛ̀ndìyɛ́lòʊ (RC)

slí·pìŋ

náis bóʊbə̀

slíːpˊ (RC)

ɔ́kʰɛ́i

náis bóʊbə̀ slí·p (SC)

ǽntə̀nì bíháindˊ bóʊbə̀ (4×)

ǽntə̀nì bìháindˊ

ὲndὲ blú blǽŋkʰὲtʳ
  (signal unintelligible)
pʰìkʰápʳ yélòy̥ blǽŋkʰὲtʳ
wὸtʳ hǽpʰὸndʳ (RC)
wέr dìdìtʳ góy̥
ìts lɔ́ktʳ
lí·vìtʳ ɔ́n | bóy̥bɔ̀ | lí·vìtʳ ɔ́n (RC)
dóy̥ntʰèi̥kʰìtʰɔ́f
tʰèi̥kʰìtʰɔ́f (2×)
ɔ́kʰéi̥
góy̥ ìndì gárdὸn | wìtʰálìs
pʰúlìn wí:dz
ìndὲgárdὸn
wìtʰálìs
wìt bóy̥bɔ̀
gòy̥ slí·pʳ ὸlrédì
góy̥ slí·pʳ
ὸrlìndὲmɔ́·rníŋ
slípʳ ɔ́rlì ìndὲ mɔ́·rnìŋ
kʰábὸs ɔ́·l dɔ́rtʰì (2×)
kʰábὸs ɔ́·l dɔ́rtʰì ìndὲ mɔ́·rnìŋ
mɔ́·rnìŋ kʰábὸs ɔ́·l dɔ́rtʰì (2×)
dɔ́rtʰì kʰábὸs ìndὲ kʰár
hwái̥ (RC)
ái̥ kʰǽntʳ
hwái̥ (2×) (RC)

SLEEP

BIBLIOGRAPHY

Abernethy, E., "The effect of changed environmental conditions upon the results of college examinations," *J. Psychol.* 10.293–301 (1940).

Albright, R. W., Joy B. Albright, "Application of descriptive linguistics to child language," *Journal of Speech and Hearing Research* 1.257–261 (1958).

Berko, J., "The child's learning of English morphology," *Word* 14.150–177 (1958).

Berko, J., R. W. Brown, "Psycholinguistic research methods" in P. H. Mussen (ed.), *Handbook of Research Methods in Child Development* (New York, 1960).

Bolinger, D. L., "Intonation levels versus configurations," *Word* 7. 199-210 (1951).

Boyd-Bowman, Peter, "Cómo obra la fonética infantil en la formación de los hipocorísticos," *Nueva Revista de Filología Hispánica* 9.337–366 (1956).

Brown, R. W., "Language and categories," Appendix in Bruner, J. S., et al. *A Study of Thinking* (New York, 1956).

Brown, R. W., "Linguistic determinism and the parts of speech," *Journal of Abnormal and Social Psychology* 55.1–5 (1957).

Brown, R. W., *Words and things* (Glencoe, 1958).

Brown, R. W., C. Fraser, W. Bellugi, "Evaluation procedures for grammars written for the speech of children." To be submitted to Child Development Monographs.

Brown, R. W., J. Berko, "Word association and the acquisition of grammar," *Child Development* 31.1–14 (1960).

Brown, R. W., E. H. Lenneberg, "A study in language and cognition," *Journal of Abnormal and Social Psychology* 49.454–462 (1954).

Bruner, J. S., E. Brunswick, L. Festinger, F. Heider, K. F. Muenzinger, C. E. Osgood, D. Rapapport, "Contemporary approaches to cognition." *A symposium held at the University of Colorado* (Cambridge, 1957).

Bruner, J. S., J. J. Goodnow, G. A. Austin, *A study of thinking* (New York, 1956).

Bühler, C., *Kindheit und Jugend* (Leipzig, 1931).

Bühler, C., *Das Märchen und die Phantasie des Kindes* (Leipzig, 1918).

Bühler, K., *Die geistige Entwicklung des Kindes* (Jena, 1930).

Bühler, K., *Sprachtheorie* (Jena, 1934).

Buxbaum, E., "The role of second language in the formation of ego and superego," *Psychoanalytic Quarterly* 18.279–289 (1949).

Carmichael, L. (ed.), *Manual of child psychology* (New York, 1946).

Carroll, J. B., "Determining and numerating adjectives in children's speech," *Child Development* 10.215–29 (1939).

Carroll, J. B., *The study of language: a survey of linguistics and related disciplines in America* (Cambridge, 1953).

Chao, Y. R., "The Cantian idiolect. An analysis of the Chinese spoken by a twenty-eight-months-old child." *Semitic and Oriental Studies* 11.27–44 (1951).

Cohen, M., "Observations sur les dernières persistances du langage enfantin", *Journal de Psychologie normale et pathologique* 30.390–399 (1933).

Cohen, M., "Sur l'étude du langage enfantin", *Enfance* 5.181–249 (1952).

Cohen, M., "Sur les langages successifs de l'enfant", *Mélanges Vendryès* 109–127 (1925).

Čukovskij, K., *Ot dvux do pjati* (Moscow, 1956).

De Camp, L. S., "Learning to talk", *American Speech* 21.23–28 (1946).

Delacroix, H., *L'enfant et le langage* (Paris, 1936).

Durand, M., "Le langage enfantin", *Conférences de l'Institut de linguistique de l'Université de Paris* 11.83–98 (1952–53).

Ervin, S. M., "Grammar and classification". Paper read at meeting of APA, 1957.

Ervin, S., and W. Miller, "Language development" (to appear in National Society for the Study of Education Yearbook: Child Psychology, Chapter 3, 1963).

French, N. R., Carter, C. W. Jr., Koenig, W. Jr., "The words and sounds of telephone conversations", *The Bell System Technical Journal*, 11.290–324 (1930).

Freud, S., "Archaic and infantile features in dreams", *A general introduction to psychoanalysis* 209–223 (1961).

Freud, S., *Jokes and their relation to the unconscious* (New York, 1960).

Freud, S., *Psychopathology of everyday life* (New York, 1951).

Fries, C. C., *The structure of English* (New York, 1952).

Goldstein, K., *Language and language disturbances* (New York, 1948).

Goodglass, H., and Berko, J., "Agrammatism and inflectional morphology in English", *Journal of Speech and Hearing Research* 3.257–267 (1960).

Grégoire, A., *L'apprentissage du langage* (Paris, 1937, 1947).

Grégoire, A., "La renaissance scientifique de la linguistique enfantine", *Lingua* 2.355–398 (1950).

Groddeck, G., *Der Mensch als Symbol* (Vienna, 1933).

Guillaume, P., "Les débuts de la phrase dans le langage de l'enfant", *Journal de Psychologie* 24.1–25 (1927).

Gvozdev, A. N., *Formirovanie u rebenka grammatičeskogo stroja russkogo jazyka* (Moscow, 1949).

Gvozdev, A. N., *Usvoenie rebenkom zvukovoj storony russkogo jazyka* (Moscow, 1948).

Hayden, R. E., "The relative frequency of phonemes in general American English", *Word* 6.217–223 (1950).

Henle, M., and M. B. Hubbell, "'Egocentricity' in adult conversation", *Journal of Social Psychology* 9.227–34 (1938).

Horn, E., "A basic writing vocabulary", *University of Iowa Monographs in Education*, No. 4 (1926).

Irwin, O. C., "Development of speech during infancy: curve of phonemic frequencies", *Journal of Experimental Psychology* 37.187–93 (1947).

Irwin, O. C., "Phonetical description of speech development in childhood", in L. Kaiser (ed.) *Manual of phonetics* 403–425, (Amsterdam, 1957).

Jakobson, R., *Kindersprache, Aphasie und allgemeine Lautgesetze* (Uppsala, 1941).

Jakobson, R., "Linguistics and poetics," in T. A. Sebeok (ed.), *Style in language* 350–357 (New York, 1960).

Jakobson, R., "Why 'Mama' and 'Papa?'," in B. Kaplan and S. Wapner (ed.), *Perspectives in psychological theory* 124–134 (New York, 1960).

Jakobson, R., C. G. M. Fant, M. Halle, *Preliminaries to speech analysis. M.I.T. Acoustics Laboratory Technical Report*, No. 13 (1952).

Jakobson, R., M. Halle, *Fundamentals of language. Janua linguarum*, No. 1 (The Hague, 1956).

Jakobson, R., M. Halle, "Phonology in relation to phonetics", in L. Kaiser (ed.), *Manual of phonetics* (Amsterdam, 1957).

Jespersen, O., *Language, its nature, development and origin* (London-New York, 1922).

Jones, D., *An outline of English phonetics* (New York, 1940).

Kahane, M. R., S. Saporta, "Development of verbal categories in child language," Indiana University Research Center of Anthropology, Folklore, and Linguistics (Bloomington 1958).

Kaper, W., *Einige Erscheinungen der kindlichen Spracherwerbung erläutert im Lichte des vom Kinde gezeigten Interesses für Sprachliches* (Groningen, 1959).

Kaverina, E. K., *O razvitii reči detej pervyx dvux let žizni* (Moscow, 1950).

Köhler, Elsa, *Die Persönlichkeit des dreijährigen Kindes* (Leipzig, 1926).

Kraepelin, E., "Über Sprachstörungen im Traume," *Psychologische Arbeiten* 5.1–104 (1910).

Krapp, G. P., *The pronunciation of standard English in America* (New York, 1919).

Leopold, W. F., "Patterning in children's language," *Language Learning* 5.1–14 (1953–54).

Leopold, W. F., *Bibliography of child language* (Evanston, 1952).

Leopold, W. F., *Speech development of a bilingual child*, Vol. 1–4 (Evanston, 1939–1949).

Lévi-Strauss, C., *La pensée sauvage* (Paris, 1962).

Lewis, M. M., *How children learn to speak* (London, 1957).

Lewis, M. M., *Infant speech* (New York, London, 1951).

Liublinskaya, A. A., "The development of children's speech and thought", in B. Simon (ed.) *Psychology in the Soviet Union*, Stanford University Press (1957).

Luria, A. R., "The directive function of speech, I: its development in early childhood," *Word* 15.341–352, (1959).

Luria, A. R., "The directive function of speech, II: its dissolution in pathological states of the brain," *Word* 15.453–466 (1959).

Luria, A. R., *Rečevye reakcii rebenka* (Moscow, 1927).

Luria, A. R., *Le rôle du langage dans la formation des processus psychiques* (Moscow, 1957).

Luria, A. R., *The role of speech in the regulation of normal and abnormal behavior* (New York, 1961).

Luria, A. R., F. Yudovich, *Speech and the development of mental processes in the child* (London, 1959).

McCarthy, D., "Language development in children," in L. Carmichael (ed.), *Manual of child psychology* 476–581 (New York, 1954).

McCarthy, D., "The language development of the preschool child," *Institute of Child Welfare Monographs* No. 4 (1930).

McGeoch, J. A., A. L. Irion, *The psychology of human learning* (New York, 1952).

Métraux, R. W., "Speech profiles of the preschool child 18 to 54 months," *Journal of Speech and Hearing Disorders* 15.37–53 (1950).

Miller, G. A., *Language and communication* (New York, 1951).

Miller, G. A., E. Galanter, K. H. Pribram, *Plans and the structure of behavior* (New York, 1960).

Miller, W., S. Ervin, "The development of grammar in child language," A paper read at the SSRC Convention (Boston, 1961).

Morley, M. E., *The development and disorders of speech in childhood* (Edinburgh, London, 1957).

Morris, C., *Signs, language and behavior* (New York, 1946).

Mowrer, O. H., "Hearing and speaking: an analysis of language learning," *Journal of Speech and Hearing Disorders* 23.143–151 (1958).

Mowrer, O. H., *Learning theory and personality dynamics; selected papers* (New York, 1950).

Ogden, C. K., I. A. Richards, *The meaning of meaning* (Cambridge, 1946).

Ohnesorg, K., *Fonetická studie o dětské řeči* (Prague, 1948).

Ohnesorg, K., *O mluvním vývoji dítěte* (Prague, 1948).

Osgood, C. E., T. E. Sebeok, *Psycholinguistics: a survey of theory and research problems* (Bloomington, 1954).

Pačesová, Jaroslava, "Contribution à l'étude de la phonétique du langage enfantin", *Sborník prací filosofické fakulty brněnské university* 8.20–30 (1959).

Pan, S., "The influence of context upon learning and recall," *Journal of Experimental Psychology* 9.468–491 (1926).

Parsons, T., R. F. Bales, *Family, socialization and interaction process* (Glencoe, 1955).

Peirce, C. S., *Collected papers of Charles Sanders Peirce*, Vol. 4 (Cambridge, 1933).

Penfield, W., "A consideration of the neurophysiological mechanism of speech and some educational consequences," *Proceedings of American Academy of Arts and Sciences* 85 (1953).

Penfield, W., L. Roberts, *Speech and brain mechanism* (Princeton, 1959).

Piaget, J., *The child's conception of number* (New York, London, 1952).

Piaget, J., *Introduction à l'épistemologie génétique*, Vols. I, II, III, (Paris, 1950).

Piaget, J., *The language and thought of the child* (New York, 1926).

Piaget, J., *The moral judgment of the child* (New York, London, 1932).

Piaget, J., *The origins of intelligence in children* (New York, 1952).

Piaget, J., *Play, dreams, and imitation in childhood* (New York, 1951).

Rapaport, D. (ed.), *Organization and pathology of thought* (New York, 1951).

Riffaterre, M., "Vers la définition linguistique du style," *Word* 17.318–344 (1961).

Roberts, A. H., *Frequencies of occurrence of segmental phonemes in American English.* Unpublished Ph.D. dissertation, University of Wisconsin (1961).

Sapir, E., "Abnormal types of speech in Nootka," *Selected Writings of Edward Sapir* 179–196 (1949).

Sapir, E., *Language* (New York, 1921).

Saporta, S. (ed.), *Psycholinguistics: a book of readings* (New York, 1961).

Šaumjan, S. K., "Nasuščnie zadači struktornoj lingvistiki," *Izvestija Akademii Nauk SSSR, Otdelenie literaturi i jazyka* 21.103–111 (1962).

Scupin, E. and G., *Bubi's erste Kindheit* (Leipzig, 1907).

Sewell, E., *The field of nonsense* (London, 1952).

Shands, H. C., "Anxiety, anaclictic object, and the sign function: comments on early developments in the use of symbols," *The American Journal of Orthopsychiatry* 24.84–97 (1954).

Skinner, B. F., *Verbal Behavior* (New York, 1957).

Slama-Cazacu, T., *Dialogul la copii* (Bucharest, 1961).

Slama-Cazacu, T., *Relaţiile dintre gîndire si limbaj în ortogeneza* (Bucharest, 1957).

Smoczyński, P., *Przyswajawie przez dziecko podstaw systemu językowego* (Lodż, 1955).

Steinitz, W., *Der Parallelismus in der finnisch-karelischen Volksdichtung* (Helsinki, 1934).

Stern, C. and W., *Die Kindersprache* (Leipzig, 1928).

Templin, M. C., *Certains language skills in children: their development and interrelationships. Institute of Child Welfare Monograph Series*, No. 26 (1957).

Trager, G. L., H. L. Smith, Jr., *An outline of English structure* (Norman, 1951).

Velten, H. V., "The growth of phonemic and lexical patterns in infant language," *Language* 19.281–92 (1943).

Vinogradov, G., *Russkij detskij fol'klor* (Irkutsk, 1930).

Voegelin, C. F., S. Adams, "A phonetic study of young children's speech," *Journal of Experimental Education* 3.107–116 (1934).

Voelker, C. H., "A sound count for the oral curriculum," *The Volta Review* 25.55–6 (1935).

Vygotskij, L. S., *Izbrannye psixologičeskie issledovanija* (Moscow, 1956).

Vygotskij, L. S., *Thought and language* (New York, 1962).

Wallon, H., *Les origines de la pensée chez l'enfant I, II* (Paris, 1945).

Whitely, P. L., "The dependence of learning and recall upon prior intellectual activities," *Journal of Experimental Psychology* 10.489–508 (1927).

Wyatt, G. L., "Stammering and language learning in early childhood," *Journal of Abnormal Psychology* 44.75–84 (1949).